THE PRESIDENTS

Text
Bill Harris

Illustrations
Bettmann/UPI
Culver Pictures, Inc
Keystone Collection
National Archives, Washington, DC

Design
Clive Dorman

Commissioning Editor
Andrew Preston

Commissioning Assistant
Edward Doling

Picture Research
Leora Kahn
Kenneth Johnston

Editorial
Jane Adams

Production
Ruth Arthur
David Proffit
Sally Connolly

Director of Production
Gerald Hughes

Director of Publishing
David Gibbon

CLB 2397
© 1990 Archive Publishing, a division of Colour Library Books Ltd,
Godalming, Surrey, England.
All rights reserved.
This edition published 1990 by Portland House, a division of dilithium Press, Ltd,
distributed by Outlet Book Company, Inc, a Random House Company,
225 Park Avenue South, New York, New York 10003.
Printed and bound in Italy.
ISBN 0 517 03382 8
8 7 6 5 4 3 2 1

THE
PRESIDENTS

BILL HARRIS

PORTLAND HOUSE

Introduction

In the summer of 1787, forty-five men argued among themselves for four months over how the new American nation ought to be governed. The country had been limping along under its Articles of Confederation, but the time had come to make some changes.

There were some things they felt shouldn't be changed, though, and one of them was that the United States had been governed by a council and not a single person. When a delegate from Pennsylvania suggested that what this country really needed was a strong individual at the top, the room fell silent, except for some embarrassed throat-clearing here and there. It was the most revolutionary idea they'd heard. Hadn't they just fought a long, expensive war to keep kings from meddling in their lives?

But in spite of their misgivings, they incorporated the idea of a president into their new Constitution. They also left the ultimate decision up to the states by requiring ratification by at least nine of the thirteen new states. And that's when the real debate began.

In Virginia, George Mason said that a single president would be "directed by minions and favorites, or he will become a tool of the Senate." Patrick Henry said that the proposal "squinted toward monarchy." And Thomas Jefferson wrote from Paris that a president "possessing the military force of the union … would not be easily dethroned." He advised that the chief executive should be forever ineligible for a second term at the end of four years.

New York's Governor George Clinton said that even four years was too long. "If the president is possessed of ambition, he has power and time sufficient to ruin his country." He also predicted that the president's "unrestrained power of granting pardons for treason … may be used to screen from punishment those whom he has secretly instigated to commit the crime, and thereby prevent a discovery of his own guilt." And a Philadelphia pamphleteer went so far as to charge that the framers of the Constitution had come up with the idea "in hopes of obtaining some lucrative employment, or of receiving a little more homage from the rest of their fellow creatures."

But there were strong arguments on the other side, too. In the *Federalist Papers*, Alexander Hamilton wrote: "Talents for low intrigue and the little arts of popularity may suffice to elevate a man to the governorship of a state, but it will require other talents and a different kind of merit to establish him in the esteem and confidence of the whole Union. It will not be too strong to say that there will be a constant probability of seeing the station filled by characters preeminent for ability and virtue."

The Constitution, which was ratified in spite of the naysayers, spells out the basic duties of the president, but it doesn't offer any advice on how to find characters with the right abilities and virtues. That is the job of the people. All the Constitution says is that the people's choice should be "a natural born citizen … neither shall any person be eligible to that office who shall not have attained the age of thirty-five years, and been fourteen years a resident within the United States."

Because of it, the idea that anybody's child could become president is the centerpiece of the American Dream. As each Administration reaches the end of its first year, a PR blitz begins to gather attention for any number of people the columnists and commentators tell us are beginning to look "presidential." Then, during the long campaigns to separate the wheat from the chaff, the voters look them over and attempt to decide which of them would make a "good president." But if the Constitution is vague about the kinds of personal background they should be looking for, history isn't much help, either. The forty men who have become president of the United States actually have very little in common with each other. And their routes to the presidency have been as different as their genealogical roots and their career backgrounds.

The Founding Fathers had their eye on George Washington as the kind of man who should run the country and establish the pattern for his successors.

They had also created the office of vice president, and decided that the job should go to the man with the second-highest number of electoral votes. It followed that the vice president would succeed his president in the next election, if not through death. It worked that way in the case of Washington's Vice President, John Adams, and his Vice President, Thomas Jefferson. Then the pattern changed. The next three succeeded to the presidency from the office of Secretary of State. The Constitution had been amended in 1804 to require a separate candidate for vice president, and the politicians responded by picking men not for their ability but to "balance the ticket," with the result that in all the years since, only two vice presidents, Martin Van Buren and George Bush, were able to become president on their own. The death of a president elevated eight others.

In the beginning of the republic, the people had a dread of monarchs and the opposition to the creation of the presidency came directly from that fear. But in the years since, we have come to regard our presidents as something close to kings. Inauguration ceremonies have all the trappings of coronations, and the social life of the President and First Lady is watched with the same awe as the Royal Family of Britain. But if the President enjoys the life of royalty, the job is also that of a prime minister. He's the head of state, but he's also the head of the government and of a political party.

Our ancestors might be shocked if they knew what's become of the office they created. But they'd probably be pleased at the amazing cross section of America that has been represented in the office in the last two hundred years.

The 1st President
GEORGE WASHINGTON
(1789-1797)

The Father of His Country had no children of his own, but his wife, Martha, the widow of Colonel Daniel Parke Custis, brought her son Parke, and daughter Eleanor to Mount Vernon.

ngland's King George II was one of the first important people to consider George Washington as a Colonial with a future. After the twenty-two year old Virginia planter took on the French and their Indian allies in Western Pennsylvania in 1754, his flowery report of the victory reached the King, who beamed with pride and admiration. The following year, when Washington volunteered to serve on General Braddock's staff for an expedition to drive the French from Fort Duquesne, on the site of present-day Pittsburgh, he was welcomed with open arms and the customary fee for the commission was waived in favor of his experience in the service of the King.

As it turned out, the expedition was a disaster. Braddock was killed and his army routed. But young George Washington came back a hero, and was made commander of the Virginia militia, such as it was. Over the next three years he served on the frontier, where his reputation increased, and he began a personal campaign for a commission in the British Army, which required honing his political skills. The men who could reward him with a red coat weren't

impressed, but important men in the Colonies took notice. Eventually another English king named George would take notice, too.

Young George Washington became the squire of a Virginia plantation at the age of eleven when his father died. By the time he was of a legal age to administer it, he was also well on his way to expanding it. He had been made county surveyor at seventeen and over the next two years he speculated in the land he surveyed, adding thousands of virgin acres to his holdings. Long before he was old enough to call himself one, George Washington had all the attributes of a country gentleman.

His military activities enhanced his status, and then in 1759, after announcing his retirement from the militia, he married Martha Custis, a member of one of Virginia's most influential families, and settled down on his estate at Mount Vernon determined to make his own family name as impressive as any in the colony.

As a farmer and businessman and a member of the Virginia House of Burgesses, he succeeded admirably. And when men in the other colonies began protesting about English taxation and restrictions, he joined the cause with a passion, becoming one of Virginia's seven delegates to the First Continental Congress.

He was an impressive man. At six feet two inches, Washington was much taller than most of his contemporaries, and his regal posture made him look taller still. A contemporary description said, "his head is well shaped … gracefully poised on a superb neck … blue-gray penetrating eyes, widely separated and overhung with a heavy brow…. A pleasing countenance … all the muscles of his face under perfect control…. In conversation, he looks you full in the face … his voice is agreeable rather than strong. His demeanor is at all times composed and dignified." But possibly most important of all was that George Washington was a man of few words. In the fervor of the times, the revolutionaries had a tendency to make long, impassioned speeches, often calling attention to nothing more important than themselves. When Washington spoke, it was usually because he had something to say. And the other delegates listened.

None of his early military exploits were especially noteworthy, and though he was credited with organizing a dignified retreat after Braddock's defeat, the battle itself was one most people preferred to forget. But many important men remembered George Washington as a hero and his physical appearance reinforced their memories.

When the Minutemen were attacked by the British at Lexington and Concord, the Second Continental Congress began debating the merits of a half-dozen different men to become the Commander-in-Chief of its army. There was no contest. George Washington was clearly the man for the job. Some delegates had reservations about it, but the only one to express them was Washington himself, who told Congress, "I do not think myself equal to the command." Even though George Washington was well known as a man who couldn't tell a lie, nobody believed him. On Sunday, July 2, 1775, he took command of the American troops at Cambridge, Massachusetts.

After organizing the patriots into an army, he was eventually able to drive the British from Boston and within a year most of the King's men had retreated into Canada. The time was ripe for Congress to declare America's independence from England and King George III, but in the months that followed, there must have been moments when George Washington wished they hadn't. Within a few weeks of the Declaration of Independence in the summer of 1776, Washington's army was on the run northward from New York, and as winter set in they were still retreating. Even the most dedicated rebels among them were conceding that they might be British subjects again before time for spring planting.

The British thought so, too, and after establishing a chain of winter camps across New Jersey, General Howe and his men settled down for a long winter's nap. General Washington, meanwhile, went to Philadelphia to report that "the game is pretty near up." Then he went back to his own winter camp and began planning an offensive. On Christmas night, 1776, he led his men on a surprise attack at Trenton, across the Delaware River. It was his first important victory, and by spring he had scored several more. As

One of the most dramatic moments in Washington's career was his farewell to the officers who had served him in the Revolutionary War. He thought it would be his last public act.

the weather began improving, so did the Continental Army. New recruits began reporting for duty, its officers had gained experience and confidence, and so had General Washington himself. By the end of 1777, Washington was more than just a hero, and some members of Congress began worrying among themselves that they had created a "deity" when they made him Commander-in-Chief.

But for all his successes, General Washington spent the second winter of the war at Valley Forge among starving, freezing and demoralized troops. The fact that he shared the hardships with his men is the most frequently cited reason that they not only survived, but picked up a new resolve to fight. They also joined their officers in absolute trust of Washington. The French were impressed, too, and agreed to join the fight against their old enemy. And the British were impressed enough to replace their own commander and withdraw from Philadelphia without a fight.

By the time the war ended, six years after it had begun, George Washington had, indeed, become something of a deity in America. But he was weary of war and retired in triumph to his plantation at Mount Vernon. He retired from politics, too. But in 1787, Washington was persuaded to join Virginia's delegation to a convention called to revise the Articles of Confederation that loosely joined the new United States. As it turned out, they drafted an entirely new Constitution. Washington, who had been named president of the convention, personally submitted the document to Congress for ratification by each of the states, then he retired to his farm again. But he knew it was only a matter of time before the office of President of the United States, established by the new set of laws, would be offered to him. When the call finally came on April 14, 1789, the former General answered it with feelings he said were "not unlike those of a culprit who is going to the place of his execution." The place was New York, the temporary capital of the new nation. The journey there from Mount Vernon was marked by the greatest outpouring of love and respect America has ever shown any man.

He was known by then as "the father of his country," a mark of affection formerly reserved for England's kings. His birthday was declared a holiday, just as the English had honored their monarchs. But though many observers had worried that Washington would use his popularity to become a dictator, he himself had led discussions at the Constitutional Convention to make sure that the powers of the presidency would be limited and that titles of nobility were strictly prohibited. After he became Washington's Vice President, John Adams proposed that he and the President should be addressed as "His Highness." Washington put down the notion and suggested instead that he should be called, simply, "Mr. President." But if he was thoroughly dedicated to republican principles, George and Martha Washington lived like royalty, first in New York and then in Philadelphia after the capital was moved there in 1790. Their house was staffed with more than twenty servants and they were driven from place to place in a gilded coach drawn by six white horses. They entertained stylishly and often, and held a formal reception at least once a week during the whole eight years of his presidency.

During his first year in office, he worked with Congress to prepare a dozen amendments to the new Constitution to clarify individual and states' rights. Ten of them were ratified by the state legislatures by the end of 1791 and became known as the Bill of Rights. The Constitution had also neglected to establish certain departments of the new government, and Washington and Congress worked together to establish four of them. They also created a judiciary system and a Supreme Court. George Washington's choice of men to head the new departments was nothing short of brilliant. Thomas Jefferson became his Secretary of State, Alexander Hamilton Secretary of the Treasury. Henry Knox was made Secretary of War, Edmund Randolph Attorney General and John Jay Chief Justice. Excepting Jay, but including Vice President Adams, they formed the President's Cabinet, a body of advisers Washington established by custom rather than by law.

The first Cabinet meetings were potentially stormy affairs. Jefferson and Hamilton were both men of strong will and totally different opinions on how the country should be run. But Washington, who admired both of them, was able to get them to work together, and actually made their differences work to the benefit of the country.

Not much conflict of any kind arose during the first years of the Washington Administration, and he spent a great deal of time traveling throughout the states, mostly to encourage better farming techniques. In the process, his personal popularity increased, and many of the homes and inns he slept in, even for one night, became local shrines. Some of them still are.

But his presidency wasn't all a bed of roses. There was a battle among the states over Hamilton's ideas

The Constitution does not provide for advisors to the President, but Washington invented the Cabinet and staffed it with brilliant men. From left to right are President Washington, Secretary of War Henry Knox, Secretary of the Treasury Alexander Hamilton, Secretary of State Thomas Jefferson, and Attorney General Edmund Randolph.

for paying off the national debt. There was still trouble with the Indians west of the Appalachians. Political parties were beginning to air their differences, sometimes at the expense of the president himself. The individual states were having problems adjusting to their new marriage, which gave the Father of His Country problems of his own. And when his first term came to an end, he needed to be talked into accepting a second. He reluctantly agreed, only because he was convinced that rivalry between the two political parties, the Republicans and Federalists, would tear the country apart without him. Both parties supported his candidacy and he was unanimously reelected.

The political wars continued in his second administration, and the Indian wars heated up. The rough and ready settlers on the frontier rebelled against the central government, more often than not over Federal taxes on whiskey. And on the other side of the world, America's foreign policy was faced with its first serious challenge as the French revolted against their king. Many of the men who had helped America

One of the turning points of the Revolutionary War was Washington's surprise attack on Trenton, an attack made after he had moved his army across the ice-choked Delaware River in the winter of 1776.

during its own revolution, including the Marquis de Lafayette, became victims of the upheaval, and many Americans were strongly opposed to the Reign of Terror that followed it. On the other hand, America had demonstrated to the world that it was opposed to the idea of monarchy and didn't care to be put in the position of siding against other such revolutionaries. The debate that raged in the American Government was the hottest any of its participants had seen. But though Washington had held firm on a policy of neutrality, an attempt to restore the French monarchy made that impossible. The French republicans, citing a treaty negotiated during the American Revolution, and reminding the Americans of the help they had delivered at the time, asked for help in return. The United States needed to act to protect its shipping, which was being threatened by the British, who had gone to war against France. Spain, which was also at war with France, seemed in danger of losing the last of its possessions in Louisiana. Washington cooled the situation in his own country by issuing a proclamation of neutrality. But it was easier said than done. Both the French and the British routinely attacked American ships and pressed the sailors into their own navies. Washington was determined to keep America out of the war, but agreed to the building of six warships, which eventually became the backbone of the American Navy. He sent John Jay to England to negotiate a treaty that became one of the hardest tests of his personal popularity. Most Americans regarded it as pro-British and began to suspect that their President had something other than their best interests at heart. But Washington signed it anyway. Soon after, another treaty was negotiated with Spain, giving the Americans the right to traffic on the Mississippi River, among other important matters. Washington's popularity rating improved dramatically, as often happens in politics.

But the man was weary. In 1797, he pulled out the farewell address he had prepared four years earlier, dusted it off and delivered it to Congress. On March 8, after saying his farewells to old friends, he and Martha rode off to retirement at Mount Vernon. He made it a point to let the new President run the ship of state without interference. As President, he had tried to stay above politics, and usually succeeded, but in his last years he broke with Jefferson and his Republicans, openly endorsing the Federalists.

But in retirement, Washington's most important interest was his Virginia plantation. He was forced to sell off huge pieces of it to make ends meet, but he managed to maintain the lifestyle of a country gentleman for the rest of his life. In late December 1799, he became ill after riding through rain and snow over his lands, and within a few days he was dead of a streptococcus infection, an ailment easily cured in our own times.

Of all the tributes that poured in from around the country and around the world, the one that stood out above the rest came from England's King William IV, the son of George III, who called Washington "the greatest man who ever lived."

JOHN ADAMS

The 2nd President
JOHN ADAMS
(1797-1801)

He's often regarded as one of the more patrician of our presidents, but John Adams was born in the early New England version of a log cabin at Braintree, Massachusetts. His father was a hard-working farmer whose own father had been one of the founders of the town. He was a man, his son would later say, whose "sphere of life was not very extensive." But if he wasn't a well-educated landowner with a Georgian mansion full of servants, he was highly regarded within his little sphere, and had high hopes for his eldest son. Though he needed the boy's help to support the family, he sent John to school to start him on the road to becoming a clergyman. The road eventually led to Harvard College, which young Adams entered at the age of fifteen. Though he had mastered his Latin grammar and could read the New Testament in Greek, he was still considered a rough country boy and was treated like one by his fellow students.

But unlike his fellow students, who were scandalizing Cambridge at the time with their "habits of frequenting taverns and alehouses," and even "addressing the female sex," John Adams was, if anything, overly serious about his studies. He was considered one of the most brilliant scholars in his class and the day he graduated he was offered the job of Latin master in the grammar school at Worcester. Adams considered it a dead-end job, but it was also one that allowed him time to consider his future and to continue his education on his own. In the process he decided to abandon his family's dream that he would become a minister and decided instead to study law.

In the New England of the 1750s, lawyers ranked a slim notch above shoemakers on the social scale and were considered beneath contempt by most men of substance. But John Adams saw it as a higher calling and spent two years under the wing of the local lawyer, earning his way by pouring Latin into the heads of Worcester youngsters with "scolding, then flattering, then thwacking."

At the end of his apprenticeship he went back to Braintree to become a country lawyer. He had the only practice in a town that was becoming known as the most litigious in Massachusetts. But he still had time to read and discuss philosophy and history. He also found time to court the daughter of Parson Smith of nearby Weymouth, and in 1764, after thinking it over for three years, he asked the cleric for permission to marry Abigail. The parson put aside his doubts and, ignoring the opinion of his parishioners that the girl was marrying beneath her station, performed the ceremony himself.

Adams's law practice was thriving by then, and he seemed destined to become a family man and a pillar of the Braintree community. But there was a different kind of destiny in the New England air in 1764. He had always divided his time between Braintree and Boston, and the big city was buzzing with dissent

As America's first Ambassador to Britain, John Adams was also one of the few rebels to have a face-to-face meeting with the hated King George III.

against the Mother Country. In spite of the fact that his second cousin, Samuel Adams, was among the most vocal of the dissenters, John Adams was determined to stay aloof. When the citizens of Boston destroyed the home of the Provincial Secretary to protest the English stamp tax, he was horrified at what he called "the blind, undistinguished rage of the rabble." But when the stamps themselves arrived in spite of the protests, John Adams seems to have had a change of heart. He wrote and circulated a strong petition denouncing taxation without representation. His words were published in newspapers all over Massachusetts, and overnight John Adams became an important part of the revolutionary movement. He was invited into the homes of Boston's most influential merchants and he mingled with the lower classes, too, through the Sons of Liberty who welcomed him as one of their own.

It was inevitable that he and Abigail and their year-old son, John Quincy, would eventually move to Boston. They had no sooner settled down than he was offered a high post in the Royal Courts of Admiralty. It represented an opportunity for power and influence, not to mention financial security, but he refused the offer and in the process he sent a signal to the revolutionaries that he was one of them. But it was a mixed signal. When British soldiers were provoked into firing on a mob in Boston Common, killing five of them, the soldiers were arrested and their captain ordered to defend himself in court. No lawyer in the city would touch the case, but Adams agreed to help gather the evidence that would guarantee him a fair trail. It could have meant the end of a bright legal career, but he became convinced that the officer was innocent and eventually convinced the judges, too.

There were rumors among the Patriots that he had sold out, but most Bostonians knew that instead he had defended the rule of law and, especially among the upper classes, John Adams became something of a hero.

He scrupulously avoided politics, until the call came to become a member of the Massachusetts delegation to the first Continental Congress, which he answered willingly. On the other hand, when Congress adjourned, he was happy to go home again, proud that he he done his duty but determined not to repeat the experience.

His determination was short-lived. After the confrontation between the Minutemen and British soldiers at Lexington and Concord, he knew he couldn't stay above the battle and when Congress reconvened, he left his sick bed to be there. This time he had a personal stake in their deliberations. His wife and four children were in a city filled with hostile troops, and he knew that there wasn't any time to be wasted. He led the movement to appoint George Washington commander of the Continental Army and worked tirelessly to convince Congress to support the army and of the necessity of establishing a navy. He was among the hardest-working of all the delegates, in fact, and eventually the strain took its toll. After four years of service, he asked to be relieved of his duties and went back to Boston to pick up the pieces of his life. But less than a month later he accepted an appointment to become Ambassador to France.

By the time he arrived, Benjamin Franklin had already established himself at the Court of Versailles and the French had little time for the comparatively dull scholar. When Congress made Franklin its Minister to France a few months later, Adams felt that his services as Ambassador were redundant and asked to be recalled. Then, without even waiting for his request to be approved, he sailed for Massachusetts on the next available ship.

He was no sooner home than he was elected to join a committee to write a constitution for the Commonwealth. The resulting document was almost entirely his own work. And as soon as the work was completed and approved, he turned his attention to the national scene again. In the fall of 1779 he went back to Paris to begin negotiating a treaty of peace with Great Britain. He sailed immediately after receiving the commission, without any instructions from Congress, whose instincts he didn't trust. He preferred, he said, to "trust events to Heaven."

Those events kept him in Europe, shuttling between Paris, Amsterdam and London, until 1785, when word reached him that he had been made America's first representative at the Court of St. James. He was welcomed to England with a newspaper headline that read: *An Ambassador From America! Good Heavens What a Sound!* And that was just the beginning. The British were not amused that the upstarts from across the ocean were beginning to feel like their equals. The Adamses themselves found life in London expensive and dreary compared to Paris, and they were insulted

When Adams began working on the Massachusetts Consititution, his wife, Abigail, cautioned him to "remember the ladies and be more generous and favorable to them than your ancestors."

when they were asked to pay import duty on the wine cellar they had brought with them. But the Minister from America had plenty to take his mind off the expense, the inconveniences and the snubs. And when he wasn't dealing with America's foreign policy interests, he busied himself collecting and digesting books on history and political science. In the process, he became the world's leading authority on the art of government and put that knowledge together in a treatise on *Defence of the Constitutions of Government of the United States*. It became the major reference work for the framers of the American Constitution when they met at Philadelphia the following year.

Adams arrived back in America three days before New Hampshire's ratification made the new Constitution official on June 21, 1788. He had talked of retirement, but was elected to the new Congress long before his ship cleared the port of Boston. With characteristic stubbornness he refused to go to New York to take his seat. But his supporters had other things in mind anyway. When the Electoral College met to cast all of its votes for George Washington as the first president, thirty four of the sixty nine electors cast their votes for John Adams to become the first Vice President.

The Constitution had been silent on what was expected of a Vice President, and Adams reveled in the job of establishing precedents for future generations. As president of a Senate that was often split over regional and political interests, he held the power of breaking tie votes. As a pedant, he also took it upon himself to lecture his colleagues on how they should behave. He didn't always win his points and he had more than his share of political enemies. But Vice President John Adams was a very happy man.

At the end of Washington's first term, he ran unopposed for a second. But Adams had serious rivals for the number two spot, and his candidacy gave America its first opportunity for a national election campaign. But, as would often happen in the future, the politicians were more passionate than the voters, who found they had better things to do than vote on election day. Adams beat his nearest rival, George Clinton of New York, by twenty-seven electoral votes.

Four years later, most Americans considered Adams Washington's heir apparent, but Thomas Jefferson had other ideas and though neither he nor Adams actively campaigned for the office, their supporters managed to keep the pot boiling with charges, countercharges and mudslinging. The Republicans said Adams was an elitist determined to take government out of the hands of the people. The Federalists said that Jefferson was a warmonger, though a coward who had deserted under fire, and an atheist. And rumors were circulated that he had an unnatural fascination with the anatomy of negroes. When the votes were counted, Vice President Adams reported to the Senate that he had won the higher office by just three electoral votes. His rival, Jefferson, who gathered the second-largest number of votes, succeeded him as Vice President.

Adams's narrow electoral margin haunted him during his years as President. The country was divided over its relations with France and Britain and, like Washington before him, Adams was convinced that neutrality was the only answer. In spite of charges that, unlike Washington, he was not the president of all the people, he won his point in the end, but at great expense to his own popularity and political power.

After the battles of Lexington and Concord, Adams led the movement to appoint George Washington commander in chief of the Continental Army.

A memorial to John Adams and his son, John Quincy Adams, was created by an act of Congress to honor the second and sixth Presidents and was erected at their home in Quincy, Massachusetts.

He had never regarded himself as a politician, but he was a man surrounded by them. The infighting took its toll and by the middle of his administration Adams had decided that it was time to think of retirement. When George Washington died in 1799, he wrote to a friend, "I feel myself alone, bereaved of my last brother." Even his own party had deserted him. His fellow Federalist, Alexander Hamilton, wrote, "he does not possess the talents adapted to the administration of government."

Hamilton notwithstanding, the Federalists named Adams their candidate in the 1800 election. He was defeated, but retired to Massachusetts with his head high. He had kept his country out of the European war, made peace with the French and paved the way for his successor to concentrate on the expansion of his country. He was sixty-five years old and eager for the pleasures of his farm and family.

As far as his New England neighbors were concerned, the pleasure was all theirs. They sought his opinion on every subject from the proliferation of grog shops to the British habit of kidnapping their subjects from American ships. He enjoyed the role of elder statesman, and delighted in writing political pamphlets, as well as letters to newspapers. He settled his old differences with Jefferson, who in his own retirement wrote to his predecessor: "we rode through the storm with heart and hand and made a happy port." For his part, Adams, calling his former Vice President and old adversary "my friend," wrote wishing him "an easy journey to heaven, which I wish may be delayed as long as life is agreeable to him."

Adams found his own life more than just agreeable. At the age of seventy-five, he walked at least four miles each day and rode regularly, "but rarely more than ten or fifteen miles." He could say that he had never seen a day without more pleasure than pain. And to add to his pleasure, he had thirteen grandchildren and four great-grandchildren at his knee, "disarranging my writing table."

As a local hero, John Adams was on hand for every public occasion during his years in retirement. And when the town began making plans to celebrate the fiftieth anniversary of the signing of the Declaration of Independence on July 4, 1826, they considered themselves fortunate to have the oldest signer of the document in their midst. But the old man had slowed down by then. He had given up his daily walks in favor of sitting in his window. He was still very much alert, and more weary than ill. He had agreed to appear for the Fourth of July festivities, but said he would limit his participation to delivering a single toast honoring "Independence Forever." As it happened, he never lifted the glass. He spent most of that day in his armchair listening to the music and the salutes outside his window. But before the day was over, John Adams was dead. It was reported that his last words were, "Thomas Jefferson still survives," but Jefferson himself had died just a few hours earlier.

Of all the so-called "founding fathers," Adams probably understood human nature best. His study of history convinced him that the whims of the masses were just as dangerous to a society as the whims of a ruling class. In his later years, as he and Adams debated their philosophies, Jefferson began to temper some of his own populist leanings, and between them they created the political theories that we still celebrate every year on July Fourth as The American Way.

The 3rd President
THOMAS JEFFERSON
(1801-1809)

Before he died, Thomas Jefferson designed the marker for his own grave and insisted on "The following inscription and not a word more: 'Here was buried Thomas Jefferson, Author of the Declaration of Independence, of the Statute of Virginia for religious freedom, & the Father of the University of Virginia.' Because by these, as testimonials that I have lived, I wish most to be remembered."

It wasn't a case of false modesty. A list of Thomas Jefferson's accomplishments could have kept the stone cutters busy for months, and he was proud of every one of them. But he explained that these three were things he had given to the people. All the others, from membership of the Virginia House of Burgesses to the presidency, he said were things the people had given him.

Jefferson was a champion of the common man, but he was probably the most uncommon man America has ever produced.

His father was among the first men to move inland from Tidewater Virginia and he established a huge plantation in the Piedmont. His mother was a descendant of William Randolph, one of the colony's original settlers and founder of an aristocratic dynasty that had become first among the First Families of Virginia. As the eldest of their two sons and six daughters, young Tom was heir to their estate and was educated in a style that matched the responsibility.

He was fourteen when his father died, and when he went to the College of William and Mary three years later he was already well-established a country squire. His family connections, his personal charm and his already well-developed intellect made him an important young man at Williamsburg, where he often dined with the Governor and was invited to join in evening discussions with his professors, who found his eagerness to learn stimulating.

It was during these salons that he developed his fascination with philosophy, with architecture and the law. His future as a planter was relatively secure; he had already written a book on farming and another on gardening, but he decided to quit college after two years to study law. His apprenticeship was slowed by the day-to-day operation of his farm and his research into improving its crop yield. But he was admitted to the bar at the age of twenty-four and a year later was elected to the Virginia House of Burgesses.

Jefferson took his seat in the legislature in the midst of a heated discussion over the British treatment of the Massachusetts colonists. He joined the faction led by Patrick Henry in drafting a protest to Parliament, and when the Royal Governor disbanded the assembly in protest, he followed them to the local tavern, where they set up their own unofficial council to make a protest of their own. After calling for a boycott of British imports, they took their case to the voters and to a man were reelected. There was no doubt about where Thomas Jefferson stood on the issue of colonial rights.

The following year he was instrumental in establishing the first Committee of Correspondence outside New England and, though the Governor once again disbanded the Burgesses for their effrontery, the idea took hold and the colonies were united for the first time with a formal communications network. It was used by the Virginia rebels to issue the first call for a Continental Congress.

Jefferson himself was not a delegate to its first sessions, but he provided Patrick Henry with a document outlining "A Summary View of Rights of British America," which ultimately reached London, prompting Parliament to add his name to a list of twenty men it considered the most dangerous radicals in the colonies. By then he had become a member of Congress and seemed bent on pushing his name to the top of the list by working with John Adams, Benjamin Franklin and his fellow Virginian, Richard Henry Lee, to draft a call to arms against the British.

After fighting actually broke out, Congress dragged its feet on calling for a break with the Mother Country. It was nearly a year later, when the Second Continental Congress convened with its majority sympathetic to the rebels, that it was decided the time had finally come for the Colonies to declare their independence. The committee charged with the job of drafting the document chose Jefferson actually to write it. Using George Mason's Declaration of Rights as his guide, he worked on it for nearly a month, and when it was submitted to Congress for approval, his fellow committee members had hardly changed a word. Congress itself deleted a paragraph or two, including one calling for an end to slavery, but Jefferson's words put the world on notice that a revolution was under way and a new nation, quite unlike anything the world had ever seen, had been born.

When his term in Congress expired, Jefferson was reelected, but he was also elected to serve in the House of Burgesses again and opted to go to Williamsburg rather than Philadelphia. Over the next two years he worked to change completely the code of laws that regulated the colony. The principles he had outlined in his Declaration of Independence were changed into statutes that would become the model for the other new states to follow. He also lobbied to have the state capital moved from Williamsburg to the more central Richmond, and then designed a building for them to meet in. When they met there for the first time, Thomas Jefferson was their Governor.

He wasn't comfortable in the role, and retired to his farm and his beloved Monticello in 1781 after a single term. His wife, Martha, died less than a year later, soon after he completed his book, *Notes on Virginia*, which earned him an international reputation as one of the great thinkers of an era that produced more than its share of them. But as much as he loved the home he created with a "sea view" of his fields, it was empty without Martha, and when he was asked to serve in Congress again, he welcomed the opportunity. It gave him a chance to advance the cause of men like himself who had settled the interior, and he wrote laws to organize the expansion of the west. But his destiny was in an entirely different direction.

In 1784 he was asked to go to Paris to work with his old friends, Benjamin Franklin and John Adams, negotiating trade agreements with the European powers. He accepted with enthusiasm, especially pleased for the opportunity it gave his eleven year-old daughter, Patsy, to get a Continental education.

Among all the words Thomas Jefferson wrote, the Declaration of Indpendence stands out as his greatest monument. Among the first to hear those words was his old friend Benjamin Franklin.

But expanding his own education proved most pleasing of all. Jefferson replaced Franklin as Minister to France less than a year later, but before the old man went home he had introduced his successor to all the intellectual stimulation that Paris had to offer during those years of the glorious Enlightenment. He discussed the ideas of Voltaire and Rousseau with men who were keeping those ideas alive. He was sought-after by Lafayette and other leaders who were planning a revolution. He also found time to tour the Continent, to learn more about farming techniques, to study architecture, to acquire new tastes. On a sojourn to Italy, he carefully copied the recipe for Parmesan cheese, which he introduced to America, and he smuggled out samples of a type of rice he knew would thrive back in Virginia.

He was an eyewitness to the Revolution that began in Paris with the storming of the Bastille in 1789, but he refused to become involved beyond allowing his home to be used as a meeting place for leaders of the Patriot Party developing a plan for their country's future. His own Declaration of Independence served as a model for their Declaration of Rights and he advised Lafayette in preparing it, but his actual words were carefully avoided.

A few months later, Jefferson was on his way back to America after five years abroad. His plan was to return to Paris again, possibly permanently. But as he was crossing the ocean, President Washington made a decision that would change his plans completely. By the time he landed, nearly everyone in the United States knew what Jefferson himself had yet to find out. He had been appointed America's first Secretary of State.

It took some arm-twisting by his friend James Madison and the President himself, but he finally agreed to accept the job. But though he served with distinction, he couldn't avoid confrontations with Alexander Hamilton and the Federalists, and at the end of the first Washington Administration he handed in his resignation. The President would have none of it. He wanted nothing more than retirement himself, he said, but that they both owed it to the country to remain in its service.

In agreeing to stay on, Jefferson left the door open to resubmit his resignation after another year. But a year later, the country was steering a course between France and Britain and trying desperately to stay out of a war in Europe. Jefferson, as Secretary of State, was at the center of the controversy and it was clear that his services were needed more than ever. His heart was on the side of the French, but Ambassador Edmond Charles Genêt managed to defuse his affection. Citizen Genêt arrived with an anti-British propaganda campaign that offended most Americans, and when he armed privateers to attack British coastal shipping from American ports, Washington was forced to ask for his recall. Jefferson, who admired the principles of the French Revolution, and had warmly welcomed the Republic's ambassador, was embarrassed politically. In spite of it, he still couldn't support the other side, and at the end of the year he resigned and went back to Monticello, both to finish building the house employing architectural ideas he had discovered in Europe, and to make his farm more productive.

Thomas Jefferson hated politics, but even in retirement he found them hard to avoid. He felt that Hamilton and the Federalists were taking the country down a path that threatened his own principles, and Washington's support of what he considered a demeaning treaty with Britain made him begin to reconsider his resolve to stay down on the farm. When the parties were drawing up strategies for the 1796 election, he allowed his name to be placed in nomination, along with Aaron Burr, as the Republican candidate for president. It was a nasty campaign, ultimately won by John Adams, and when all the votes were counted, Jefferson, with the second-largest majority, had become Vice President.

He went to Philadelphia determined to be "a servant of the Senate," keeping politics out of the office. But the climate had changed. He noticed that "men who have been intimate all their lives cross the street to avoid meeting," and discovered that if he had any principles at all he had to fight for them in the political arena. It made for a stormy vice presidency, but the gutter fighting only strengthened his resolve to keep up the battle for his ideas of democracy.

The presidential election of 1800 was a classic example of democracy gone mad. Jefferson won the popular vote by a comfortable margin, but when the state electors began casting their ballots, the Federalists made political deals to give the election to John Adams, while the Republicans countered by sacrificing votes for Aaron Burr to help Jefferson. Then the Federalists concocted a scheme to arrange a tie between Burr and Jefferson, which gave the final choice to the House of Representatives, which they controlled. Fortunately for Jefferson, one Congressman refused to go along with the plot, and after an incredible thirty-five ballots, he finally cast the deciding vote in Jefferson's favor. Jefferson himself was philosophical about it. The politicians had made him President by one vote, but he knew that the people themselves had elected him. He had scored a victory for democracy.

As the first president to serve in the new "Federal City" of Washington, D.C., Jefferson was able easily to sweep away some of the imperial trappings of the presidency. He dressed more simply and entertained more modestly, and was more accessible to the people than his predecessors. And he was able to concentrate more on the needs of the people. The war in Europe had settled down, and Napoleon had placed himself in control of France's destiny. He felt that Americans didn't deserve his attention, but when Jefferson sent James Monroe to Paris to negotiate the purchase of New Orleans, the Emperor decided that it was time to sell the whole colony. The price was $16 million. The prize was a territory that doubled the size of the country with a stroke of the pen. No one knew how vast it was until Jefferson commissioned his secretary, Captain Meriwether Lewis, and William Clark to explore it. When they reported back two-and-a-half years later, they had covered more than 9,000 miles, but only saw a small part of the new country.

In spite of Jefferson's accomplishments, the politicians kept up their attacks against him, but when he ran for a second term in 1804, he won the electoral votes of every state except Connecticut and Delaware. With the exception of James Monroe, no other president would score such an overwhelming victory for a hundred and thirty years. It helped to take the wind out of the opposition's sails, and weakened the Federalists almost beyond recovery. But Jefferson's second term was as frustrating as his first and he retired to Monticello at the end of it more eager than ever for the life of a country gentleman.

He lived that life for the next seventeen years, enjoying the respect of his neighbors and corresponding with the men who had shared his dreams. When the British attacked Washington in 1814 and burned the Library of Congress, most of whose books Jefferson had personally selected, he offered to sell his own personal library, probably the most extensive in America, to the Government. And the following year, he worked for the establishment of the University of Virginia, whose campus and buildings at Charlottesville he designed himself. It became his consuming passion for the rest of his life. But he had one more crisis to meet.

Jefferson had never been a rich man, in spite of his land holdings, and he was forced to accept the idea of a lottery to sell off his land to pay his creditors. The lottery was a failure and he died leaving a debt of well over $100,000. But in the end, America was in his debt. And the people whose lives he had touched knew it.

His legacy was the American idea that government isn't an impersonal thing, that it should operate for the benefit of the people rather than their representatives. He was first to point out that all men are created equal, a radical idea at the time, but an idea he spent all his life defending.

Jefferson's neighbor, James Madison, worked closely with him and was one of his earliest and greatest admirers.

The 4th President
JAMES MADISON
(1809-1817)

James Madison was possibly the most fair-minded and even-tempered of all the presidents. But he could get a little testy if anyone called him the "Father of the Constitution," as many did in his lifetime. "You give me credit to which I have no claim," he once protested. "This was not, like the fabled Goddess of Wisdom, the offspring of a single brain." Yet no other brain involved in the framing of the Constitution had accumulated as much insight into the differences between the individual states and the historical experiences of other nations. And few were as eloquent about what should be done to make this nation the beneficiary of the best ideas in the cumulative history of mankind. The debate that resulted in the Constitution lasted non-stop for eighty-six days, and "the Great Little Madison" made important speeches during all but fifteen of them. He later wrote that he was at his front-row seat every single day and "not absent … more than a casual fragment of an hour in any day." And at the end of each day, he transcribed his shorthand notes into the only complete written record of the squabbles and compromises that took place during the secret sessions.

Beneath it all Madison was basically a shy man, and when the Constitutional Convention began its deliberations, he was intimidated by the fact that of the fifty-five delegates who assembled at Philadelphia in 1787, thirty-four were lawyers and he was not. He wasn't a forceful speaker, either, but one of his fellow delegates pointed out that he was a man with a "remarkable sweet temper," and went on to say that, "he is easy and unreserved, and has a most agreeable style of conversation." He was also a man who understood better than almost any of the others that if they didn't succeed, the states would never be united and the war they had fought a decade earlier would have been a waste of time.

Most of the leading political figures of the day, including his mentor, Thomas Jefferson, had never quite gotten used to the idea that it was more important to be an American than a citizen of their home state. Each of the former colonies put its own independence first and the tug of their special interests was pulling the country apart. When the new Constitution was presented to them for their approval, Madison said

that the fact it existed at all was "impossible to consider as less than a miracle." But the real miracle would be to get the individual state conventions to ratify it. James Madison knew it couldn't be done without him, and he began working to produce a second miracle.

He went from Philadelphia to New York, where he was to take his seat in the Continental Congress, but before his bags were packed, other leaders were already talking about making drastic changes to the proposed Constitution. Many were calling for a new convention and some were in favor of scuttling the whole idea. Madison landed in New York running. He joined forces with Alexander Hamilton to begin a series of essays they called the Federalist Papers, published anonymously to give the impression they reflected the opinion of a thoughtful, public-spirited citizen aloof from politics. But the thought behind them was to persuade New Yorkers to push their representatives off the fence and behind the Constitution. Madison himself wrote twenty-nine of the papers, which Jefferson said was "the best commentary on the principles of government which ever was written."

Madison went beyond the written word to rally support for ratification. He personally talked with delegates in uncertain states, including his own Virginia, digging in his heels at suggestions of compromise and quietly persuading them to support the document as it was presented. One by one the states fell into line. While Madison was mending fences in the South, Hamilton kept up the fight for New York's important vote, and when he succeeded the opposition began to crumble. There was still a groundswell to hold a second convention, and Madison had a new fight on his hands. He knew that if the debate raged much longer, it would be put off until the following year and they would be faced with the problem of starting all over again. He finally prevailed and the job of amending the Constitution fell to the first Congress. And in spite of a bitter campaign in Virginia to prevent him from being a part of it, James Madison was on hand in New York when the debate began. The legislature, which appointed Senators in those days, succeeded in denying him an upper house seat, but he was elected to the House of Representatives, which he felt gave him a mandate to look out for the interests of the people. It was appropriate. James Madison was committed to a bill of rights and he believed that such an idea was doomed if it were left to men with political debts to pay.

Madison was a busy Congressman. And while he was earning the admiration of his colleagues during Congressional sessions, he was doing his homework on what the various states had indicated they wanted in an amended Constitution. The list was a long one, but he finally boiled them down to nine points which he felt summed up the basic rights of an American citizen. Congress debated the points and added three of their own before passing them along to the states for approval. When they were finally accepted, two of them, dealing with election and pay scales of Congressmen, had been forgotten. America had a Bill of Rights, and the author of the Constitution had been given the opportunity to improve on his own work.

Madison had a broader view of America than most of his contemporaries because he was one of the few young men of his time to leave his home state to get an education. It was often said that he was a frail youngster, and his father didn't think it would be good for his health to spend time in the Tidewater city of Williamsburg where, besides, the students at William and Mary College were given to drinking and carousing. But there was a better reason. When he was quite young, Madison had developed a passionate opposition to the idea of state-supported churches and chose the College of New Jersey, now called Princeton, because it was notorious for its views on religious freedom. The experience helped cement his own opinion, but it also brought him into contact with young men from the northern colonies, which gave him new ideas that were unheard of back home. He also developed more political awareness and became a founding member of the American Whig Society, a campus club supporting the idea of revolution. His Princeton education, based mainly on the classics, made him well suited to become a minister, as most of his fellow graduates did. But his weak speaking voice made that choice impossible. His voice also prompted him to decide against becoming a lawyer, but, because of his love of public affairs, he studied law to master the art of governing.

After his graduation, he went back to his father's plantation, Montpelier, in the Virginia Piedmont, convinced that his poor health would prevent him from ever using his education in the service of his state or country. He was certain, in fact, that he only had a few more years to live. As it turned out, he lived to the ripe old age of eighty-five. But in spite of his premonition, he kept expanding his education on his own, and when the first Continental Congress convened two years after his graduation, there was no more interested observer than James Madison. It had no sooner adjourned than he formally entered politics as a member of a newly-created county committee. And in 1776, he was sent to Williamsburg

to serve on the historic convention that petitioned Congress to call for complete independence and to establish a bill of rights for all Americans. Young Madison, overshadowed by such greats as George Mason and Patrick Henry, made a name for himself with an unprecedented call for freedom of religion, far stronger than anything the other men had considered.

But the most important thing that happened to James Madison in 1776 was meeting Thomas Jefferson. Their friendship blossomed three years later when Jefferson was Virginia's Governor and Madison a member of his Executive Council. Madison had spent his post-college years building his personal library, but it was nothing compared to the books available to him through his new-found friend. He had also devoted his time to self-education, but Jefferson opened new doors he had never noticed. Individually they were ranked among America's greatest intellects, but together they were formidable. Their close

Madison's Virginia plantation, for a time known as the Old Woman's Home, has been preserved as the home of the last of the Founding Fathers.

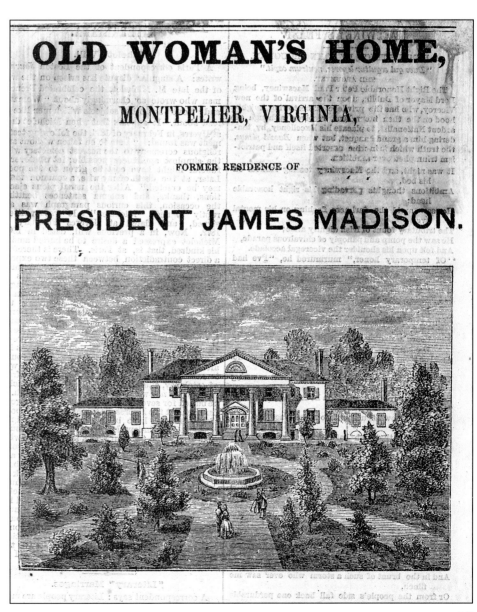

OLD WOMAN'S HOME,

MONTPELIER, VIRGINIA,

FORMER RESIDENCE OF

PRESIDENT JAMES MADISON.

friendship lasted until Jefferson's death fifty years later.

Like Jefferson, Madison spent much of his public career dreaming of eventual retirement to his beloved plantation in the foothills of Virginia's Blue Ridge Mountains. When President Washington's second term ended, his own career as a Congressman came to an end and he began gathering his effects to go back to Montpelier. But the new President, John Adams, knew his retirement would be only temporary. "Madison is to be President," he said. "It is marvellous how political plants grow in the shade."

Jefferson's correspondence and quiet conversations between the two men kept Madison's political interests alive, and he finally agreed to go back to the Virginia legislature in 1799. It gave him a base to work for Jefferson and his Republican Party, while freeing the Vice President himself for a lofty stance above political battles. And when Jefferson became President himself, James Madison was his natural choice for Secretary of State.

It brought the two men together on a day-to-day basis, and because Jefferson was a widower, he relied on Madison's wife, Dolley, to help him with the social obligations of the presidency. Eight years later, when she officially became the First Lady, she was more than ready for the job. And her husband, the new President, was also thoroughly familiar with all the things that were expected of a chief executive.

During the Jefferson Administration, his opponents had begun calling Madison "America's Prime Minister." But in spite of his experience, and the warm backing he was given by the founder of the party, the Republicans selected three different candidates to run against each other in the 1808 presidential election. In spite of the Federalist's hope that their single candidate would probably win by default, Madison won handily.

His first term was marked by British attempts to restore trade with America on its own terms and Napoleon's political moves to keep down an English threat in the Atlantic. Closer to home, settlers in Florida were rebelling against the Spanish. Each of the situations could have resulted in war, but the country had a tiny army, a practically non-existent navy, and no money to improve either one. Madison managed to convince Congress of the dangers the country faced, but he was counting on diplomacy to defuse them.

But as he was preparing himself for the 1812 election, he called on Congress to declare war on Britain, which he said was bent on a policy of world monopoly in commerce. What became known as "Mr. Madison's War" began on June 18 and raged for close to three years. The country was clearly unprepared, and the idea was considered preposterous. In spite of it, Madison was reelected, but probably because of it, he lost all of the northern and coastal states except Vermont. Significantly, the war was taking place near the Canadian border, and it wasn't going at all well. It came home to Madison in 1814, when British troops marched on Washington itself and set fire to public

Dolley Madison, recognized as one of the greatest of the White House hostesses, brought experience to the job. She had already helped Thomas Jefferson by acting as his hostess at social events, since Jefferson was a widower.

buildings, including the capitol and the White House. The Madisons were forced to run for their lives, but not before Dolley scurried about the White House, rescuing historic artifacts. Fortunately, a heavy rainfall diminished the fires and cooled the enthusiasm of looters, and when James and Dolley Madison went back to Washington the following day the damage was less than either of them thought they had a right to expect.

But if the executive mansion was spared, the political fortunes of the chief executive were scorched. Individual states began reinterpreting the Constitution in an effort to keep their tax money at home rather than fueling a war machine, and the Federalists took advantage of the situation by openly calling for Madison's resignation. The tide turned for the President a few months later with Andrew Jackson's stunning victory over the British at New Orleans, ending the war with a flourish. Madison's fortunes turned so completely that his former opponents were beginning to tell each other that the war had brought the country together and had renewed the spirit of the Revolution. More important to many of them, it had pushed aside the country's aversion to a strong military establishment and done away with opposition to taxing the people directly to pay for it.

The country was prosperous during the last years of the Madison Administration. The British and French weren't pushing America around any longer. And the general mood was almost euphoric. The Madisons reflected it in their lavish entertainments, the like of which hadn't been seen since Washington's day, and when they finally retired to Montpelier, the man whose resignation they had called for three years earlier was considered, even by his political enemies, as the most popular president the country had seen, including Washington himself.

In retirement, he became an elder statesman. He was the only survivor of the Constitutional Convention and of the 1776 Virginia Convention. He was the last of the Founding Fathers, and in the opinion of many he was the Founding Father. It was only natural that important leaders from all over the country actively sought his advice. But they had to go to him to get it. He was determined never to leave his Virginia plantation again. He was among old friends like Jefferson, whom he succeeded as Rector of the University of Virginia. And he was busy editing the notes he had made during the Constitution Convention. He considered it his legacy to the country, more than the Constitution itself, and he was hopeful that publication of the documents would also see Dolley through a comfortable old age. And while he was reviewing the past, he had his eye on the country's future. He was worried about what would become of it when men of the soil would no longer be in the majority, but he didn't waste much energy wringing his hands. He was confident that no problem would ever arise that the system he had helped create couldn't solve. And with that in mind, his final advice to Americans was that above all, "the Union of the States be cherished and perpetuated."

The 5th President
JAMES MONROE
(1817-1825)

As the last of the presidents to come from the landed gentry of colonial Virginia, James Monroe's name is usually added to lists of the "Founding Fathers." But although he knew all of them, he was a lad of eighteen when Thomas Jefferson wrote the Declaration of Independence. Monroe was a student at the College of William and Mary at the time, and was one of the first to get rid of his tailor-made clothes in favor of the homespun that was considered the mark of a patriot, and he was one of the first to begin drilling on campus as a member of the Continental Army's version of today's Reserve Officer Training Corps. By the time he joined the army itself, he was enrolled as a lieutenant, and was shipped to New York, where General Washington and his men were on the run from the British after the Battle of Long Island.

Monroe followed the army's retreat and saw his first action against the British at the 1776 Battle of White Plains, after which he took part in Washington's bold crossing of the Delaware River and the successful attack on Trenton. He was given a battlefield promotion to captain, but he was also wounded and left behind. He was out of action for nearly six months, but after rejoining Washington in time for the defense of Philadelphia in 1777, he was promoted to major and made an official aide to Lord Stirling, one of the key American generals. They wintered together at Valley Forge, and in the spring, young James Monroe became Stirling's acting adjutant general during the

The Monroe Doctrine, one of the building blocks of American foreign policy, made European potentates sit up and take notice of the American Government.

19

Battle of Monmouth. When the Continentals fought their way north again, Monroe began longing for the south, and in 1779, he resigned his commission and headed back to Virginia, armed with glowing letters of praise from General Washington, not to mention his aide, Alexander Hamilton, and from Lord Stirling. As a gentleman army officer, Monroe had taken care of all his own expenses, and he needed time to cover his losses. It had also become obvious that the war would eventually spread into Virginia, and he wanted to be there when it did.

The war got there ahead of him, but the Virginia Legislature had no funds to recruit new militia regiments, so his service as an officer wasn't needed. He decided to stay in Williamsburg to be on hand for the next available opening and to use the time to study law. His teacher was no ordinary lawyer. James Monroe had accepted an appointment as aide to Governor Thomas Jefferson.

In 1780, the Governor gave his student the assignment of establishing communications between the government and the Virginia militia, which was faced with a British advance after the fall of Charleston. And when the war finally arrived at their doorstep, Monroe was among the fighting men waiting for them. At the end of 1781, after Lord Cornwallis had surrendered at Yorktown, the former law student wrote to his teacher that he was planning to sail for France. "I have read all the books you mention on the study of law," he wrote, and added that his life had become "sedentary."

But before his ship sailed, Monroe's neighbors gave the twenty-three year old a new lease on life by electing him to the Virginia General Assembly. A year later, at the end of his first term as a state legislator, they sent him to Congress, where he represented his state as one of its youngest members. Like so many men in those postwar years, he considered himself a Virginian rather than an American, but his experiences as a Congressman changed his outlook. He became an important influence in convincing the states to cede their western territories to the Federal Government so they could be open for orderly settlement and the creation of new states. He also became the first Congressman to travel through those territories on a personal tour that made him one of the few real authorities on the possibilities of westward expansion.

He retired after three terms as a Congressman and went home to Virginia with his new bride, the former Elizabeth Kortright, the daughter of a socially-prominent New Yorker. He established a law practice at Fredericksburg, where he was elected to the town council and seemed destined to spend the rest of his days as a big fish in a small pond. But he was still interested in the world beyond. He kept in touch with the world of ideas through correspondence with his former teacher, Thomas Jefferson, and his friend James Madison.

Monroe died in this New York house on the Fourth of July, 1831. The building itself died an ignominious death a generation later.

Eventually, with Jefferson's encouragement, he bought a tract of land at Charlottesville and moved his law practice there. Not long afterward, he bought the plantation next to Jefferson's Monticello and asked his new neighbor to design a "cabin castle" worthy of the site. The move into the Piedmont was symbolic of Monroe's interest in the West. He was pleased to say that he had left the influence of "hard-drinking, fox-hunting imitators of English squires" back in the Tidewater, and had come home to be among "hard-working, hard-thinking men who wrestled with nature as with their consciences." And he was ready to serve them in Congress again. This time he went to Philadelphia as a United States Senator.

Little by little his fascination with politics overshadowed everything else, and he became one of Jefferson's chief lieutenants in establishing the strategies of the new anti-Federalist movement which they called the Republican Party, but eventually came down to us as the Democratic Party. The Federalist philosophy was to preserve the order of things, and its leaders gravitated toward the English system. The Republicans were dedicated to personal liberty, and in the years surrounding the French Revolution, they were unabashed Francophiles. George Washington's government was doggedly determined to steer a neutral course, and men like Monroe were a thorn in his side. Yet when the French Government demanded the recall of the American Ambassador, Gouverneur Morris, President Washington surprised everyone, including James Monroe himself, by sending his fellow Virginian to Paris.

He landed in France to a hero's welcome, and the first reports of French enthusiasm and Monroe's own public statements made Washington wonder if he hadn't made a mistake. In a way he had. Monroe was able to placate the French in the face of an American treaty with Britain, but the opposition at home kept up the attack that the Ambassador had become a bit too Frenchified. And when the French Government finally filed an official protest of the treaty, the attacks intensified on the grounds that Monroe had failed miserably in conveying America's official stand. The President finally admitted his own "uneasiness and dissatisfaction," and James Monroe was on his way home, bitter and angry and with the French farewell ringing in his ears. After a less than diplomatic reference to America's condescension to the suggestions of her former tyrants, the French President told the departing Ambassador of his hope that "the successors of Columbus, Raleigh and Penn, always proud of liberty, will never forget that they owe it to France."

Back home, Monroe found that the American people, at least those of the Federalist persuasion, didn't quite agree that they were in France's debt for their liberties, and he was forced to bear the brunt of their displeasure. He spent the summer of 1797 trying to clear his name in a battle of charges and countercharges with Alexander Hamilton that resulted in a challenge to a duel between the two men. Ironically, Monroe named Aaron Burr as his second,

and instructed the man who would later kill Hamilton in a duel to postpone the encounter for a few weeks until he could vindicate himself over his recall. The affair eventually cooled as the Federalists lost power, the duel with Hamilton was cancelled, and by 1799 James Monroe had become Governor of Virginia. And when his term ended three years later, President Jefferson gave him an opportunity for a new diplomatic post and a new chance to reestablish himself as a champion of westward expansion.

Jefferson, who didn't take a back seat even to Monroe in his admiration of the French, had taken a turn against them when Napoleon made a deal with the Spanish to take control of Florida and the Louisiana territory. He needed a good man for a special mission to Paris, and proposed Monroe's name as a special minister to France. In spite of Monroe's track record in Franco-American affairs, the Senate confirmed the appointment almost without debate. This time James Monroe wasn't going to Paris for a love feast. He was

Of all the presidents, only James Monroe is honored with the name of the capital of a foreign country. The first African republic, Liberia, named its capital Monrovia in 1822 in gratitude for his support.

armed with a tough message to the French that the Americans weren't too pleased with their activities around New Orleans. He was authorized to tell Napoleon that Jefferson was prepared to send troops down the Mississippi, and that his government would ally itself with Britain to prevent the western part of the American continent from developing a French accent. Napoleon had reasons of his own for giving up his claim, and by the time Monroe arrived in France, he had outlined a plan to sell the whole colony to America. The job of working out the details and negotiating a fair price fell to Monroe and the American Minister, Robert Livingston.

Monroe's foreign mission took him to London and to Madrid to make sure that the purchase would be concluded peacefully, and to negotiate with the Spanish for Florida, which had become a rather useless appendage in their empire. In the political battle that followed in Congress, both Jefferson and his Secretary of State, James Madison, were attacked but Monroe was singled out for high praise, the direct opposite of his earlier foreign experience. But it was a Federalist plot to deny Madison the presidency. Monroe was among the first to see through the scheme, and though Congressional leaders tempted him with the possibility that he could become president if he would come home and work for it, he resisted. James Monroe understood politics. He could wait.

During the five years he spent abroad, Monroe had drifted away from the influence of Jefferson and felt that his old friend wanted him out of the way. When the President offered him the governorship of the new Louisiana Territory, saying it was the second most important job in America, he viewed it as an offer of exile. When James Madison passed him over for a cabinet post in the new administration, he was sure his political career was over. But the tide turned when Madison's Secretary of State was forced to resign and the President turned to Monroe as the only possible successor. He accepted the job, but when war broke out with Britain, he tried to resign the post to take command of the army.

Before his resignation was accepted, the British attacked Washington, and he took charge of the city's defenses. When the battle was over, he was in charge of the War Department itself. As the head of two Federal Departments, he finally had an opportunity to show the country what he could do, and passed the test with flying colors. On the one hand he directed the negotiators working for a peace treaty, and on the other he persuaded General Jackson to abandon a mission in Florida to meet the enemy at New Orleans. The results of both moves were spectacular victories for the American cause and for the political fortunes of James Monroe.

Two years later, he was President of the United States. The White House wasn't quite ready to be reoccupied after the burning by the British, and Monroe took advantage of the opportunity to take a Grand Tour of the United States, a fifteen-week trip that took him in a great circle from Washington, D.C., to Portland, Maine, and west to Detroit. The trip broke down the last of the country's prejudices that he was a Southerner cool to the needs of the Northeast. The trip set the pace for eight years of prosperity and growth that was remembered as the "Era of Good Feeling." Florida was added to the Union after twenty-five years of negotiation. He was able to steer the country through the crisis over whether Missouri should become a state free of slavery. And as the West opened up, he gave Federal support for a better transportation network to help it grow. At the same time, he gave close personal attention to foreign affairs, especially the relationship between Spain and her South- and Central-American colonies. It eventually resulted in the Monroe Doctrine, which has been at the bottom of American foreign policy ever since. Stating the belief that America could never be sure of her own freedom in a world where other men were enslaved, he put the European powers on notice that the Western Hemisphere was off-limits to colonization and the introduction of European systems of government. He promised that Americans wouldn't interfere with already-established colonial enterprises, but said that he hoped other world powers would have the good sense to leave the affairs of other countries to themselves.

As his Administration came to an end, Monroe's successor, John Quincy Adams, summed up his incredibly successful shoring up of the Union and the enhancement of America's international image by saying that "he is entitled to say, like Augustus Caesar of his imperial city, that he found her built of brick and left her constructed of marble."

But, like so many other former presidents, he retired with the acclaim of the people but completely without their financial blessings. He was deep in debt, and Congress turned a deaf ear to his pleas for reimbursement for his expenses on his various missions to Europe or even for his army service. Among the congratulatory letters he received on his retirement, one from John Jacob Astor wished him a long life "to witness the prosperity of the country to which you have so generously contributed." Then the letter demanded payment of a loan the Great Man had made to him.

He managed to support himself, and pay off most of his debts, by selling some of his land, and Congress finally agreed to partial payment of his claim. But Monroe never felt he had received the thanks of a grateful nation, and turned again to the service of his home state. He became regent of the University of Virginia, served as a county magistrate and accepted membership of a convention to amend the state constitution.

Like John Adams and Thomas Jefferson before him, the fifth president died on the Fourth of July. His financial difficulties had forced him to sell his plantation and he died at the home of his daughter in New York. His remains were taken home to Virginia twenty-seven years later. He was the last of the old line of Virginia patricians, and the first of them to consider himself an American first and foremost. But his heart never really left Virginia.

The 6th President
JOHN QUINCY ADAMS
(1825-1829)

I f America ever had anything resembling a crown prince, John Quincy Adams was that person. When he was born in 1767, the idea that there would ever be such thing as the United States, or that it would be headed by a president, was still very much up in the air. But his father made up his mind that whatever they decided to call the man in charge, history would record that his name was John Quincy Adams.

The name was one to reckon with. The Adams family had been important members of the Massachusetts colony for a century and a half. The new baby was named for his great-grandfather, John Quincy, who had served in the colony's legislature. His grandfather, the first John Adams, was a town selectman, a deacon of the church, a lieutenant in the militia; and he had married the granddaughter of one of the first surgeons in the colony, making the Adams name important in the society of New England. His father's cousin, Samuel Adams, a founder of the Sons

After leaving the White House, John Quincy Adams became a member of the House of Representatives and served there for nineteen years.

of Liberty, was already working hard to change New England society. And John Adams himself was well on his way to becoming an influential part of it.

But his influence on his eldest son involved something much more than providing footsteps for him to follow. John Adams had no way of knowing that he himself would eventually become president. From the day he became a father, he dreamed a dream for his son's future that many American fathers after him would feel. But dreaming was one of the things that self-respecting New Englanders denied themselves in the 18th century. Latter-day American fathers would spend their time taking their kids to ballgames and working to develop their competitive impulses. But John Adams dedicated himself to guiding his son down the paths of virtue. When he left home to serve in the Continental Congress, he left behind careful instructions for his wife, Abigail, to make sure that their daughter and three sons should "consider every vice as shameful." He gave her the responsibility of developing their ambition to be useful and to feel nothing less than contempt for frivolous activities.

By the time he was ten, John Quincy Adams was well on his way. He had read most of the English classics from Milton to Shakespeare by then, and he understood what he was reading. He admitted in a letter to his father that his mind often drifted to trifles, but said that with his mother's help he was able to keep "steady." His father responded with the suggestion that he spend his time learning to read the Greek classics in their original language. He also added that the boy should make careful observations on the conduct of the war that had come to Boston because one day he may be required to make decisions about war and peace. As the family of a traitor to Britain, Abigail and her children were in mortal danger, but she made the decision to stay in Boston to follow her husband's second order, and their ten-year-old son followed the first. Destiny demanded it.

John Quincy Adams was ten when destiny decreed that his father should go to Paris to represent his country. He made it a point to take the lad with him to give him the advantage of a European education. The mission lasted less than a year, but when his father went back to Europe a second time, young John Quincy was at his side, eventually enrolling in the University of Leyden in the Netherlands, which he left at the age of fourteen to become secretary to the American minister at St. Petersburg, Russia. Three years later, when his father became Ambassador to Great Britain, the whole family was reunited in London, and began giving serious thought to John Quincy's education. It didn't matter that he had seen the major capitols of Europe, had mastered five languages, and conversed with all the leading minds of his day from Thomas Jefferson to William Pitt. In 1785, eighteen year-old John Quincy Adams was enrolled at Harvard University.

After eight years in Europe, he was what they called in those days a "macaroni" – young men who considered Old World ways superior and substituted such things as Italian spaghetti for the meat and potatoes of their less cultured neighbors. He also wore European-style clothes, and even carried a sword in the fashion of the nobility. But few of his fellow students were impressed, and he quickly altered his style, going completely in the opposite direction, and for the rest of his life he was seldom seen in anything but American-made clothes, preferably black. He hadn't gone to Harvard to makes a fashion statement, anyway, and when he graduated fifteen months later, he was second in his class and had been made a charter member of a new society called Phi Beta Kappa.

His next step was to study law, and John Quincy dutifully followed his father's wishes to serve as a clerk under the most prestigious lawyer in Massachusetts. He found the experience boring, and

At a ball given by Mrs. John Quincy Adams at the White House, the President is standing on the left, while future President, Andrew Jackson, is shown as a guest.

when he finally hung out his own shingle in Boston he found the reality of practicing law financially unrewarding. His parents agreed to support him while he struggled to establish himself, which, of course, kept him tightly in their control. He wasn't able to get out from under it until four years later, when the new President, George Washington, appointed him Minister to the Netherlands. His father, the Vice President, had accepted the honor for him, and was clearly more pleased by it than his son. But John Quincy Adams never told his diary that he didn't want to give up the law for public service. The fact is, he never turned back. He stayed in the service of his country for the next fifty-four years. The new job paid more than the old one, too, and more than financial independence, it gave him an opportunity to get five thousand miles, and several weeks by mail, away from his parents.

After a few months in the Hague, he was reassigned to London, where he courted and married Louisa Johnson, the daughter of an American family living abroad. His parents learned of the marriage by reading the newspapers. Three months later, the newlyweds were on the move again: John Quincy Adams had been appointed by his father, the President, to the post of America's Minister to the Prussian Court at Berlin. They wouldn't go home for nearly four more years, and for Louisa it was her first look at America since she was three years old.

The Adams family welcomed her as warmly as was possible for New Englanders, and they were especially pleased that she had brought them a representative of the next generation, ten-week-old George Washington Adams. But Louisa found America a strange place where people seemed to talk through their noses, where church meetings lasted past four in the afternoon, and where people found her fashionable, slender figure a sign of weakness. But she was stronger than she looked and survived their suspicion and reserve. She had other things to think about. Within a year she was undergoing her seventh pregnancy, and on July 4, 1803, gave birth to her second son, John Adams II. Her husband was not at her side. He was on his way to take his seat as United States Senator from Massachusetts, a reward from the state legislature for faithful service.

As a Senator, John Quincy Adams broke with his party and the men who had sent him to Washington to support Thomas Jefferson, whom had known and admired since boyhood. Eventually his New England benefactors found a way to force his retirement. But his public career was far from over. In 1809, on a visit to Washington, he was called to the White House for an audience with the new President, James Monroe. He was given exactly thirty minutes to decided to accept the post of Ambassador to Russia. He accepted in less time, and a month later the young Adams family was on its way to the Court of Alexander.

His experiences in the opulence of 18th-century Berlin hardly prepared him for the splendors he found at St. Petersburg. He wasn't prepared for the massive bureaucracy of the Czar's government, or its elaborate spy system, either. But the endless round of parties at night and the equally endless intrigues by day all contributed to expanding the education of John Quincy Adams.

In 1814 he was sent to Ghent to take part in negotiations with the British to end the war that had been raging in America for two years, and the following spring, after the peace treaty was signed, he was made Minister to Great Britain. His main job was to heal the wounds of war, and over the next two years the Adams family lived a relatively quiet life in a London suburb. It was a life they hoped would never end, but in 1817, duty called again and they were on their way back to Washington. John Quincy Adams had been appointed Secretary of State.

It was a job he took seriously. Over the next seven and a half years almost no detail of the State Department escaped him. He involved himself in everything, from personally changed its filing system to insisting on reading every document, something his predecessors hadn't bothered to do. During Adams's days in Russia, his friend Czar Alexander had three hundred people running his foreign ministry. Adams's own staff consisted of himself and eight clerks. The routine he established left almost no time for the self-education that had always been an important part of his life, but the job was an education in itself, and it was well known by then as a stepping stone to the presidency. John Quincy Adams wanted to be president, but it was important to him that the office sought him rather than the other way around.

Even before the end of James Monroe's first term, Adams began a quiet campaign to replace him. Taking a statesmanlike approach, he let the other contenders fight among themselves while his wife, Louisa, began a round of lobbying important men by socializing with their wives. At the end of his busy days, he joined her in the social whirl, quietly cultivating Congressmen who had it in their power to make or break his candidacy. The campaign went on non-stop for almost six years. It wasn't easy for the dour New Englander whose impressive education had overlooked the social graces. Even in St. Petersburg he had been described as a "bulldog among spaniels."

When the 1824 election finally rolled around, the result was a three-way split of the electoral votes among Adams, Andrew Jackson and former Treasury Secretary William Crawford. The choice fell to the House of Representatives, and the old bulldog came out fighting. He made deals, called in favors and even forced himself to smile a bit. It paid off. On February 9, 1825, the conferees did their duty and elected John Q. Adams president on the first ballot.

He had been preparing for the presidency all his life, and had developed grand ideas for reforming the office. But Congress felt it had done enough by making him president in the first place, and seemed to take delight in rejecting all of his ideas. He had made some important enemies on the road to the White House, and when he called for a stronger Federal Government they brushed him aside with ridicule. After less than a year in office, he realized he could never be elected to a second term, and over the next three years he became more and more withdrawn. The prize he had worked so long for didn't seem worth it after all.

But he tried anyway, running against Andrew Jackson in 1828. It was one of the nastiest campaigns the country has ever seen, before or since. The Jackson supporters charged that Adams had become rich by stealing public funds, and horrified the voters by saying that the President was fond of playing billiards like some young lounge lizard whose life was being destroyed in a cloud of cigar smoke. Whether the charges annoyed or only amused the electorate will never be known. But in the end, Andrew Jackson was swept into office. The Adamses responded with the biggest White House party they had given in their entire four years. Then they went back to Massachusetts, billiard table and all, with their heads held high.

But Washington hadn't seen the last of John Quincy Adams. Back home in Quincy his neighbors talked him into running for Congress, and in 1829 he was swept into the House of Representatives by a vote of 1,817 compared to 373 for his nearest opponent. Ironically, at the age of sixty-four it was the first time in his career that the people had actually elected him to any office. They did it again eight more times. In all, he served in the House for seventeen years.

Adams had made only two public speeches during his years in the White House, and one of them was the obligatory inaugural address. But as a Congressman, his supporters often called him "Old Man Eloquent." Hardly a day went by that he didn't get to his feet to make his feelings known. His Southern colleagues felt his wrath over the issue of slavery. American women, who were beginning to speak out for their rights, found a willing voice in Congressman Adams. And the more he fought, the tougher he got. He fought for five straight years against the so-called "Gag Rule," which had been instituted to prohibit the very mention of slavery in the House of Representatives. Even he was surprised when Congress finally passed his resolution against it. He had worn them down, but he wasn't worn out himself. He spent his seventy-ninth birthday railing against the Mexican War and the annexation of Texas as a slave-holding state. And even at the age of eighty, he was one of the few Congressmen in the history of the institution who was in his seat for every single session.

On February 21, 1848, after shouting a ringing "no!" to the roll-call vote on giving medals to heroic officers of the Mexican War, he slumped over in his chair and fell to the floor. The Government of the United States came to a stop for two days as the old man lay dying. When his body was taken back to Massachusetts, it was accompanied by an honor guard of one Congressman from every state and territory in the Union, including a young representative named Abraham Lincoln. They had called his Congressional service a "second career," but it was just a continuation of the first. John Quincy Adams had been trained from boyhood to serve his country and it was all he knew how to do.

The 7th President
ANDREW JACKSON
(1829-1837)

"He's tough as hickory," they said when General Andy Jackson led 2,500 Tennessee volunteers through the wilderness after their unit was disbanded eight hundred miles from home. The men in charge had suggested that he should encourage his men to enlist in the regular army, and wished him "pleasant weather" for his own trip home. It was obvious they wanted to get rid of him – he never had been an easy man to deal with. But instead, they made a hero of Andrew Jackson, and Old Hickory became one of the most talked-about military men in the United States without firing a shot or organizing a battle.

Jackson was forty-six years old at the time, and had never quite decided what he'd like to be when he grew up. His father died before he was born, and when the Revolutionary War reached the North Carolina backwoods where the Jacksons lived, his two brothers and his mother were killed. When the redcoats passed on, he was left completely alone at

In 1831, Andrew Jackson's Cabinet resigned over the Peggy O'Neill affair and cartoonists had a field day.

the age of fourteen. All he knew for sure was that he hated the English.

The widow Jackson and her sons had lived with her sister's family, and the boys' education wasn't neglected. No one accused Andy of being bookish, but he learned to read and write. He was much more adept at learning the tricks of cockfighting and horse trading, and at fourteen he was a recognized authority on both. He was able to keep body and soul together, at least, gambling on one or the other.When the boy was fifteen, his grandfather died in Ireland and left him the relative fortune of four hundred pounds. He had already inherited a small farm from his mother, and his future couldn't have been brighter. But he had to go to the big city of Charleston to claim his grandfather's money. Before he left for home again, the money was almost gone. There was enough left for a little more schooling, and even though he was regarded as "the most roaring, rollicking, game-cocking, horse-racing, card-playing, mischievous fellow that ever lived," a local lawyer agreed to take Andy under his wing.

His heart wasn't in it, but studying law or preparing for the ministry was expected of ambitious young men in the 1780s. Andy Jackson knew he wasn't cut out to be a man of the cloth, and if he wasn't fired with ambition to be a lawyer, he knew by then that he didn't want to be a farmer. In 1788, he managed an appointment to become the Public Prosecutor in the Western North Carolina Territory, which he himself less then ten years later would rename Tennessee. He was part of the special convention formed to write a constitution for the proposed state at the time, and when Congress reluctantly agreed to confer statehood on the rugged frontier territory, Andy Jackson was elected to go to Philadelphia as its representative.

Except for his hell-raising sojourn in Charleston, it was the first time Jackson ever had a taste of what could be called a sophisticated community. He was thirty years old by then, and had presumably sown his wild oats. But except for the fact that he was one of the few members of Congress who openly opposed President Washington, his record in Philadelphia was dim. He did cultivate some important friends, and acquired a taste for city clothes and fine wines;

but his heart never really left Tennessee and he was happy go back less than two years later when he was appointed judge of the State Superior Court.

When he went to Nashville as a new lawyer in 1788, he waded into what had been a relatively lawless community and quickly saw the advantage of defending property owners' rights against their debtors. More often than not, he collected his fees in land rather than cash, and quickly became one of the Territory's most important landowners himself. But in his early years he preferred to live in a boarding house. Among the reasons was the landlady's youngest daughter, Rachel Robards. Rachel was married, but was, as they say, estranged from her husband. But when her husband accused her of being a bit too starry-eyed with her mother's star boarder, Andy Jackson moved out. He stayed in the neighborhood, though, and when Captain Robards finally left the Territory with a promise never to return, Andy married Rachel. Robards and she had originally been married under the laws of Virginia, which didn't allow divorce, but after leaving her, the Captain had petitioned the Virginia Legislature to allow him to divorce her in Kentucky. The request was granted and Jackson assumed it meant she was free to marry him. But Robards didn't bother to take his petition to Kentucky for two more years. To the people on the frontier, it meant that Andy and Rachel had been living in sin for all that time, and though

they were remarried when they found out about it, the scandal would follow Jackson through the entire thirty years of his marriage. He was single-minded about his love for Rachel, and was always ready with dueling pistols for anyone who even hinted that she was not a virtuous woman.

Jackson had accumulated a nice little nest egg by the time he rose to the Superior Court bench. He owned huge tracts of undeveloped land that had been worth ten cents an acre in Territorial days, but were now worth five dollars an acre in the brand-new State. He was an important man in his own society, and anyone who said otherwise violated the frontier code of honor. Even though Jackson was a lawyer and a judge, he was likely to settle personal affronts with his fists, a horsewhip or a pistol. It enhanced his reputation among his neighbors, but it was a reputation that was used against him time after time later in his life.

Jackson hadn't especially enjoyed the study of law, didn't care much for politics and the life of a judge wasn't his cup of tea, either. In 1804 he retired and became a planter and a storekeeper. It may have been a case of wound-licking. When he heard about the Louisiana Purchase in 1803, Jackson made a trip to Washington to convince President Jefferson that he was a perfect choice to be Governor of the new territory. Jefferson was cordial, but non-committal, and Jackson didn't get the job. The President never explained why. But years later, when Jackson was a hero and President

Four presidents have been the victims of assassinations, but the first ever assassination attempt on a president was made on Andrew Jackson in 1835, when Richard Lawrence decided that the President was depriving him of his right to be King of America. Both his pistols misfired.

Jackson was the first president the people thought of as one of their own and they came out in their thousands to wish him well on his inauguration day.

Monroe thought of rewarding him with an ambassadorship, Jefferson warned him, "He would breed you a quarrel before he had been there a month!"

Jackson spent the next several years making money, earning the respect of other frontier individualists and building the Nashville plantation he called the Hermitage. He bred quite a few quarrels, too, but he celebrated his forty-fifth birthday without any goals beyond the ones he'd already reached.

After Jefferson passed over his request for a governorship, Jackson joined a radical wing of the political party the President had founded. When James Madison moved into the White House, Jackson's was among the strongest voices favoring going to war against the hated British. And when war was declared, Andy Jackson rounded up 2,500 men he assured the War Secretary had "no constitutional scruples," and offered their services. They were sent to Natchez to wait for orders, but before the orders came, Jackson's private war with the officers over him resulted in the dismissal of his troops and General Jackson marched them home at his own expense. It was worth every penny it cost. Andrew Jackson became a local hero.

It was only natural that when an Indian war broke out a few months later, the Tennesseans would look to Jackson as their leader. When he was appointed to head their militia, he was flat on his back recovering from a wound he had received in a duel, but as soon as he could stand, General Jackson was in the field. He proved a brilliant Indian fighter as well as an inspiring leader, and when the short war was over, Jackson was the man of the hour. The U.S. Army, which had sent him home less than a year earlier, welcomed him back into the fold and made him Commander of the South. Andrew Jackson was about to become a national hero.

He made his base at Mobile and enhanced his reputation with a daring raid on Pensacola that would have been one of the more important victories of the war if Jackson hadn't outdone himself three months later at New Orleans. His life-long hatred of the English, coupled with an obsession that American territory should never be invaded, made him a formidable enemy. From the moment he arrived to take charge at New Orleans, his energy level reached a fever pitch and he communicated it to his troops. They attacked before the enemy could, and from the moment the first shot was fired, it was obvious that Jackson's outnumbered force had the upper hand. When the English withdrew, they had lost 2,000 men. Jackson had lost seven.

It was a brilliant personal victory for General Jackson, but except for the boost it gave American morale, the Battle of New Orleans was completely unnecessary. Two weeks before the engagement began, a peace treaty had been signed in Europe and the war was over.

But General Jackson's fighting days were far from over. In 1818 he went to Florida to help free it from the Spanish and to end the Indian menace there. There is no record that his Commander-in-Chief had approved the mission, and Jackson raised his own troops because the Governor was out of town when he allegedly received his marching orders. But by the time he marched into Florida itself, he had popular support at least. Five months later, Jackson had conquered Florida, brought the Indians in line and secured peace on the border. He had violated neutral territory, he had created an international incident by executing two Englishmen who got in his way, and he had fought a war that had never been officially declared. The inevitable Congressional inquiry condemned Jackson, but it was just as inevitable that action was never taken against the man who had captured America's imagination.

He was rewarded instead. He was appointed Governor of Florida. But in spite of his conquest and the subsequent purchase of the Territory, Jackson wasn't the only man in charge. Congress had approved the purchase, but adjourned before it could establish a government. The former Spanish Governor, who hadn't been recalled, was hostile to the new man, who could carry a grudge with the best of them. The result was a mess. And after discussing the pros and cons of the situation for weeks, the Administration solved the problem by offering to make Jackson Ambassador to Mexico. He refused and went back to Tennessee to think about his future.

His future was being discussed in political circles, too. Andrew Jackson was looking very presidential to a group of insiders headed by his friend and neighbor, William Lewis. Their campaign began when they engineered Jackson's election to the U.S. Senate in 1823, and they didn't stop pulling strings and controlling events until their man won his second presidential election six years later. During all that time, Lewis and his cohorts didn't make a move that wasn't calculated to move Jackson closer to the White House, but they were careful enough that not even Jackson himself completely understood what they were doing. He was far from a reluctant candidate, but Old Hickory was very much his own man. He was the people's man, too. He got a majority of the votes in the 1824 election, but lost the presidency to John Quincy Adams in Congress. There was nothing for it but to look for a bigger majority in '28.

Jackson himself, who had been lukewarm to the idea of running in the first place, felt that the decision was a personal affront and began running to replace Adams even before the man took his oath of office. By the time the campaign officially began, well-organized political clubs had sprung up all over the country, partisan newspapers had come into existence and the stage was set for a blitz of character assassination, half-truth and innuendo and out-and-out lies, the like of which hadn't been seen before. A historian wrote fifty years later that "one is driven to wonder whether the American people of that day were such that all this drivel and vulgarity could affect their votes." It obviously could. Jackson won handily and his supporters called him the first "reform" president.

He was a president of the people and they loved him for it. His mentor, Lewis, turned out to be completely selfless. Jackson surrounded himself with cronies who superseded the Cabinet, and made all the important decisions of his Administration. Jackson pleaded with his old friend to become one of them, but Lewis said all he wanted was a job that didn't require any work. He was made a Treasury Auditor. Beyond that, Jackson rewarded his friends and punished his enemies. He had plenty of both and by the time he ran for a second term, he had accumulated some new enemies. He had tacitly voided Indian treaties, and went against decisions of the Supreme Court. He had interpreted the Constitution to suit his own purposes. He had vetoed public works, and had nearly bankrupted the Bank of the United States by dividing public money among state banks. But when he was reelected, he felt the slate had been wiped clean and his second Administration was completely personal. He could be spiteful, petty, prejudiced and blindly emotional, and some historians claim that whatever good he may have done for the country in those years was probably accidental.

Fortunately for Jackson, the country was prosperous and growing richer, possibly in spite of him. But it was also a violent time. There were more brawls, duels, riots and incidents of mob rule than at any other time in American history, and some historians say the people were really following the lead of their President. Blacks were hanged in the South, Catholic priests murdered in New England, and in 1835 the first attempted presidential assassination was directed at Jackson himself.

He brushed it off as a plot by his political enemies. But they had a better weapon. He was denied a third term in 1836. Congressman John Q. Adams said that he was a victim of the wearying "sordid subserviency of his supporters." He retired to the Hermitage still immensely popular with the people who had elected him. When he left Washington, his health had deteriorated, and most of his friends were convinced his days were numbered. But he lived eight more years, long enough to see most of his enemies either defeated at the polls or dead.

Jackson was one of twenty-four presidents to be a lawyer by profession, but though he cut a fine figure in a courtroom, he found the law dull.

The 8th President
MARTIN VAN BUREN
(1837-1841)

When he wrote his autobiography, Martin Van Buren said that his main purpose was to help the young men of the country profit by the example of the "rise and progress of one who, without the aid of powerful family connections, and with but few of the adventitious facilities for the acquisition of political power had been elevated by his countrymen to a succession of official trusts, not exceeded, perhaps, either in number, in dignity or responsibility by any that have ever been been committed to the hands of one man." Modesty was not Mr. Van Buren's long suit. But, like so many public servants, he hid his his real talent behind a lofty word. In this case, the word "adventitious," which he used to indicate that in acquiring political power, he left nothing to chance. It was the key to his style. Martin Van Buren was a master politician.

His assessment of his own political career was not an idle boast. He had served as a county surrogate, a state senator, Attorney General and Governor of New York. He had been appointed to revise his state's constitution, and elected to serve as its United States Senator. He was Secretary of State, Minister to England, Vice President and President of the United States.

It was true that he had no powerful family connections. Even in Kinderhook, New York, where he was born in his father's tavern, the Van Burens were far from the local elite. By the time he was born in 1782, New Englanders had moved into the Hudson Valley and were beginning to change its accent. But in Kinderhook, they still spoke Dutch among themselves, and though most local families had been Americans for as many as six generations, they hadn't seen a need to make a break from the Old Country. Van Buren, whose own family was Dutch on both sides, was pleased to say that "there has not been a single intermarriage with one of different extraction from the time of the arrival of the first emigrant to that of the marriage of my eldest son, embracing a period of over two centuries."

Over those two hundred years, there had been a good deal of intermarriage among local families, and most were related to one another. But Van Buren's father had contrived to make himself something of an outcast by opposing the local preference for the Federalist cause. His neighbors seem to have considered it an eccentricity. They made Abraham Van Buren their town clerk. He had married the widow Van Alen and ended a long bachelorhood as the stepfather of her three children. In time, they had six more of their own and, counting the hired help, seventeen souls were crowded into the living quarters of his tavern. Among them, their third child, Martin, was everybody's favorite. He worked as hard as any kid in town, harder than most, but he never seemed to get dirty. He never stopped smiling, either, and he completely charmed all the important adults in Kinderhook, who probably wondered why their own children couldn't be as neat and sweet as little Martin Van Buren. But if the comparisons offended the town's younger set, they couldn't help admiring him themselves.

His family was too poor to send him to college, but a local lawyer, who was also part-owner of the general store, agreed to guide him into the mysteries of the law in return for working in the store and serving as a clerk in his law office. When he was seventeen Van Buren was appointed to represent his county at a state convention of Thomas Jefferson's new Republican party, and he never looked back. He flexed his new-found political muscle by engineering the nomination and election of his friend John Van Ness to Congress. The Congressman, whose most notable act in Washington was marrying an heiress, rewarded him with a loan that allowed him to go down the river to New York City to learn more about the law and, more importantly, to indulge his love of politics.

It was the best possible place to be, and the timing couldn't have been better. Aaron Burr and DeWitt Clinton were locked in battle like bull elks at rutting time over who would control New York's political machinery. Burr's star was declining at the time, but Van Buren's friends were fiercely loyal to him and encouraged the newcomer to join them. He did, but he was careful not to take a stand. Martin Van Buren couldn't predict the future, but he knew a lot about the past and a great deal about human nature. When he was admitted to the bar in 1803, he quietly left New York without having made a commitment to either side. When the voters took a stand against Burr,

Governor Clinton saw Van Buren as a possible supporter with friends in the opposition camp and made him a surrogate judge. It was a boost for his law practice, and it gave him influence and some power in local circles. It gave him a stronger taste for politics, too, and he used his spare time to boost the political fortunes of the Governor. But DeWitt Clinton was a controversial man, and when he broke with the national party and destroyed his own political career, the men around him were badly burned. Martin Van Buren, who had learned long before to keep his ears open and his mouth shut, survived the storm and went back to his law practice apparently determined to forget politics. It was what he wanted everyone to think. Over the next four years, he carefully avoided giving an opinion on anything political except to defend his own fierce loyalty to the Party itself.

He was elected to the State Senate by a narrow two hundred votes, but the victory was filled with symbolism that wasn't lost on his constituents. It seemed to be a triumph over special interests, opportunism and corruption. Van Buren told the voters that he was dedicated to "correct principles," and the fact that even such a slim majority of them agreed with him amounted to a political breakthrough. At the age of thirty, he had become a major figure in a major state and it gave him a chance to make his way into national politics. But first he had to conquer New York State.

He was completely loyal to Jefferson's Republican Party, and when he realized that Governor Clinton was willing to make deals with Federalists to further his own career, Van Buren broke his ties with the Party's leader and a few years later took control of a faction of New York City's Tammany Hall, known as the Bucktails, who were fanatic on the subject of DeWitt Clinton. Van Buren had been serving as the State Attorney General for four years and was dumped from the job by the Governor in retaliation. But when Clinton lost control of the legislature, the Bucktails gleefully claimed the spoils of victory in the form of about 16,000 patronage jobs.

It gave Van Buren the power and the will to set up a political machine of his own. His Albany Regency gave him the means of extending his influence into every city and hamlet in the State of New York. The Regency swept the state elections in 1823, and once they were in complete control Van Buren went to work to solidify his control over the Party organization. There wasn't a local issue anywhere in the state that didn't concern them. The machine was sensitive to the needs of the people at the most basic levels, and the people responded with loyalty at the polls. And under Van Buren's rule, every arm of the machine was rigidly loyal to the organization.

Van Buren himself had been elected to the United States Senate in 1821, and when he arrived in Washington, he was appalled at the lack of discipline in party ranks, and he appointed himself to fight the system in hopes of changing it. He believed strongly that the Federal Government could draw energy from the states, but what he saw was a President whose own energies were wasted in bickering with Congress. The only way out of the dilemma, as he saw it, was a complete return to the principles of Thomas Jefferson. But right or wrong, the system was the system, and fighting it has always been a discouraging business.

Meanwhile, when Van Buren's back was turned, the Albany Regency outsmarted itself in a move to discredit Clinton and he took control of the state government again. When they roundly defeated Van Buren's presidential choice in 1824, Van Buren said he was "as completely broken down a politician as my bitterest enemies could desire." But he was still a politician and a very good one. The election of John Quincy Adams had split the Republicans, and the confusion provided a perfect opportunity for Van Buren the reformer. But Van Buren the political animal knew that he needed to shore up the Albany Regency as his power base. He worked at it for two more years before he was sure DeWitt Clinton's influence had been broken and felt free to get on with his national career.

He began by hitching his wagon to Andrew Jackson's star. He saw the hero of New Orleans as the perfect agent to rally the people against the Federalist enemy. His efforts in the 1828 election revolved completely around shoring up the Party rather than promoting its candidate. In fact, he was himself running in that same election to become Governor of New York. Both men won, and Martin Van Buren was convinced that the people had spoken out in favor of cooperation between the states and the Federal Government. But a few months later he removed himself from the state level when he accepted Jackson's offer to become Secretary of State.

Van Buren was the first vice president to go on to be elected to the presidency afterwards. It wouldn't happen again for another 152 years.

Van Buren was fiercely proud of his Dutch heritage and spoke Dutch among his neighbors in Kinderhook, New York. But he was actually the first president to be born a citizen of the United States. All of his predecessors had been born before the Articles of Confederation were ratified in 1781.

Van Buren had never been sure of Jackson's own party loyalty. When he got to Washington, he discovered that his suspicions may have been accurate, and rather than concentrating on foreign affairs, he spent most of his first weeks ironing out intra-party squabbles over patronage. And he spent the rest of his career as Secretary of State feuding with Vice President John C. Calhoun, over which of them would eventually succeed Old Hickory and which would control the destiny of the Democratic Party. When Van Buren sailed away to become Minister to Great Britain, it seemed to nearly everyone that he had won both battles. The new assignment took Van Buren out of the public eye as President Jackson took on the Bank of the United States with an eye to destroying it.

But Van Buren wasn't gone long enough. Within six months, his old enemy Calhoun blocked his appointment and Van Buren came home jobless and a complete underdog in the public eye. Calhoun had tried to destroy him, but only succeeded in making a martyr of him, and in the election of 1832 Jackson was swept back into office, and Martin Van Buren, rather than John Calhoun, was the Vice President.

In his second Administration, Jackson was, if anything, less the Party man than he had been in the first. Van Buren found himself torn between loyalty to his President and the position of self-appointed builder of the Democratic Party. He finally compromised with Jackson, agreeing to support him in removing deposits from the Bank of the United States. It went against the principles of the Party, smacked of Presidential tyranny and threatened to widen the gulf with Congress. But Van Buren was willing to risk the fallout in the name of loyalty. More than party loyalty was at stake. He had also made up his mind that he was going to be the next President of the United States.

In 1836, he combined his loyalty to a popular president with his ability to keep the state political machines in line, and won the presidential election by a comfortable margin. Ironically, the man who had dedicated his life to promoting states' rights was perceived as the only "national" candidate in the field. And the man who had championed the rebirth of the Jeffersonian party found it in disarray when he moved into the White House. Worse, because for all his faults, Jackson retired from the lists as popular among the people as he had ever been, and he was a very tough act to follow. Van Buren was perceived as the professional politician he was, and though he was admiringly called a "magician," he was a politician nonetheless, and it was a profession Americans never have learned to respect. He went to his inauguration hoping to be a peacemaker. But there was some unfinished Jackson business that made him wish he had stayed in Kinderhook.

Jackson's schemes to revolutionize the economy eventually came back to haunt Van Buren, and he had no sooner taken his oath of office than banks all over the country began closing their doors. Factories closed, farmers and merchants went bankrupt. The country had never seen such a crisis, and the new Administration's plans for stopping the hemorrhaging were seen as too short-sighted to do any good. The panic went unchecked for more than four months before Congress began debating ways to stop it, and before the debate ended, the interstate combine of political organizations that Van Buren had built was swept away. Worse, the Whigs in New York used the panic issue to defeat the Albany Regency, and with it any hope Van Buren might have had to be elected to a second term. It took him the rest of his term to get a bill passed in Congress that seemed to be the way to put the panic to rest. But by the time he signed it into law, election day was less than four months away.

The Democratic Convention made him their standard-bearer in 1840, but it was his last victory. He lost the election and the organization he had built disappeared. He had hopes of redeeming himself four years later, but the Democrats turned their backs on him. Four years after that, he ran as a third party candidate and the voters turned their backs on him.

After he left Washington, he sailed up the Hudson River in a steamboat to be welcomed back to Kinderhook with ringing church bells and cannon salutes. He rode into town on horseback every day, calling out cheerful greetings to old friends in Dutch. The man who had set out to change his country was pleased to find little was changed in the Hudson River Valley. When he arrived back home, he told his cheering former neighbors that he was a "satisfied and contented man." Except for a few months he spent in an Italian Villa writing his memoirs, he never left home again. He died there in 1862 at the ripe old age of seventy-nine.

The 9th President
WILLIAM HENRY HARRISON (1841)

Americans have a romantic notion that a majority of the early presidents were born in log cabins. Some were, but of the first eight, only Andrew Jackson had the dubious honor, and there is some debate about that. William Henry Harrison, who was one of the perpetrators of the myth of humble birth, was actually born in a sixteen-room Virginia plantation house that stood on land that had been granted to his ancestors by England's King James.

Yet he was elected president with almost nothing else to recommend him other than the claim that he was a farmer from North Bend, Ohio, reduced to a hardscrabble existence in a humble log cabin. It was true that he had been an Ohio farmer, and during his first two years on the frontier he did, indeed, live in a log house. But long before he ran for president, his house had been faced in clapboard and expanded to a comfortable sixteen rooms. He had gone to Ohio from Vincennes, Indiana, where he had lived in a mansion, the first brick structure in town, designed to resemble the family homestead back in Tidewater Virginia.

Why the log cabin? When Harrison was nominated by the Whigs to oppose Martin Van Buren in the 1840 election, a newspaper editorial said that with a nice pension and a barrel of hard cider, "... he'll spend the rest of his days in a log cabin studying moral philosophy." Somebody connected with the campaign, a man who had probably sat at the feet of the great P.T. Barnum, turned the insult around and presented the Whig candidate as a man of the people, at the same time characterizing his opponent as a man who wore corsets and eau de Cologne.

Harrison made very few speeches during the campaign. It was considered bad form among early presidential candidates. But the beat was kept going through log cabin headquarters in every major town, with hoe-downs, rallies and song-fests. The local campaigners provided gallon after gallon of hard cider, which they served in teacups molded in the form of log cabins. They marketed brands of tobacco and whiskey with log cabins on the label. And when they weren't selling humble beginnings, they promoted Harrison's war record, especially his

defense, as Governor of the Indiana Territory, of the settlement at Prophetstown in the famous battle of Tippecanoe. It gave rise to the most enduring campaign slogans in American political history, exhorting voters to cast their ballots for "Tippecanoe and Tyler, too," which also made John Tyler history's most visible vice presidential candidate.

Though Tippecanoe was an important battle, Harrison scored an even more impressive victory at the Battle of The Thames where, as Commander of American forces in the West during the War of 1812, he defeated the British, eliminated the opposition of the Indian Chief Tecumseh, and made the West safe for expansion. But somehow, Tippecanoe had a better ring to it, and Whig campaign literature often referred to Harrison as "Old Tip." The Democrats loved it. It gave them a chance to call him "Old Tip-ler," a not-so-veiled reference to the idea that the presidential hopeful may have a drinking problem. He didn't. But he wasn't born in a log cabin, either.

As it turned out, the voters liked the Whig brand of campaigning better and more people turned out to vote in the 1840 presidential election than any other that had been held up to that point. Nearly double the number of voters participated than had shown up at the polls eight years earlier to re-elect Andrew Jackson, the self-proclaimed president of the people and another hero of the War of 1812.

During the campaign, the Whig hierarchy had issued an order cautioning its lieutenants not to let the candidate make any public statements. It was an insulting piece of writing that said, "... Let the use of pen and ink be wholly forbidden as though he were a mad poet in Bedlam." But after the election, he was the biggest Whig of all. He retired to the room where he had been born in Virginia, put pen and ink to paper and went up to Washington to read it at his inauguration. He had a lot to say. The speech lasted almost two hours on a cold, windy March day, during which time the 68 year-old President stood hatless and coatless. He contracted pneumonia a few days later and exactly a month after becoming President, William Henry Harrison was dead.

The Whigs had chosen to hide his real record as they were scheming to make him president. But it wasn't as though he didn't have one. If he was elected because he had been a war hero and the personification of the common man, William Henry Harrison had been a professional politician most of his life. But as a youthful aristocrat in Virginia, he had originally wanted to be a doctor. He began his training at Richmond and eventually went to Philadelphia where, at the age of seventeen, he suddenly joined the army and was shipped off to Pittsburgh for training. Within a year he had become a sharpshooter and an expert with a tomahawk and scalping knife, and he joined General "Mad Anthony" Wayne's expedition against the Indians with the rank of lieutenant.

The expedition took them into the part of the Northwest Territory now called Ohio, where he found a whole new life, not to mention a wife, the daughter of a local judge who was also one of the Territory's biggest land speculators. Soon after, he was promoted to captain and put in charge of a frontier outpost. But Wayne and his men had done their job too well. The Indians were quiet, and so was the life of a frontier soldier. Harrison resigned his commission and bought a distillery, a potentially profitable enterprise in a place where hard drinking was a way of life. At the same time, he decided on a political career and used his family's influence to become Secretary of the Territory. It was a quick step from there to run for election as its first representative in Congress. He ran against the Governor's son, but won by a vote of eleven to ten. At Philadelphia, he worked hardest for legislation to redefine the boundaries and the government of the Northwest Territory, which extended at the time from Pennsylvania to the Mississippi River. When his bill creating the more geographically manageable Territory of Indiana was signed into law, Harrison was rewarded with its

· *William Henry Harrison made a name for himself fighting Indians on the Indiana frontier, beginning at the battle of Tippecanoe.*

governorship. He was reappointed three times and held the job for the next twelve years. He had control of every appointment, from county clerks and sheriffs to justices of the peace. He was also the final arbiter of disputes, land claims and local laws in an area that included all of the present states of Indiana, Illinois and Wisconsin and big chunks of Michigan and Minnesota.

In his spare time he ran a large farm on the outskirts of Vincennes, the territorial capital. He speculated in real estate, too, and he was pleased to say that he usually spent half of each day hunting and fishing. As the population grew, his leisure time naturally decreased, and just as naturally, his problems with the Indians intensified. William Henry Harrison was also the local Superintendent of Indian Affairs, the Great White Father himself to an estimated hundred thousand Red Men.

But the Indian problem mostly revolved around the White Man. When Harrison arrived on the scene, most of the Indians had been reduced to poverty, their hunting lands had already been carved up by the new farmers in their midst, they were regularly victimized by traders and the laws against selling whiskey to them were as regularly disregarded as automobile parking rules are today. Harrison was single-mindedly dedicated to Thomas Jefferson's ideas of treating the native Americans with dignity and respect, but he was also responsible for enforcing the President's policy of making more and more land available for more and more westward-bound settlers.

The first signs of trouble came in 1806, when the formerly docile Indians began raiding farms and settlements. Harrison blamed it on the British, but he really had himself to blame. He had negotiated with the Indian leaders, but it was well-known on both sides that he carefully selected the leaders he knew would be easy to deal with, and had added more than fifty million acres to the public lands. The Indians weren't paid, of course, but the official Government price to white settlers was two dollars an acre. By 1809 it didn't matter who was to blame. The Indians, led by the Shawnee known as Prophet, were on the warpath. Harrison had made a treaty with the Miami tribe for two and a half million acres of rich farmland along the Wabash River. But Prophet and his brother, Tecumseh, saw it as the last straw and set up a village in the middle of the tract to stop surveyors and any settlers who may be brave enough to move in. In 1811, Harrison moved in on them with a thousand soldiers. They spent most of the fall building fortifications and on November 7, as they were preparing to attack Prophetstown, the Indians attacked first. Harrison's army had them outnumbered by about three to one and easily turned the tide, but not without heavy casualties.

The battle of Tippecanoe didn't change anything. Indian raids continued and Prophet and Tecumseh were still at large. Harrison's political enemies were saying he was a failure as a military man, and he decided to prove them wrong by asking President Madison to declare and all-out war on the Indians.

But Madison had other fish to fry. On June 18, 1812, he declared war on Great Britain.

At the same time, he ignored Harrison's request to rejoin the army as a brigadier general. But Harrison was Governor of a Territory that promised to become one of the battlegrounds, and by late summer he placed himself in command of the Indiana and Kentucky militia units assigned to the regular army. By the following spring, after months of Indian fighting, he had his commission and control of a military district that covered the western frontier from Kentucky to the south and Missouri to the west. He was also asked to invade Canada. But there was a catch. He was forced to give up his governorship.

Harrison proved to be a brilliant commander and one of the genuine heroes of the war. His victory at the Battle of The Thames, which defeated the British Army retreating after Commodore Perry's destruction of the English fleet on Lake Erie, effectively ended Indian involvement in the war and put the British out of action in the Northwest. It also allowed the recapture of Detroit, a dramatic morale-booster in every part of the country.

The war was effectively over in his part of the country, and Harrison resigned from the army to get back to the business of running his farm and managing his land. As a war hero and former governor with a reputation as the warmest host in the West, it was only natural that he would drift back into politics. At the end of 1816, he went back to Congress representing the State of Ohio. He was reelected to a second term and in 1819 went back home to serve as a Senator in the Ohio legislature. After two terms he went back to his farm, but he made a try for the United States Senate in 1822 and for the House of Representatives later the same year. He lost both elections. But he tried again and took a seat in the Senate at the end of 1825.

He was a strong supporter of President John Quincy Adams, and he lobbied hard for the vice presidential spot on the ticket when Adams was preparing to run for a second term. But Harrison wasn't the kind of man Adams could possibly like. He was open, friendly, liked an evening of hard drinking among old friends and, in general, enjoyed life. Mr. Adams, the tight-lipped New Englander, found him "obstinate, self-willed, garrulous and without sense." He put Harrison out of the way by making him Ambassador to Colombia. He arrived at Bogota in time to see President Simon Bolivar declare himself dictator. The Liberator thought, not without good reason, that Americans were meddlers in his country's affairs, and before Harrison was recalled at the beginning of the Jackson Administration, he was accused of having hatched a plot to assassinate several high Colombian officials. He was able to prove that the charges weren't true, and nobody in official Washington believed them anyway, but there were no public posts waiting for him when Harrison arrived back home. He went back to his farm deeply in debt. There was talk of making him Governor of Ohio, and he ran for the Senate again. But it looked for all the world like William Henry Harrison was a man without a future. He even

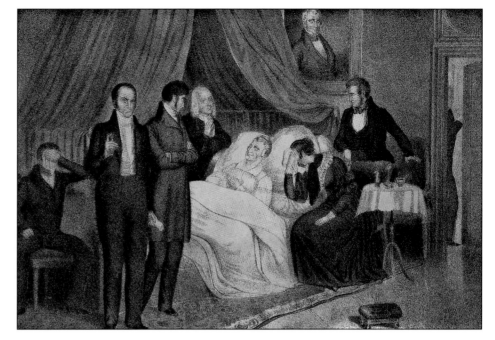

refused to take part in a celebration of the Battle of The Thames.

But if he was gone from the public eye, he wasn't forgotten. At the end of 1834, a Pennsylvania newspaper suggested that he might be the man to beat "King Andrew" Jackson two years later. Harrison was overjoyed. Jackson didn't run for a third term, as it turned out, and his protégé, Martin Van Buren, beat Harrison by a small margin. But as Harrison's supporters told him, "brighter prospects are now before us." The Whigs had four years to get their act together and they didn't waste a minute. As Daniel Webster told them, "I look for severer distresses, for extreme difficulties, for far greater inconveniences." One man's inconvenience is another man's opportunity, and in 1838, opportunity knocked again for William Henry Harrison.

He wasn't without his opponents. Henry Clay wanted to be president and, in addition to the fact that he was probably better-qualified, he had strong support. Another wing of the party was boosting the candidacy of General Winfield Scott, who had recently led a "Patriot Army" to make the Niagara Frontier safe from the Canadians. But Harrison took the nomination after two days of balloting, thanks to the newly-contrived "unit rule" that decreed that all the votes of individual state delegations needed to go to a single candidate.

Then they haggled over the vice presidential candidate, but finally compromised by making it "Tyler, too." But in the end, there was no consensus in the party that their convention had picked the right men. Fortunately, the Democrats were more scornful of Harrison than anyone, and for the next several months they spent more energy attacking Harrison than defending their own candidate. In the end, as far as the Whigs were concerned, it was like being handed the key to the White House. Every knock was a boost for Old Tippecanoe. And Tyler, too.

Harrison was the first president to die in office. His death after just thirty-two days in office also made his the shortest ever Administration.

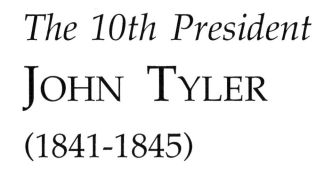

The 10th President
JOHN TYLER
(1841-1845)

The Constitution is quite specific: "In case of the removal of the President from office, or his death ... the powers and duties of said office ... the same shall devolve on the Vice President." But Henry Clay didn't quite see it that way.

When death removed William Henry Harrison from the presidency, Clay saw it as a personal affront. The undisputed leader of the Whigs had extracted a promise from the compromise candidate that he wouldn't run for a second term. Clay himself wanted to become its candidate in 1844. John Tyler, the Vice President, was picked to balance the ticket and squeeze extra votes for the main man. Even though Harrison arrived in Washington as President-elect on his sixty-eighth birthday, it never dawned on anyone that John Tyler would ever succeed him. Tyler represented the South, Harrison was a man of the West. Harrison was in favor of a new charter for the Bank of the United States, Tyler was against it. Tyler was also against distributing the profits of Federal land sales to the individual states, and he was just as determined not to raise tariffs. Harrison was in favor of both. In short, William Henry Harrison was a loyal Whig, John Tyler was not. He had been a Democrat all his life, in fact. He went over to the other side of the political fence in a protest against the Jackson Administration.

Henry Clay had a problem, and its name was John Tyler. At first he orchestrated a war of words, or, more specifically, a single word. When the framers of the Constitution had said that "the same shall devolve on the Vice President," Clay wondered, what did they mean by "same"? Were they referring to the office itself or just the duties of the presidency? Was Tyler required to embrace the policies of his predecessor or was he, God forbid, his own man?

Tyler answered the question even before Harrison was laid to rest. During his first meeting with the Cabinet, which had been selected by his predecessor, the man people were calling "His Accidency" was told that Harrison had intended to make all of his policy decisions through a majority vote of his advisers. But Tyler had some advice for them. "I am the President," he said, "and I shall be held responsible for my Administration." Then he added, "I shall be pleased to avail myself of your counsel and advice.

But I can never consent to being dictated to ... When you think otherwise, your resignations will be accepted."

He first locked horns with Clay over a banking bill. When Clay rammed his ideas through Congress, Tyler vetoed it. But it was not for nothing that Henry Clay was known as "The Great Compromiser." He tinkered with his bill and ran it through Congress again, but the President still wasn't satisfied. He vetoed it again. All of Washington was shocked. There was a near-riot on the floor of the Senate, a mob armed with shotguns stormed the White House, and the new President was burned in effigy across the street. The next day, Clay made it clear that Mr. Tyler was no longer a friend of his or of the Whigs who had given him the power of the presidency in the first place. There was talk of impeachment, but Senator Clay had another plan.

A few days later, Tyler's entire cabinet resigned. The Congressional term was about to expire and it would be six months before new candidates could be confirmed. Faced with the prospect of running the Government without department heads, the reasoning went, "Old Veto" would have no choice but to resign himself. But Tyler was ready for them with a full slate of new Cabinet members, each carefully chosen to be above Congressional rejection.

Henry Clay wasn't dead yet. He had a backup plan. He called a meeting of all the Whig Congressmen to adopt a document informing the American people that President Tyler was no longer allied with the Whig cause and that they no longer considered him one of the boys. The Democrats, meanwhile, thought of him as a traitor for abandoning their cause.

But if he didn't have a political base, John Tyler had political problems. The Clay-led Congress regularly served up bad legislation, and when the President vetoed it, they accused him of treason. The Government came to a virtual standstill until the people had their say in the 1842 Congressional elections and altered the balance of power.

Meanwhile, the President had a trick up his own sleeve. Like modern chief executives faced with problems at home, he decided to rise above them and make a place for himself on the world stage.

Statesmanship has always been considered better than partisanship, and skill at diplomacy the mark of a gentleman. John Tyler was a Virginia gentleman, and he knew that if he were to be elected to his own term of office, which he sincerely wanted to be, he'd better start acting like one. He sent a trade mission to China that came back with a treaty allowing Americans to do business there. But closer to home, he chose an unlikely pair of foreign countries to test his diplomatic skills. He kept the hotheads at bay over the Oregon issue, and where the northwestern border of the United States ought to be. And in the last years of his Administration, John Tyler became single-minded about American relations with the Republic of Texas.

The Republic had been formed after an 1836 revolution against Mexico, and its leaders had applied for annexation into the United States a year later. But the slavery issue kept the request bottled up until 1843, when the Texans withdrew it and began talking with Mexico and England about becoming a completely independent country. Tyler set out to head them off at the pass. He began secret negotiations that produced a treaty, but when it went to the Senate for approval, the Whigs and back-sliding Democrats killed it by a vote of more than two to one. But the Texans had been rebuffed twice before, and now that Sam Houston knew he had an ally in the White House, he decided to try again. His ally had a better plan. Annexation by treaty would require a two-thirds majority vote in the Senate, but a joint resolution initiated by the President could pass with a simple majority in both houses. Tyler came up with one demanding the "reannexation" of Texas, on the grounds that the Lone Star Republic had been a part of the Louisiana Purchase, and asking for U.S. support in the disputes between Texas and Mexico based on the provisions of the Monroe Doctrine. Tyler signed it into law on March 2, 1845, two days before the inauguration of his successor, James Knox Polk. Then he and his wife, Julia, hosted the most lavish party Washington had ever seen.

Even Dolley Madison, the acknowledged queen of Washington party-givers, who was among the guests, had to admit that, no matter what anybody said, John Tyler would not go down in history as a President without a party.

The Tylers were possibly the greatest party-givers in the history of the presidency. But the first of his legendary White House entertainments didn't take place until June 28, 1844. It was the President's own wedding reception. Not long after he became President, Tyler's wife, Letitia, died, and after waiting a respectable length of time, he went to New York to marry Julia Gardiner, the twenty-three-year-old daughter of a socially prominent family. The President himself was fifty-four. Four of his seven surviving children were older than their new stepmother. But Julia captivated all of them, and though Washington society was a bit scandalized, Julia won them over, too. She was the first First Lady to hire a social secretary and he earned every penny of his salary. They had a party at the White House every evening, and during the day "the Presidentess," as they called her, seemed to be everywhere, mostly in Washington's finer shops. She was an irrepressible flirt, which made her a perfect lobbyist for her husband's point of view, but there was never any doubt that she loved John Tyler. Her mother saw fit to tell her, "Let your husband work during business hours … reserve your caressing for private leisure." And her sister scolded, "You spend so much time in kissing, things of more importance are left undone."

John Tyler was informed that he had become President by a messenger who delivered the news of Harrison's death to Tyler's Virginia plantation. It touched off a crisis among politicians, who were unable to agree on what the Constitution meant about transferring the powers of the presidency to the vice president.

Julia traced her American ancestry back to Lion Gardiner, who arrived from England in 1635 and founded a family dynasty that still retains a thirty-three-hundred-acre island off the coast of Long Island that he bought from the Indians four years later. But the Tylers weren't exactly newcomers themselves. The family was established in Tidewater Virginia by Henry Tyler in 1653. It had produced, in John Tyler, Sr., a Governor of Virginia who was also a delegate to the Annapolis Convention, which set the stage for the country's first Constitution. The future President became a member of the Virginia House of Delegates at the age of twenty-one, and began an impressive career as a lawyer at the same time. He was clearly marked for greater things. One of his colleagues, Jefferson Davis, who was marked for greater things himself, said that he was "among the most felicitous orators I have known." Tyler knew how to use words and emotions to sway a jury, and he knew how to use them to equal advantage in the legislature. He joined the local militia as a captain during the War of 1812, but the only action he and his men saw was a comic opera call to arms that sent them all tumbling down a flight of stairs on their way to a battle that turned out to be a false alarm.

Even if Tyler couldn't claim to be a war hero, he was elected to the House of Representatives in 1816, and cut a swath through the Washington social scene. He served as a Congressman for four years, fighting hard against the Federalists and for the preservation of the Constitution. But by 1820, he felt that it was a battle nobody could win and he resigned to support his growing family. But the lure of politics was too strong. Three years later he was back in the House of Delegates, and in two more years he followed in his father's footsteps to become Governor of Virginia.

He became a United States Senator in 1827. At first, he was openly critical of President Adams and scandalized many of his fellow Virginia gentlemen by supporting the candidacy of Andrew Jackson. But he eventually redeemed himself by opposing Jackson, even though it meant that he became a Whig in the process.

By the time his presidency ended, he was no longer a Whig, of course. But he had formed his own party by then. His Democratic-Republicans held their 1844 nominating convention in Baltimore, just down the street from the hall where the Democrats were meeting. They nominated Tyler, but he didn't have any illusions that a third party could help him renew his lease on the White House. What he was really after was support for his views on Texas. Henry Clay was already the Whig candidate, and he had said that the time wasn't yet propitious for bringing Texas under the American wing. The Democrats seemed certain to nominate Martin Van Buren again, and he was cautious about Texas, too. The noise from Tyler's convention drowned out the pro-Van Buren oratory, and Old Kinderhook, who had almost, but not quite, enough votes to carry the nomination, found the Democrats deadlocked after seven ballots. They compromised with James Knox Polk, a staunch Jackson ally, who shared Old Hickory's view that Texas should be welcomed with open arms. John Tyler may have left Baltimore with the prospect of a losing battle. But he had won the war for Texas.

When Polk was inaugurated, the Tylers didn't wait around for the inaugural ball. It didn't promise to be as good as the one they had themselves given to celebrate the Texas victory, and they were anxious to get home again to Sherwood Forest, the Virginia estate the President had bought the same year he married Julia. His aristocratic neighbors along the James River weren't too pleased to have him there. To a man they were Clay-supporting Whigs, and when Tyler had rejected his third-party candidacy to support Polk, who was not only opposing Clay, but was a protégé of the hated Jackson, it was too much for them to bear. But politics come in a lot of different forms. They were curious about their neighbor's rich Yankee wife, and when they met Julia they instantly forgot that they had a grudge against her husband.

The former President busied himself with scientific farming, collecting legal fees that dated back to his early years, and making the plantation house even more attractive. Among the additions he made was a 68-foot ballroom, so he'd have plenty of room to dance the Virginia reel. He and Julia danced there often during the seventeen years they'd have together to share the house with the seven children they had together.

They spent part of each summer at White Sulphur Springs, the posh resort that was a mecca for the Virginia gentry. Julia would have preferred the society of Newport, but her husband hadn't forgotten his political roots, and preferred to water them at the Springs. The local Whigs, who thought they were being funny, had made him county commissioner of roads, but he had the last laugh by using their slaves to do the work. Meanwhile, his influence in Washington, as a man without a party, deteriorated. But he kept his hand in the controversies over abolition of slavery, and his open opposition to the Fugitive Slave Act pushed him back into national politics, though it didn't do his reputation much good in many circles. Nonetheless, he provided a voice for moderation on the slavery issue and people listened to him.

But action often speaks louder than words. When John Brown took the fort at Harper's Ferry in 1850 and called for a revolt of all the slaves in the State of Virginia, John Tyler was shocked almost beyond words and predicted that "disunion must soon come." He began to support proposals he would have considered unthinkable before then.

When the Virginians finally decided to secede from the Union, Tyler was among the men who led them. He wrote the legislation to put Virginia's Militia in the service of the Confederacy, and he served on a commission to set up the Confederate Government. And in 1862 he was elected to the Confederate House of Representatives. It was his last election. Like the man he replaced as President, John Tyler died after a month in office.

The 11th President
JAMES KNOX POLK
(1845-1849)

During the 1844 election campaign, the Whigs' principal theme was "Who is James K. Polk?" On his inauguration day in 1845 official Washington began to find out.

I n these days of television and presidential campaigns that can last as long as eight years, it's hard to imagine a political convention nominating a "dark horse." But James K. Polk was the first of them, and if he was shadowy then, many of the shadows seem to have deepened over time. Yet he was the first President of a coast-to-coast United States. During his Administration, more than 800,000 square miles of territory were added to the country. He was the first President to put the Executive branch in charge of establishing the Federal budget, and to centralize the chief executive's role as the real head of the Government. And though he wasn't a military man, as some of his predecessors had been, he was the first actually to control the Navy and War Departments and establish his successors as the real Commander-in-Chief of the country's armed forces.

When the Democrats nominated him to run for the presidency in 1844, a lot of Americans got the news by

telegraph. Most of them were sure the device had made some sort of mistake. It was a new-fangled machine, after all. But it wasn't as though no one had ever heard of Mr. Polk. He was the Speaker of the House of Representatives and a veteran of seven terms in Congress. He had been Governor of Tennessee, too, and a close associate of Andrew Jackson. But nobody seemed to know exactly who he was. Henry Clay, the Whig candidate, took advantage of the anonymity by making his major campaign slogan, "Who is James K. Polk?" But the more he asked the question, the more people remembered the name. Today, James Knox Polk is remembered as the eleventh President of the United States and Henry Clay forgotten as a three-time also-ran.

When the Democrats assembled in Baltimore to choose their candidate for the 1844 campaign, they expected that they'd spend the week sipping whiskey and puffing cigars and then, about mid-week, cast their ballots for former President Martin Van Buren, who had let it be known that he'd like another shot at the White House. The majority of the delegates were willing to give it to him, but the Democrats had a rule that two-thirds of them had to approve. Van Buren was close, but not close enough. Close by, President Tyler was orchestrating a convention of his own to drum up support for the annexation of Texas, a prospect that didn't thrill Van Buren. But the message got through to the Democrats, and after seven ballots Van Buren not only hadn't put together a two-thirds majority, but other potential candidates were beginning to take votes away from him. He finally agreed to step aside in favor of James Knox Polk, a Southerner and a Jackson man, and a strong supporter of the re-occupation of Oregon and the re-annexation of Texas. It was a string of liabilities as far Van Buren was concerned, but Polk had something in his favor that pleased the old man. Alone among the other hopefuls, James Knox Polk was a Locofoco.

If the name Locofoco sounds like an insult, so it did to nearly everybody but urban Democrats in the mid-19th century. But it was music to the ears of a man like Martin Van Buren of New York. The name, which literally means "self-moving fire," came from the newly-invented friction matches that produced a flame

against a hard surface. The movement itself was started in New York in the 1830s by working class people who felt it ought to be against the law to put debtors in jail and to use prisoners to take work away from men who paid their debts. It was a radical viewpoint back then, and as times got tougher, the Locofocos got tougher, too. They were in favor of labor unions and against monopolies; they thought that prices were too high and wages too low. The Whigs were horrified that anyone could think such things, let alone air their thoughts in polite society. But Martin Van Buren took the radicals to his bosom. He didn't do much for them as President, but he never stopped saying that he believed in everything they stood for. That the prospective candidate believed in their philosophies, too, made his views on domestic matters OK with Old Kinderhook. James Knox Polk was nominated on the ninth ballot.

Polk had come into national politics from Middle Tennessee via the State Legislature, where he was one of only two or three members who had been to college, and where as a young law student he had served as a clerk, earning two dollars a day more than the legislators themselves. Among his colleagues at Murphreesborough, where the lawmakers met in 1823, was Colonel Davy Crockett, the hero of the Western frontier. And when Polk went to Washington to serve in Congress two years later, Davy was right behind him. They didn't agree on every issue, in fact, they soon became political enemies. But as freshman Congressmen, they were four-square on the side of fanning Andrew Jackson's presidential campaign fire.

The Congressional election of 1827 swept in a majority of like-minded Jacksonians, and Polk, who was reelected that year, became a member of the powerful House Foreign Affairs Committee. Not much

Of all the men who have taken the oath as president, Polk did most to shape the modern view of the office's responsibilities.

was happening in the realm of foreign affairs except the problem with Great Britain over the status of the Oregon territory, and though Jackson was in favor of moving in and taking Oregon by force if necessary, Polk sided with John Quincy Adams to let time heal the wounds first. Twenty years later, during his own campaign to become President, he called for stronger action on the Oregon Territory with his campaign slogan, "54-40 or Fight!," which was comparable to a kid drawing a line in the dust and challenging anyone to cross it. In the end he negotiated rather than fought, and settled for the 49th parallel rather than the 54th, as the line between Oregon and Vancouver. But in the early years of Polk's career, his stand on the Oregon question was one of the very few times that he didn't completely agree with the philosophies of Andrew Jackson. It was not for nothing that he was known as "Young Hickory."

When Jackson was first bitten by the presidential bug, he kept in touch with Washington affairs through his protégé, Congressman Sam Houston, who would eventually move on to Texas. But when Houston left Washington to become Governor of Tennessee, Old Hickory turned to James Polk as his political ear in the Capitol. Polk did his work well, but his star reached the stratosphere during the election itself. Old Hickory thought he was entitled to a sweep of Tennessee, but there was a strong pocket of opposition in Polk's home district. The Congressman turned the tide with a little arm-twisting and even a brawl or two, and a grateful Jackson never forgot him for it.

By the middle of the Jackson Administration, Congressman Polk was one of the most influential men on the Hill. His intimacy with the President was only one reason. He had a reputation for fairness that went far beyond politics, and a flair for parliamentary procedure that forced an uncommon efficiency on the House of Representatives.

In the great battle over the Second National Bank, Polk led the Democrats in championing the President's point of view, and when they won the first important round, the Congressman was almost as much a national hero as Jackson himself, who said "Polk deserves not only a golden medal, but the gratitude of the whole country." But neither gold medals nor public gratitude are always enough in the world of politics. During the second four years of Jackson's presidency, the Democrats began to split apart over his banking policies and the rift was strongest back home in Tennessee. Polk was chairman of the powerful House Ways and Means Committee and had hopes of becoming Speaker of the House. But his hopes were dashed when the post went to Congressman John Bell. It was bad enough that Bell was a fellow-Democrat. He was also from Tennessee. For what it was worth, the President wasn't pleased, either. The day after the election, the White House doorkeeper told a visitor that it would be better "to put your fingers into a candle as to go in there, for he is in a miserable bad humor."

James Knox Polk finally became Speaker of the House in 1835, but it turned out to be a thankless job.

He was surrounded by enemies, Whigs as well as Democrats, and he found himself at the center of the controversy between the pro-slavery interests and the abolitionists. Polk was a lightning rod between them and, because the issue hadn't come before Congress before then, he had no precedents to follow. He made up rules as he went along, and more often that not was attacked for his decisions, both on the floor of the House and in the press. Because of their wrangling and in-fighting, Congress adjourned in 1837 having accomplished almost nothing. When Congress reconvened, Polk was elected Speaker again, but his man Jackson was no longer in the White House and the Democratic majority in the House had been reduced. At the end of the session he announced that he was retiring from Congress and he and his wife, Sarah, packed their bags to go back to Tennessee after fourteen years as important members of Washington society.

The Whigs had taken control of Tennessee politics by then, which was bad for local Democrats but good, as it turned out, for Mr. Polk. When he got back to Nashville, he found himself the most important Democrat in the state. He had spent his spare time in Washington rebuilding the state party structure, and when he got home he landed running to put the pieces in place. He was running for Governor.

He won the election by a narrow margin, but Democratic candidates for both houses of the legislature were swept in on his coattails. Tennessee's Congressional delegation was tilted into the Democratic column, too. Democrats everywhere were impressed. Way out west in Michigan, a newspaper said that his campaign was "the best-planned and the most valiantly-fought that ever distinguished a popular election." Back home, his opponents had been saying that Polk didn't really want to be Governor of Tennessee, but was planning to use it as a stepping stone to the Vice Presidential nomination. After his victory, his supporters stopped denying it and their advice to the Governor was "go for it!"

Polk did. And his chances were outstanding until the Whigs nominated William Henry Harrison and John Tyler as their candidates. The Democrats, who were committed to Martin Van Buren as their presidential candidate, felt the need for a running mate who could cancel some of Harrison's appeal in the Northwest. Polk lost the nomination, but he still had a political future. Some of his closest friends had advised against running for the vice presidency in the first place, pointing out that he was still too young for such things. James Knox Polk was forty-four years old.

Besides, he had work to do at home. It was up to him to carry Tennessee for Van Buren, and the Whigs, who had never paid much attention to the common man, announced that they were going to "out-locofoco Van." As it turned out, their hard cider, log cabin campaign did the trick. In spite of Polk's best efforts, the Whigs took Tennessee, and the Governor was faced with the biggest challenge of his career. He rolled up his sleeves and set out to rebuild his party a second time. He was only partly successful. When he ran for governor again, he lost the election. But he had cut the Whig majority to a quarter of what it had been, and he was proud to point out to his fellow Democrats that though they may have been cast down, they were far from destroyed.

He retired to his plantation and went back to his law practice, but he kept his eye on the political scene and worked for the Democratic candidates and served as a one-man "truth squad," comparing Whig promises with Whig accomplishments. And finally, in 1844, he was handed the opportunity to produce some accomplishments of his own.

When he got to the White House, it was clear he had some ideas of his own about what it meant to be President of the Unites States. He was determined to be the chief executive in every sense of both words. When one of his Cabinet members attempted to control some of his appointments, he said that he couldn't "yield up the Government into his hands and suffer him to be, in effect, President." But he was also a strong believer in the separation of powers. He refused to intercede in the deliberations of the Federal courts, which had been customary in earlier administrations. And when the Supreme Court affirmed the right of the Mormons to live in any state they pleased, Polk brushed aside a public call for him to do something about it by pointing out that the President had "no power to prevent or check the emigration."

But of all his accomplishments as President, James Knox Polk probably deserves the most credit for determining what has become the modern view of the office itself. The ten men who preceded him had each contributed to the concept of the presidency, but none of them had Polk's vision of the future combined with a sense of history. In his last message to Congress on the State of the Union, he described the role of the president in terms we take for granted today. But the men who heard his words considered them an almost revolutionary pronouncement:

"The people, by the Constitution, have commanded the President, as much as they have commanded the Legislative branch of the Government, to execute their will." he told the legislators. "If it has been said that the Representatives in the popular branch of Congress are chosen directly by the people, it is answered, the people elect the President. If both Houses represent the States and the people, so does the President. The President represents in the Executive department the whole people of the United States as each member of the Legislative department represents portions of them."

They knew he believed what he said. During his Administration, James Polk had led them to accept his programs without their customary inclination to put politics ahead of what needed to be done. But if he was able to control Congress and restrain his Cabinet, and in the process accomplish more for the country than most other presidents of any era, Polk lost control of his party during his presidential years and lost the chance for nomination to a second term in 1848. The divided Democrats lost the election.

The 12th President
ZACHARY TAYLOR
(1849-1850)

By the time Congress declared war on Mexico in 1846, General Zachary Taylor had already won two battles against the Mexican army and there was a strong groundswell all over the United States to change his rank from General to Commander-in-Chief.

But in spite of all the mass meetings and high-sounding editorializing, nobody thought of asking Taylor if he wanted to be president. When someone finally did, the General thanked him kindly and replied that his duty called him to finish the job at hand. A few weeks later, he told a friend, "in no case can I permit myself to be the candidate of any party or yield myself to party schemes." But neither statement put out the fire. When a political rally actually nominated him, it was pointed out that it required an official national party convention to do that. But the man who led the movement shouted, "Conventions be damned! I tell you General Taylor is going to be elected by spontaneous combustion!"

No one had given much thought to Taylor's politics, either. He hadn't seemed too interested in any party, and had never voted in any election. Although he was apolitical, he was also a strong admirer of the perennial presidential candidate, Henry Clay, and even if he did want to be President himself, he wouldn't have dreamed of standing in the Senator's way. But little by little the spontaneous combustion moved the General and, citing a soldier's sense of duty, he eventually allowed that if nominated he would run but only "without promises, pledges or bargains." And he finally confessed to being a Whig, though he said it was more a matter of his admiration for Clay than for party principles.

At about the same time he also said that he thought that the Constitutional role of the president was a "coordinator" of the Government rather than a law-making executive, and pledged never to use the power of the veto except to protect Congress from unreasonable demands of the people. Congressmen laboring under the yoke of a strong president with direct opposite views were overjoyed. Abraham Lincoln told his House colleagues: "The people say to General Taylor: 'If you are elected, shall we have a national bank?' He answers, 'Your will, gentlemen,

not mine.' 'What about the tariff?' 'Say yourselves.' 'Shall our rivers and harbors be improved?' 'Just as you please. If you desire a bank, an alteration in the tariff, internal improvements, any or all, I will not hinder you. If you do not desire them, I will not attempt to force them on you.'" General Taylor was going to be the answer to a Congressman's dream.

When the Whigs met in Philadelphia to pick their standard-bearer for the 1848 election, Taylor was in the lead from the first ballot, and after the fourth he was nominated by acclamation. But the General himself wasn't there to hear the cheering. He was at home in far-off Baton Rouge. The Convention appointed a committee to notify the candidate, but several weeks passed without a word from the General. They had written him a letter, but mailed it with postage due. When it arrived, Taylor didn't bother to pick it up at the post office because he had gotten letters from political parties before, and he was sure the extra postage on this one would be just the first cost. The committee posted a second letter and, just to make sure the message didn't go astray, they also sent him a telegram, which was delivered by steamboat from Memphis.

Taylor accepted the honor with regrets that Clay had lost it. But Clay was less gracious. The Big Whig refused to support his party's choice, claiming that Taylor had shown too much "instability and vacillation." Others in the party agreed. The New York delegation called a meeting to repudiate him, and Congressional candidate Horace Greeley said "I cannot pretend to support him." To make matters worse, there were four other candidates in the race. The Democrats had nominated General Lewis Cass, a hero of the War of 1812, former President Martin Van Buren was the candidate of the Free Soil Party, the Liberty Party candidate called for immediate emancipation of all slaves, and the American Party, until recently known as the "Know-Nothings," called for the exclusion from politics of anyone who hadn't been born here.

But for all that, it was the quietest presidential election campaign anyone could remember, and when the votes were counted General Taylor had become President Taylor. He should have been a happy man, but he didn't seem to be. His wife, Peggy, had moved with him from one army post to another during their marriage, and wasn't looking forward to moving again from their Baton Rouge retirement home with its sweeping lawn and river view. He told his neighbors that "Had I consulted my own wishes, I should much have preferred to remain among you."

His journey to Washington produced an outpouring of popular affection that hadn't been seen since George Washington himself went to New York to become President. But this President-elect was more embarrassed than pleased. Zachary Taylor hated attention. When he retired, he was one of America's most popular war heroes, and he said that he bought the four-room, rose-covered cottage at Baton Rouge because it was off the beaten path and out of reach of his adoring public. His neighbors respected his wishes to be treated like the ordinary man he sincerely believed himself to be. Even when he was on active duty, Taylor almost never wore a uniform, even though he was in command of thousands of men. Time after time, young officers treated him like the simple farmer he appeared to be, only to discover to their chagrin that they had been lording it over the Old Man himself.

Before he left for Washington, Taylor's wife insisted that he get a new suit. He grudgingly followed her orders and bought two, carefully ordering them a size too large, "for comfort," he said. While he was at it, he bought a tall silk hat in hopes, probably, of looking more "presidential." But he insisted on wearing it pushed to the back of his head, and when he walked the streets of Washington, which was one of the great pleasures of his life there, he was more often mistaken for a rube on his first visit to the big city than the President of the United States.

His first act as President was to name a Cabinet, which, predictably, was composed almost entirely of Whig party hacks. His second was to turn them loose to dispense patronage on their own. Before spring, thousands of Democrats were fired from appointive jobs and replaced by Whigs. Taylor himself stayed blissfully above the battle, but he took the heat when it was turned on him. When one of the men who had become unemployed complained to the White House that the Administration was firing only Democrats, the President said, "Who else could I turn out? All the office-holders were of your party."

He was true to his promise of letting Congress make its own decisions. But it was a time when the decision-making process could tax the wisdom of Solomon. The country had grown by leaps and bounds, and the balance of power between slave and free states was behaving like a see-saw. When the Taylor Administration began, they were equally balanced at fifteen to fifteen. But California was about to be admitted to the Union as a free state, and the pro-slavery interests were looking for a balance. Taylor himself was a slave-owning southerner, and most were sure they knew where he stood. But the presidency can change a man's outlook. Zachary Taylor represented all the people and he knew it. His job was to preserve the Union and he knew that, too. He surprised everyone by taking a stand.

He proposed that California be admitted on the side of the free states, which its citizens wanted to do, and that other territories applying for statehood after that should be allowed to make up their own minds as well. Then, after announcing that his own mind was made up, he set up military governments in California and New Mexico while they themselves decided their own destiny. The man who everybody had thought

Twelve of the presidents also served as generals, and some, like Zachary Taylor, who earned the name "Old Rough and Ready" as a major general in the Mexican War, were more comfortable on the battlefield than in the White House.

would make politics as usual easier than ever, had taken politics out of the most explosive issue of the day. The politicians made a counterproposal, but Taylor stood his ground, quietly telling them that what they were trying to do was wreck the Union. He called that treason and hinted that he was ready to treat traitors with the punishment they deserved. Taylor won the first round, but the compromise that Congress proposed eventually destroyed the Whig party. Worse, from Taylor's personal point of view, it destroyed his personal ties with life-long friends in the South. But he had taken a stand, defused a crisis and, at least temporarily, had separated slavery from politics.

His problems didn't end there, of course. When a border war was threatened between the Texas and New Mexico Territories, he ordered reinforcements sent in to prevent it. And when his War Secretary refused to sign the order he signed it himself. When he was told the army's officers wouldn't lead a fight against fellow-Southerners, he thundered that he'd lead the troops personally if they didn't. With that, Southern Congressmen suggested that Taylor should be impeached. Both threats were idle ones, but once again the President the politicians thought they would be able to manipulate showed them that he was very much his own man.

But the man's days were numbered. On the Fourth of July, 1850, he appeared on the Mall to officiate at ceremonies on the Washington Monument construction site. It was a hot day, even by Washington standards, and the hero of the Mexican War said he had never been so troubled by the temperature. But there were speeches to listen to, and one he had to make himself, and the President kept relatively cool drinking pitcher after pitcher of ice water. He also seemed determined to eat everything in sight, and when he got back to the White House that evening, he began complaining of indigestion. His doctor tried all the standard remedies, but nothing seemed to help. Two days later, his condition was even worse, and it soon became apparent that he wasn't going to survive. The doctors didn't seem to understand that Zachary Taylor had probably had a heart attack. On the evening of July 9, Vice President Millard Fillmore became the thirteenth President of the United States.

Congressman Abraham Lincoln, who delivered the eulogy at Taylor's military funeral, said, prophetically, "The presidency, even to the most experienced politicians, is no bed of roses; and General Taylor, like others, found thorns within it." He pointed out that "It did not happen to General Taylor, once in his life, to fight a battle on equal terms, or on terms advantageous to himself, and yet he was never beaten and he never retreated."

The General's life had begun sixty-six years earlier in Virginia. But even before he was born, his father had gone to the Kentucky frontier, where the boy was raised. When the country went to war against Britain in 1812, he became an infantry lieutenant, assigned to General William Henry Harrison's force of Indian-fighters, and became, along with the General, a local hero in the Northwest Territory. By the time the war was over, he had been promoted to major and had made a decision to make the military his career. In 1837, he was promoted to the rank of brigadier general, and earned the name "Old Rough and Ready," after a brilliant rout of the Indians during the battle of Lake Okeechobee in the Florida war. Less than ten years later, he was in command of all the American forces in the Southwest, an army that that would soon fight a war against Mexico.

The fighting began when Mexican forces attacked one of Taylor's units on the Rio Grande across from Matamoros. Though hopelessly outnumbered and cut off from his supply lines, Taylor ordered his green troops to counterattack. When they pushed the enemy back into their own territory, Taylor followed them. Eventually, his force of a handful more than five thousand came face-to-face with the main Mexican force of twenty thousand led by the legendary general, Santa Anna. The battle raged for two days before the enemy was thrown back into the desert. But the Americans themselves were deep in enemy territory. They had no communications with the rest of their army, and when no word was heard from them for several weeks, it was assumed that Taylor and his men had lost the battle and were either dead or, worse, prisoners of Santa Anna. It wasn't the case, and when Zachary Taylor appeared on the horizon one day at the head of his troops, the national mood changed from despair to euphoria. It was Taylor's last battle, but he had scored a dramatic victory that no American of his time ever forgot.

He had the distinction of being the first president who was financially comfortable. When he was called out of retirement to run for office, his career as a farmer had made him relatively prosperous. He had owned three different plantations in Louisiana before settling down in his Baton Rouge cottage, and was worth an estimated $200,000. At a time when slavery was such a burning issue, less than two-thousand planters owned more than one hundred slaves each, and General Taylor was one of them. But possibly the best reason why he had such a tidy nest-egg was that Zachary Taylor had never bothered to get used to life's luxuries. Even as commander of the army, he lived in a tent with almost no more amenities than his men enjoyed. He was well-known for patching his own clothes and wearing them until they couldn't be patched any longer. In fact, P.T. Barnum offered to buy a pair of his trousers to display in his American Museum, and Taylor was pleased to take his money. Chances are the General didn't use the money to buy a new pair. As one of his soldiers said at the time, "he always wears an old cap, dusty green coat, a frightful pair of trousers, and on horseback he looks like a toad."

It was all part of his charm, and even if he hadn't been a war hero, Zachary Taylor probably could have had a grand career in politics. He was a natural leader with a broad appeal. But in this age of televised charisma, it isn't easy to imagine a leader getting any place at all working hard to look like a toad.

The 13th President

MILLARD FILLMORE

(1850-1853)

A few weeks after he moved into the White House, Millard Fillmore's father came to pay a visit. "Nice place you have here," he said, "but not as nice as your place in Buffalo."

The old man was exaggerating, but his son did have one of the finest mansions in New York State's westernmost city, and had been one of the richest men in an extremely prosperous town. One of his neighbors said that the Fillmore house was "like its proprietor, plain and unostentatious ... exceedingly neat and handsome." But for all that, Millard Fillmore was the first American President who could honestly say that he had started life with nothing.

The Fillmore family had gone to upstate New York from Vermont in 1800, the year the future President, the first of their nine children, was born. They lived in a small cabin four miles from their nearest neighbor, making the best of farming land that could never produce enough to feed the family. The elder Fillmore did the best he could and the experience made him determined that his oldest son should never be a farmer himself. But he needed the boy's help, and though young Millard was enrolled in a local school, his education was limited to the three winter months.

By the time he was fourteen, his younger brothers were able to do their share of the farm work, and he was apprenticed to a local tailor so he could learn a trade. When he wasn't hefting bolts of cloth and handling a needle, he continued his education on his own by reading everything he could get his hands on. His apprenticeship ended within a few months, and he went back to the farm. Young Fillmore didn't want to be a tailor. But he didn't want to be a farmer, either, and he continued his self-education. Two years later he became an apprentice tailor again, but this time he stayed closer to home so he could divide his time between helping his father and learning a trade. Over the next few years he learned more than just the clothing business, becoming an expert bookkeeper among other things. But he still didn't want to be a tailor.

When he was eighteen, though still bound to his apprenticeship, and though he himself had spent very little time in school, he decided to open one. As a schoolmaster, he could earn ten dollars a month and

get free room and board. There were no schools for miles around, and his enterprise was a huge success. It also gave him status in the community that neither a tailor nor a farmer could hope for. And it gave him an opportunity to expand his own education.

Among the local people who were impressed was a lawyer who suggested to young Fillmore the idea of studying with him. The tailor thought he was making a foolish mistake, but finally agreed to let the young man buy out his apprenticeship and Millard Fillmore was on his way. He continued teaching to keep from going into debt, but his heart was in the law office and two years later he moved on to Buffalo and bigger things.

Buffalo in 1822 was clearly a city with a bright future, and the new kid in town hitched his star to it. He went to work for the city's most successful lawyer and took advantage of the availability of books he had never dreamed existed. He was admitted to the bar the following year, and then made one of the most interesting decisions any lawyer has ever reached. The Buffalo courts were busy and lawyers from every part of the state were relocating there to take advantage of opportunities for steady fees. But even though young Fillmore had a chance to work in an established firm with a head start on the newcomers, he was intimidated by the array of legal talent around him and decided to move a few miles inland to the village of Aurora. His practice there thrived over the next seven years, although at first he had to take a job as a teacher to support himself and his new bride, the former Abigail Powers, daughter of the local minister. Eventually his reputation spread back to Buffalo, where the attorneys were much more intimidated by him than he had been by them.

His reputation spread throughout the state after 1829, when he was admitted as a counsellor in the State Supreme Court. It was time to move back to Buffalo, and this time he arrived with a name to be reckoned with. It wasn't long before he was elected to the State Legislature. And from that he became the natural leader of the Whigs in Western New York. As a community leader who worked doggedly to improve his new home town, his neighbors overwhelmingly elected him to Congress in 1832, and while he was in

Washington he improved his status as a lawyer by securing permission to practice before the Supreme Court.

After refusing to run for a second term, he was eventually reelected to Congress for three terms and became Chairman of the powerful House Ways and Means Committee, but he preferred life in Buffalo and he ultimately went back home to his law practice. But he stayed active in politics, and became a strong voice against the Democrats, who he said were running the country for the benefit of the South.

In 1847 he became State Comptroller and his reputation increased. Unlike almost every other politician in the United States, he was a man with hardly an enemy in the world. Men in both parties admired him and the people he represented worshipped him. Still, no one was more surprised than Millard Fillmore when the Whigs nominated him for Vice President in 1848.

He was picked to balance the ticket. The presidential candidate, Zachary Taylor, was a popular war hero, but he was a slave-owning Southerner. But Fillmore was also the right choice because he had managed to work his way up through the Byzantine maze of New York politics and remain a highly-regarded public servant, a rare accomplishment anywhere in the country in those days.

Although Fillmore had few enemies, chief among them was New York Senator William H. Seward, a close friend of the new President, who managed to convince Taylor that he, and not Fillmore, should decide on patronage within New York State. It left the Vice President politically toothless. Even his own law partner was denied a job in the new Administration. And if he hadn't had any enemies before, he began building a portfolio of them back home, where New Yorkers of the Whig persuasion blamed him when they were passed over. It wasn't easy for the Vice President to explain why the number two Whig had no influence.

But in spite of his humiliation, Fillmore stuck with the President, telling himself that Taylor himself had very little to say about dispensing political favors. But the President added insult to injury by making it a point not to consult Fillmore on any of his decisions. As Vice President, he was President of the Senate, but the upper house was a lion's den filled with strong egos, and Fillmore's opinion wasn't required there, either. But he never missed a session, and when he became President himself, he had some opinions that mattered. He knew what made the Senate tick, and he knew how its members thought.

When Taylor died in 1850, Fillmore had already decided that he wouldn't stay in Washington after his unexpired term was over. But there was work to be done in the meantime, and he began by steering Congress through the labyrinth of the compromise they had devised to confound Taylor over the admission of new Territories. He supported Taylor's order to defend the rights of New Mexico by force if necessary. In general, he was prepared to follow all of his predecessor's policies. In the process, he was accused of leaning in the direction of the South, but Mr. Fillmore had been sent to Washington in the first place to give a Northern balance to the Taylor Administration. In reality, his goal was to do what he could to prevent a civil war, which by then seemed a foregone conclusion.

And if he was dedicated to the principles of his predecessors, he was his own man, and in his three years in the White House he disproved the popular image that had been revealed to him by a carriage salesman in his first weeks there. When he decided to buy a new carriage to match his new station in life, the best on the lot was a used one. When he asked the salesman if it would be proper for the President of the United States to ride around Washington in a second-hand carriage, the answer was, "Mr. Fillmore, you are a second-hand President."

But he was not an unpopular President, even though he was the only one until that time, except Jackson, to receive death threats. And no less a person than the great Daniel Webster said he was "a good-tempered, cautious, intelligent man with whom it is a pleasure to transact business. He is very diligent, and what he does not know, he quickly learns." But what Millard Fillmore had learned in Washington was that he didn't want to be President for another four years.

The Whigs, on the other hand, weren't prepared to take his announcement lying down. And when they met in 1852 to pick their candidate, Fillmore's old enemy, Seward, was supporting General Winfield Scott, an avowed enemy of the Southern interests, and others were leaning toward Daniel Webster, who was visibly old and tired by then. After forty-six ballots, the majority, but not the required two-thirds, were still voting for Fillmore, even though he had written a strong letter asking them to "not suffer my name to be dragged into a contest for a nomination which I have never sought and do not now seek." He headed them off by openly supporting Webster, but in the end, after fifty-three ballots, the nomination went to Scott. He lost the election, and the Whig Party never fielded a candidate again.

The Fillmores were pleased to see a new President inaugurated in 1853. But Abigail Fillmore, the former President's wife of twenty-seven years, contracted pneumonia during the ceremonies, and like William Henry Harrison a few years before, died less than a month later. Fillmore sadly went back to Buffalo, where almost nothing was heard from him for more than a year.

Meanwhile, Congressman Stephen Douglas had issued a call for the repeal of the Missouri Compromise in favor of allowing Kansas and Nebraska to come into the Union on their own terms over the issue of slavery. People opposed to slavery saw it as an attempt to expand the interests of the South and used it as a platform to create the new Republican Party. Whigs and Northern Democrats alike flocked to the cause. But Fillmore was still a Whig, and he knew that if his Party were to survive at all it needed a new point of view. At the same time, the Native American Party was also being formed, and Millard Fillmore leaped to its ramparts. The Native Americans were jingoists pure and simple. They didn't like Catholics and they didn't like immigrants, and they felt that the country couldn't survive unless the government was firmly in the control of the old all-American families. Fillmore agreed that immigrants were most likely to cast their lot with the Democrats, and with old-line Whigs deserting to the Republicans, it probably seemed to him that the so-called "No-Nothings" represented a kind of Great White Hope. Ironically, the day after he announced he would accept their nomination to run for President, he sailed for a year-long visit to Europe.

In spite of his announced intentions to be the standard-bearer of the anti-Catholics, he had an audience with the Pope, and both men were highly impressed with each other. England's Queen Victoria was enchanted with him, saying he was the handsomest man she had ever seen. He charmed everyone he met, in fact, and they left their impression on him. When he arrived back in New York, he had already been selected as the Native American candidate, but he made it clear that he didn't subscribe to all of the Party's principles. He adroitly skirted the issue of stopping immigration by appealing to its America-First instincts. He said he had seen the terrible conditions people were forced to live with in Europe and thought it would be un-Christian to deny them an opportunity to find asylum in America. He refused to pay even lip service to the Know-Nothing anti-Catholic stand. But the voters, who may have been impressed with Fillmore himself, were wary of the Native American philosophies, and though Fillmore polled nearly thirty percent of the popular vote, he lost all but one state and in the process lost the election.

He gave up politics after that, married a wealthy widow and went back to his old life as the first citizen of Buffalo, New York. When the Civil War finally came, he organized a local militia of men like himself who were too old to go off to defend the Union, but might be of some help if the war happened to reach the shores of Lake Erie. They contented themselves with recruiting younger men for the Grand Army of The Republic and donating thousands of dollars to the war effort.

Fillmore lived in Buffalo with his second wife, Carolyn, for fifteen years in a style that was the envy of the society at the other end of the state. Their great Gothic palace was the scene of formal dinners and balls, teas, recitals and simple parties attended by everyone who was important on the Niagara Frontier and beyond. But the Fillmores had an iron-fast rule that each and every guest was expected to follow. As the ex-President put it to them, "This is a home of industry and temperance with plain diet, no tobacco and no swearing."

When he died an admirer wrote: "In childhood he was more moral than most children; in youth his morality was remarkable for its strictness; in manhood it presented itself to our view in noble proportions, without blemish …. From his example let little boys learn lessons of temperance and industry, and profit by putting them into practice." It was high praise in 1874, but less than a century later, in the 1960s, little boys out to change the system honored the memory of the 13th President by naming their chief indoor playgrounds in San Francisco and New York after him. But temperance and industry were far from their minds. They said they plucked Fillmore out of obscurity and those who could identify him as a one-time President considered themselves masters of trivia.

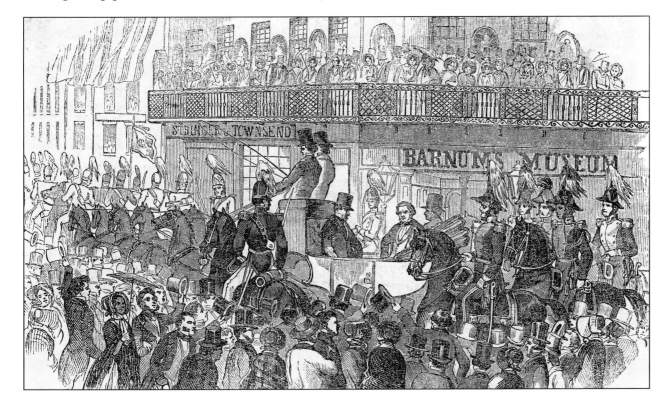

When Millard Fillmore went shopping for a carriage and preferred a secondhand one, the salesman said it was appropriate because Fillmore was "a second-hand president." Fillmore bought the carriage anyway and went on to prove the salesman wrong.

The 14th President
FRANKLIN PIERCE
(1853-1857)

It's an American tradition for fathers to dream that one day one of their children could become President of the United States. Franklin Pierce didn't mind admitting that he became President himself so that his son might have special advantages, even if he didn't ever want to follow the road to the White House. Pierce and his wife doted on their children. They lost their first son at the age of four, and after that all of their affection was centered on Benjamin, who was twelve when his father was elected President. But the boy didn't live to see the inauguration.

After the 1852 election, the family went to Boston for the holidays. The train that was taking them back home to New Hampshire crashed down an embankment, and young Bennie was killed instantly in front of his parents' eyes. Neither the President-elect nor his wife were physically hurt, but they never completely recovered from their mental injuries. They were both products of stern New England stock, believing that nothing good, nor anything bad, ever happens to anyone except as a sign from God. Pierce had been a politician all of his life, and now, he thought, God was punishing him for his sins. His wife had other ideas. God had done him a favor, she said, by taking away a potential distraction from the duties of the presidency. In her view, the son had been sacrificed to the father's ambition. And she never let her husband forget it. Either way, it couldn't add up to a healthy way to take on the new job Franklin Pierce had repeatedly said he didn't want in the first place.

The Democrats hadn't put much steam behind any Pierce bandwagon, either. He wasn't without his supporters, of course, and by the time the Party met to pick its candidate for the 1852 race, he had agreed to accept their mandate and politely stayed home to wait for it. But when word reached him that thirty-three ballots had been taken and his name not even mentioned, he decided to take a little vacation. He had been gone two days when a rider caught up with his carriage with the message that he had taken the nomination on the forty-ninth ballot. Before he could express his thanks, Mrs. Pierce fainted.

Franklin Pierce seemed to have all the qualifications for the job. His father had been a general in the Revolutionary War, and as a pioneer settler in the hills of New Hampshire, he was the leading citizen of Hillsborough County. Their home doubled as a inn, and as a boy, Franklin listened to fireside chats among important travelers from all over the Eastern Seaboard. General Pierce was fiercely interested in politics and, a Republican in an area surrounded by Federalists, he decided to send his second son all the way up to Maine to Bowdoin College, where the political atmosphere was healthier. Among his classmates there, Nathaniel Hawthorne became a lifelong friend, and Henry Wadsworth Longfellow an admirer. By the time he graduated in 1824, he had made up his mind to become a lawyer. And by the time he became one, his father had become Governor of New Hampshire.

The old General was swept out of office when the Jacksonians lost control of the State Legislature, but young Frank was elected President of the Hillsborough Town Meeting at the same time. It was the start of his political career, and for a dedicated apostle of Andrew Jackson, it couldn't have come at a better time. New Hampshire slipped out of the Jackson column in 1828, but General Pierce was reelected Governor and his son, Frank, was elected to the State Legislature. It gave him a forum to boost the stock of Andrew Jackson in the Granite State and the possibility of recognition for himself beyond the White Mountains. He was made Speaker in his third legislative session, and after two more terms was elected to Congress with almost no opposition.

Franklin Pierce was almost slavishly devoted to the Jackson cause, which, in a way, gave him time to think about other things. He chose to think romantic thoughts. He had fallen in love with Jane Means Appleton, daughter of the late President of Bowdoin College. Her mother was opposed to the idea of their even getting to know each other, let alone getting married. The Appletons were close relatives of the Lawrences of Boston and the Masons of Portsmouth, both aristocratic families and long-standing Federalists. Franklin Pierce was a frontiersman, rough around the edges, given to spending his evenings in taverns drinking and talking politics. Worse, his politics centered around the person of Andrew

Jackson, and that just wouldn't do. But Jane and Frank got married anyway, and when he went to Washington for his second session as a Congressman his life-style was quite different. But he was still President Jackson's man.

Mrs. Pierce was in poor health, and when he went back to Washington the following winter she stayed home with her family. It was the winter he took a stand on slavery and became known as a man with some opinions of his own. The issue had been quiet in Congress for several years, but when it came back in 1835, Congressman Pierce took to the floor and told his colleagues that the abolitionist movement in the North was concentrated among a few fanatics and that there was "not one in a hundred who does not entertain the most sacred regard for the rights of their Southern brethren … nay, not one in five hundred who would not have those rights protected at any and every hazard." They turned out to be fighting words back home, and the Abolitionist press began a counterattack which eventually reached the floor of the Senate, where he was accused of lying. He defended himself by saying that his theoretical five hundred had been "sturdy yeomen," and certainly not women and children. It got him out of the fire, but the issue would eventually come back to haunt him.

In the meantime, the New Hampshire Legislature elected him to the United States Senate and he became the youngest member of a body that included such men as Daniel Webster and Henry Clay, John Calhoun and Thomas Hart Benton. He was still a loyal party man, but life as a Senator proved as unrewarding as that of a Congressman. His law practice was suffering, and his wife hated living in Washington. She wasn't too fond of their long separations, either, and she began asking him to give up politics. They had a son by then, and that gave him an incentive to begin listening to her.

He was pushed over to her way of thinking when William Henry Harrison became president and swept a Whig majority into Congress. Senator Pierce had never been part of a minority and he didn't like it. He waited a year, but then resigned and went back to New Hampshire.

Franklin Pierce was one of New England's best trial lawyers and he went home to a lucrative practice. He considered himself retired from public life, even though he was only thirty-eight years old. But politics is a seductive game.

Among his law clients were New Hampshire farmers who claimed that railroad interests were cheating them. And among the railroad interests were important Whigs, who charged that the ex-Senator was using his political influence against them. Pierce told his wife and family that he had no other choice, and then went back into the political arena. Less than a year into his "retirement," Franklin Pierce became the leader of the radical wing of the Democratic Party in New Hampshire. Some said he was a political boss, which he probably was. One thing was sure, Franklin Pierce was firmly in charge of his party.

He had said that the New England Abolitionists were in the minority, and he still believed it. But there was another issue abroad in the land in the 1840s, and it was one that seemed to have grabbed the hearts and minds of everybody old enough to have an opinion. It was Demon Rum. Pierce had wrestled with the problem himself early in his career, but when he became a family man he had stopped drinking, and there is no evangelist more dedicated than a convert. He became Chairman of the New Hampshire State Temperance Committee. The political scene was murky, but it was clear where Franklin Pierce stood.

One of the best trial lawyers in New England, Franklin Pierce decided early in life to retire from politics, and when the Democrats suggested that he run for the presidency, he said he found the idea "utterly repugnant."

He was a moderate on the slavery issue and four-square against drunkenness.

But another issue raised its head in 1846 when Mexican troops killed Americans and President Polk called for volunteers to drive them back. Among the first to answer the call was Franklin Pierce, who turned down Polk's offer to become United States Attorney General in favor of an appointment as Brigadier General in the United States Army.

He joined General Winfield Scott's command at Vera Cruz to take part in a march on Mexico City. It was tough going, but he managed to lead his men on a month-long trek through jungles and deserts in the face of a half-dozen guerilla attacks without losing a single man. But when they met the full force of the enemy, General Pierce met a problem that would haunt him for the rest of his life. He wasn't a trained military man, and when the time came to lead his men into battle, he did what any good lawyer would do. He mounted his horse, rode to the front of the column and made an inspiring speech. Artillery shells were whistling over his head. The noise frightened his horse. The animal bolted. The General was thrown forward into the pommel of the saddle. Then he fainted. There is no question he was in pain, but when his aide was put in command, the whispering through the ranks was that "the General is a damned coward."

He had injured his knee in the fall, but when he recovered consciousness he mounted another horse and took command again, the only senior officer to stay with his men all night long. When Scott ordered him out of the field, he argued his case and had the order countermanded. But General Pierce was in pain from his wounded leg and fainted again the following morning. This time he refused any offers of help and stayed there on the ground encouraging his men as the battle raged around him. Medals of Honor have sometimes been awarded for less, but none of Pierce's officers or men thought he even remotely resembled a hero. The action shifted to a different quarter and his brigade was denied any chances for displays of heroism. There was no glory waiting for Brigadier General Franklin Pierce when the Mexican General Santa Anna asked for a truce.

In the end he had earned the respect of his men, he had led the remains of his army into Mexico City, and he had personally taken part in the negotiations that hammered out the armistice. Though he was a politician, he also earned rare high marks in the military by avoiding the politics of the barracks, which was considered a way of life for glory-seeking generals.

Back home in New Hampshire, the former General, ex-Senator, respected trial lawyer, became successful beyond his wildest dreams. His law practice flourished, and his political influence increased. In those days, when there was little else to do, attending jury trials was a popular form of public entertainment. Franklin Pierce was one of its shining stars, and if he was a master at convincing juries of the righteousness of his client's case, he was also playing to the audience behind him. His appearance ensured packed galleries and everybody, it seemed, was on his side. Especially the Democrats.

The New England states at the time were itching to see a local boy make good in the race for the presidency. But rivalries among the Democrats fragmented the chances of any single potential candidate they could think of. Pierce's name came up time and again. But the slavery issue had blossomed by then, and he was perceived by many party leaders as a Southerner in Northern clothing. Besides, he had lived in Washington before and found it wanting. Franklin Pierce told his backers that he considered the idea of running for President, or even Vice President, "utterly repugnant." He probably did. But when the convention's messenger caught up with his carriage and told him that he was the man they wanted, Franklin Pierce was probably pleased. Ironically, the man he would have to fight for the new job was General Winfield Scott, his old commanding officer.

It was a quiet campaign. Both parties basically agreed on the issues, and the candidates were able to keep most of their skeletons in their respective closets. When it was all over, Pierce had a majority of some 50,000 votes and carried all but four states. He went back to Washington to follow the precedents of Jackson and Polk, and let his advisers take care of the day-to-day running of the Government. But the men he picked didn't seem to be up to the task. They were overwhelmed, as other Administrations had been, by sweeping changes in the country. It took strength, even ruthlessness, to cope with them, and Franklin Pierce, who didn't have a ruthless bone in his body, had run out of strength.

By the end of his four years in the White House, even the New Hampshire party faithful had made up their mind that he couldn't be reelected to a second term, and when the Democrats met to pick their standard bearer in 1856, they turned to James Buchanan. But they also adopted a resolution supporting the Pierce Administration's policies.

Before they settled down in New Hampshire again, the Pierces took an extended tour of Europe. When the Civil War broke out, his own record on the slavery issue came back to haunt him again, but he was able to defend himself. From a political point of view, it wasn't necessary. Mr. Pierce was out of politics for good. But near the end of the war, when he was called upon to make a speech on the assassination of President Lincoln, a heckler in the crowd shouted, "Where is your flag?" His response was quick. "It is not necessary for me to show my devotion to the Stars and Stripes by any special exhibition upon the demand of any man," he said. "If the period in which I have served our country and state … commencing more than thirty-five years ago, has left any question of my devotion to the flag, the Constitution and the Union in doubt, it is too late now to resume it." It was Franklin Pierce's last public speech. He lived four more years in Concord, relatively forgotten, but proud to the end.

The 15th President
JAMES BUCHANAN
(1857-1861)

In the world of politics, there are thousands of qualities that add up to success, and physical appearance ranks high among them. James Buchanan, it was said, was "distinguished." He was tall and square-shouldered. He had a shock of wavy gray hair. His features were symmetrical. And he had piercing blue eyes. It was the eyes that most people remembered, but not many knew why. He couldn't see very well through one of them and he compensated for it by tilting his head sideways and slightly forward. The effect was one of rapt interest in any person he happened to be talking with, and nothing impresses anyone quite as much as what seems to be undivided attention.

In spite of impressive first impressions, and the fact that he was a remarkable politician, getting to the White House wasn't easy for Mr. Buchanan. He made up his mind that he wanted to be President when he was forty-two years old, but didn't make it until twenty-four years later.

His father, who migrated to Pennsylvania from Ireland, made up his mind that young Jimmy was going to amount to something big almost from the day he was born. He had seven other children to support and encouraged his oldest son to make something of himself in case the yoke should fall on his shoulders. He helped him to become a lawyer and helped him get established in Lancaster, which had the reputation of having the best lawyers, except for Philadelphia, of any city in the United States. Buchanan had no sooner hung out his shingle than he was appointed District Attorney. He also had the advantage of having been a lifelong Federalist, and arrived on the scene as a bright young man eager to be admitted into a party that was growing old and tired. In 1814, they sent him to the State Legislature and he acquired a taste for politics.

But James Buchanan was as thorough and thrifty as he was ambitious, and he sincerely believed that any man was a fool to get involved in politics until he had earned enough to support himself. When his term ended, he dropped out and went to work to build a nest-egg. Within four years he had a statewide reputation and an income to match. He had what amounted to an obsession for close attention to detail

and for hard work, but he also had a bit of good luck. Among the men he successfully defended was an important judge facing impeachment charges. From that moment Buchanan's future as a lawyer was nothing less than spectacular. But he had his eye on a different kind of future. When he was thirty years old, he gave up his practice and became a full-time politician.

It was also the time he made up his mind that he'd be a bachelor for the rest of his life. As a successful lawyer, he had been considered one of Lancaster's most eligible young men, and mothers all over the county schemed to have him notice their daughters. But he only had eyes for Ann Coleman, the daughter of Pennsylvania's first millionaire. And, as often happens, her family didn't approve of the match. To make matters worse, the ladies of the town began a whispering campaign that young Jimmy was more interested in the Coleman fortune than the Colemans' daughter. The rumors reached Ann, of course, and she was already upset that he seemed to spend more time tending to his business than showering attention on her. Eventually she broke off their engagement and left town for a vacation. She died mysteriously three days later. The gossips called it suicide. As for Buchanan, he wrote to her father that "I feel that happiness has fled from me forever."

By the end of the year, barrister Buchanan was Congressman Buchanan and on his way to Washington. Luck entered his life again when, in his first weeks there, he was asked to act as a substitute for a colleague who was too ill to make an important speech. It gave him the kind of attention few freshmen Congressmen could hope for, and he took advantage of the opportunity. In the meantime, the Federalist Party back in Pennsylvania was a shambles and he took advantage of that opportunity, too. By the time they renominated him for a third term in Congress, he had firm control of a radical wing of the Party and was openly supporting the presidential hopes of Andrew Jackson, the enemy of Federalists everywhere. When Jackson lost the 1824 election Buchanan quietly went to work to form an entirely new state political party in his own image.

It was a job he seemed born to do. He kept careful

notes on all of the people who needed to be dealt with. He knew where to look for strength, who to quietly recommend for patronage and appointments and who needed to be avoided. He depended on his personal style of one-on-one contacts with people who could help him as well as with people it would be politically profitable to help. By the election of 1826, he was ready to bring together an odd mixture of Federalists and Democrats loyal more to him than to their former party principles. Two years later he ran as a Democrat for the Congressional seat he had held for four terms as a Federalist. He kept his seat, and, thanks largely to Buchanan's orchestrations, Jackson carried Pennsylvania by a huge majority.

Before his career as a Congressman ended, there was a serious effort to put Buchanan on the ticket as vice presidential candidate in 1832. Partisans on both sides agreed that he'd probably at the very least be appointed to Jackson's Cabinet in the second term. But all the pundits were wrong. Old Hickory sent Buchanan off to St. Petersburg as Minister to Russia. It was another piece of good luck, as it turned out, though no one could have convinced Mr. Buchanan of it at the time. He had Pennsylvania politics to think about, not to mention his own career, and wasn't too pleased to be sent half-way around the world. But while he was gone, Jackson routinely clashed with Congress over the National Bank and the tariff issue, and many a Congressman found himself in deep trouble with his constituents. When Buchanan came home from Russia his reputation was intact. A year later he became a Senator and the talk of nominating him for the vice presidency started all over again.

But Mr. Buchanan was noncommittal. He was busy fine-tuning the political machine he had built. It was an almost impossible job, but worth the trouble because the boss of Lancaster had decided that he didn't want to be Vice President. He had his eye on the presidency itself. But he was careful not to tell anyone. He believed strongly that the office should seek the man and not the other way around. Besides, he understood the political value of being able to tell supporters that he'd walk out on them if they didn't walk the line his way. He talked frequently of retiring and everyone knew that, unlike most public servants, he could easily afford to give up his senatorial salary. But anyone who saw him in action on the floor of the Senate must have known he was only fooling. His colleagues were the giants of their day, still remembered for their skill, and Buchanan was their equal. He was a hard-working, well-ordered Senator, loyal to his party, but with a point of view of his own.

He had hopes, and so did hundreds of Pennsylvania Democrats, that he'd get the presidential nod in 1844, but after testing the waters and finding both Martin Van Buren and James Polk stronger, he decided to wait for a better day. His reward in the Polk Administration was the post of Secretary of State. It wasn't much of a reward as it turned out; Polk and Buchanan couldn't seem to agree on anything, and the President was determined to be a chief executive who made his own decisions. Buchanan stayed loyal to him, but complained that the job of running the State Department was drudgery. To make matters worse, he said, "I have no power. I feel it deeply."

But other men had used the top Cabinet post as a presidential stepping stone, and Buchanan worked for the nomination again in 1848. And again he missed

James Buchanan's Administration was plagued by a Union rapidly unraveling over the issue of slavery. Cartoonists and others found his cautious attitude unacceptable.

the brass ring. He had been in public service for thirty years by then, he was fifty-four years old and he decided it was time to make good on his threats to retire. He bought a big house in the country near Lancaster and announced that he was going to settle down. Even though he was a bachelor, he needed the space because he was the rich uncle to twenty-two nieces and nephews and half again as many of their own children. Several of them were orphans, all of them depended on Uncle Jimmy as their sole support. But he also needed room to entertain the politically influential. James Buchanan may have retired, but he still wanted to be President.

He kept the public informed about where he stood on important issues such as statehood for California and the Fugitive Slave Law by writing letters to newspapers, and he kept in touch with people who mattered over brandy and cigars in the drawing room of the mansion he called "Wheatland." He was every inch the country squire, his opinion was sought-after, his company treasured. He seemed to have hit all the right buttons to guarantee a draft when the Democrats met to pick their presidential candidate in 1852. He did well in the early ballots, but that wasn't to be his year, either. The deadlocked convention settled on Franklin Pierce. All of his supporters were certain that the intensifying storm over slavery would guarantee that the Democrats would have to look for a peacemaker in '56, and that their choice would have to be James Buchanan. He protested that he was already an "old fogy," but even though he told them that he planned to take an outside seat to observe the Great Drama, age hadn't withered his ambition to be President.

When Pierce offered to make him Ambassador to England, he refused at first, but finally agreed, and if it had been Pierce's intention to throw Old Buck out of the way, he had made a mistake. While he was in London, Buchanan began moving Anglo-American relations further ahead than they had come since the War of 1812. By the end of his own Administration, almost none of the old grudges existed any longer. He also cut a dazzling social figure in London. His niece, Harriet Lane, joined him there and together they made the rounds of all the important parties and country weekends. She flirted and he charmed and they became as welcome everywhere they went as members of the Royal Family. When the Ambassador had his final audience with Queen Victoria before leaving for home, she told him that she regretted most losing the company of "dear Miss Lane."

Buchanan's three years abroad provided him with yet another stroke of luck. While he was gone, the debate over the admission of Kansas and Nebraska into the Union had created a firestorm in Washington, and once again Mr. Buchanan was safely removed from the center of it, as he had been three times before. And when he arrived back in Pennsylvania, he found that his organization had not only held together, but grown stronger. The Whigs were in disarray over the Kansas-Nebraska fight and President Pierce didn't have a ghost of a chance of winning again for the Democrats. James Buchanan arrived home on his sixty-fifth birthday and he knew that at last his day had come.

Two months later he was given the nomination by acclamation after politicking his way through sixteen ballots. Then he went home to Wheatland after having said that there was only one issue that should concern any voter: "This race ought to be run on the question of Union or disunion." He conducted his campaign from his office at home, writing letters, conferring with individuals, keeping the party machine functioning. And when November came, James Buchanan was the man of the hour, "the most suitable man for the times." And a very happy man at that.

But the winter of 1856 was not a happy time for the United States of America. The Union was in deep trouble, and James Buchanan wasn't exaggerating when he said "the object of my Administration will be to destroy any sectional party, North or South, and harmonize all sections of the Union under a national and conservative government."

But if he had escaped the heat of controversy in the past, he found himself at the center of it now. There was trouble in "Bleeding Kansas." The country was going through a financial panic. Some Southern states had begun talking of secession. The Mormons were threatening war in Utah. And Congress seemed to have declared war on James Buchanan. Sectionalism, in spite of Buchanan's best efforts, was growing, and strong-willed politicians were eager to turn it to their own advantage.

But he managed to keep the Union intact, if not harmonized. The holocaust didn't come until after his successor had been elected. Within a day of Lincoln's election, South Carolina began making moves to remove itself from the Union. As a lame duck president, Buchanan had less control over Congress than ever, and when he turned the Government over to Mr. Lincoln, it seemed certain that the war that had been coming for a quarter-century was at hand. He told his successor, "My dear sir, if you are as happy in entering the White House as I shall feel on returning to Wheatland, you are a happy man, indeed."

When war finally came less than a month later, the retired President found himself in the center of a hate campaign. The Northern press began to print stories directly blaming Buchanan for all the country's troubles, and a bill of censure was introduced in the Senate. At first Buchanan tried to fight back as he always had, by writing letters to newspapers. But he quickly discovered that no matter what he said, it was twisted and turned against him. He responded with silence. He spent the next five years reading in the press and in his daily mail that he and he alone bore the responsibility for the Civil War.

Eventually he was able to ride out the storm, and spent his days managing his financial affairs. He entertained as he always had, enjoying his black cigars and fine whiskey. On the day before he died at the age of seventy-eight, he told a close friend, "I have no regret for any public act of my life, and history will vindicate my memory."

The 16th President
ABRAHAM LINCOLN
(1861-1865)

President Lincoln often visited the front lines during the Civil War to confer with General McClellan (right), and others. He was nearly always accompanied by the head of the new Secret Service, Allan Pinkerton (left).

"**O**young Lochinvar is come out of the west," wrote Sir Walter Scott, who described his hero as dauntless in war and added, "There never was knight like young Lochinvar." He could have been predicting the arrival of Abraham Lincoln on the American national scene, even though Mr. Lincoln hardly suited the role of a dashing young knight. His looks weren't calculated to bring a smile to the lips of fair young maidens, or a tear to their eye, and he wasn't even young. The first time most Americans outside Illinois ever heard of him, Abraham Lincoln was fifty-two years old. And he was asking them to make him their President.

Lincoln had served in Congress a dozen years earlier, but his own party refused to nominate him for a second term. He tried to become a United States Senator twice and failed both times. In fact, in the twelve years since the end of his single term in Congress, Abraham Lincoln hadn't held any public office at all. He himself said, "My name is new in the field, and I suppose I am not the first choice of a very great many. Our policy is to give no offense to others – leave them in a mood to come to us, if they shall be impelled to give up their first love." It wasn't exactly the call of a knight in shining armor, but he knew that the field was littered with men whose own armor was tarnished. Mr. Lincoln had no record to defend, and more than anyone else who wanted to be President, he had the advantage of having risen above a log-cabin birth to become one of the most successful lawyers on the frontier, and having done it all by himself. He was a man the masses could understand and admire.

But if the masses understood Abraham Lincoln, he understood them even better, and he also understood the art of politics. Once the bandwagon began rolling toward his presidential nomination, Lincoln and his men greased the wheels a bit to let the people help the delegates decide. The Republican party leaders were inclined to give the nomination to former Governor of New York and United States Senator, William H. Seward. There were other contenders, too, including Ohio's Salmon P. Chase, also a former Governor and Senator. But Lincoln had an edge and he used it. The nominating convention was held in Chicago, and Illinois was four-square behind Mr. Lincoln. During the convention's first two days, every seat was filled and the halls were jammed with Chicagoans fascinated by the process that was building Seward's strength. Balloting was scheduled to begin on the third day, and Lincoln's men secretly printed extra tickets to distribute among their supporters, with instructions that they should arrive early, stay late, and make plenty of noise every time they heard the name Lincoln mentioned. They did their job well. When Lincoln's name was placed in nomination, a reporter said their yells "made soft vesper breathings of all that preceded. A thousand steam whistles, ten acres of hotel gongs, a tribe of Comanches, headed by a choice vanguard

from pandemonium, might have mingled in the scene unnoticed."

But if their message to the delegates was that Abraham Lincoln was the people's choice, it took them three ballots to confirm it. And even then, Lincoln was short by two-and-a-half votes. The tension was broken by the Ohio delegation which suddenly switched four Chase votes into the Lincoln column, some said because of a promise that Salmon Chase could have any job he wanted in a Lincoln Administration. He later became Secretary of the Treasury.

After his term in Congress, Lincoln had given up politics in favor of building his law practice. He had served in the Illinois Legislature and his influence was valuable to the railroads that were being built at the time. Lincoln served as a lobbyist in Springfield to get a charter for the Illinois Central, and then represented the line, as well as dozens of others, often in landmark cases. In time he became one of the state's most important lawyers, a feat made all the more remarkable by the fact that he had never gone to college, and had taught himself nearly everything he knew.

He was drawn back into politics in 1854, when anti-slavery Democrats joined with disaffected Whigs to form a new Republican Party dedicated to stopping the spread of slavery into the Kansas-Nebraska territories. Lincoln himself had always been a Whig, but he had developed strong feelings against slavery, and became a Republican voice against Democrat Senator Stephen A. Douglas in Illinois. Douglas, who ultimately ran against Lincoln as one of two Democratic candidates in the 1860 presidential election, had made a name for himself by calling for the repeal of the clause in the Missouri Compromise that prohibited slavery west of the Mississippi. When his bill passed Congress, Douglas went home to Illinois to defend his actions, and everywhere he went he was met by opposition speakers, more often than not, Abraham Lincoln.

When the two men ran against each other for the Senate the following year, Lincoln went back to his pattern of following the incumbent around the state. Douglas drew big crowds, and the Republican planners knew it made sense to take advantage of them. Then Lincoln had a better idea. He challenged Douglas to a series of debates. At first the man they called "The Little Giant" refused, but he knew he didn't have a choice and plans were made for them to meet on the same platform in each Congressional district except Chicago and Springfield. They attracted as many as fifteen thousand people at each of them. Railroads put on special trains, farmers swept out their hayracks and used them to haul their neighbors into town, and some walked dozens of dusty miles to be part of it. The debates had all the earmarks of country fairs, with parades and fireworks, band concerts and outdoor feasts. The debaters themselves went at each other for as many as three hours, usually in the hot sun. And as far as appearances were concerned, it could have been a Laurel and Hardy roadshow. Lincoln was tall and thin, his clothes didn't seem to fit and his voice was high-pitched. Douglas was short and plump, his clothes were tailor-made and, at the start of each debate at least, his voice was deep and cultured. In the controlled television debates we've become accustomed to, there would have been no contest. But in 1858, voters were more interested in what a candidate had to say than what he looked like.

The candidates were followed by small army of newspaper reporters, some of whom provided their readers with verbatim reports. All of them interpreted what they saw and heard according to their own political leanings. But because of Douglas's national stature, the reports appeared all over the country and Lincoln became a national figure himself. The very fact that he had stood up to the Little Giant and gave a good accounting of himself made him a man to watch. Lincoln lost the election in spite of the effort, but as he told a friend, "The late race gave me a hearing on the great and durable question of the age … I believe I have made some marks which will tell for the cause of civil liberty long after I am gone."

After the Republicans nominated Lincoln for the presidency, the Democrats nominated Douglas and the Southern radicals marched out of the hall. They met a few weeks later and nominated their own candidate with a pro-slavery platform. Then another combine of men, disenchanted with both parties, formed a brand-new one they called the Constitutional Union, and nominated yet another candidate. Lincoln won the four-way race, but together the other three men out-polled him by more than a million votes, and

"The world will little note, nor long remember, what we say here ..." said Lincoln at Gettysburg in 1863.

Lincoln got no votes at all in many Southern districts. But he carried all the big Northern states and piled up an impressive electoral victory.

After his election, the Southern states began holding meetings to discuss their long-smouldering plans to secede from the Union. And even before Lincoln took his oath of office, seven of them took the first steps to make good on the threat. Congress rushed to lure them back with new compromises, and all eyes turned to the President-elect, who would have to deal with the problem in a matter of weeks. He had seen too many compromises fail, he said, and he told his supporters that the time had come to stand firm. One by one, the remaining eight slave-supporting states rejected the idea of dissolving the Union, and the crisis passed. At least for a while. As Lincoln was travelling from Springfield to Washington for his inauguration, former Mississippi Senator Jefferson Davis took his own oath of office as President of the Confederate States of America. A few days into the second month of the Lincoln presidency, the Confederates took the Union's Fort Sumter, and Lincoln issued a call for 75,000 troops to defend "our National Union."

His call united the solid South, and the disunion everyone had feared for so long was accomplished in a matter of weeks. More important to the waging of the Civil War that was sure to follow, the issue of slavery faded into the background. The majority of Southerners didn't own slaves anyway. They were fighting for no less a principle than their independence. But Lincoln felt there was a higher principle: the idea of democracy itself. He made it clear that human freedom was at stake, and never shrank from making decisions that might make war inevitable. And once it started, he took his role as Commander-in-Chief seriously, studying military tactics and conferring with his generals in an almost desperate effort to find the way to an elusive victory for the Grand Army of the Republic.

As the war dragged on, the strategies of the Union campaign were almost completely directed by the President. He had discovered early that he couldn't trust his generals, and devised a holding action until he could find a military man who could be a match for the Confederate leader Robert E. Lee. In the meantime, he needed to protect his political flank, to keep the support of his fellow-Republicans as well as Democrats who were united in favor of the war. He also needed to do what he could to keep the European powers from interfering on the side of the Confederacy. Keeping it all heading in the right direction required an unusually talented man, and day by day, Abraham Lincoln was proving that he was a big enough man for the job.

Still, the war went badly for the North until the battle of Antietam in 1863. It wasn't a stunning victory, but it was good enough for Lincoln. On September 21, he took a dramatic step to alter the course of the war, and of American history.

In 1861, the Lincoln family included eleven-year-old William (seated), who died the following year, nine-year-old Thomas, known as "Tad" (standing at his father's right), and the eldest son Robert, who was a student at Harvard during Lincoln's presidency.

Lincoln's wife, Mary, was at his side in the box at Washington's Ford Theater when John Wilkes Booth assassinated the President on April 14, 1865.

He had been waiting since July for the right moment to make his announcement. He knew a drastic measure was called for if he was to keep the support of his Party and somehow win the war. He felt he had a duty to protect the Constitution, no matter what the cost. But, as he told his Cabinet, "Life and limb must be protected; yet often a limb must be amputated to save a life; but a life is never wisely given to save a limb." He knew that he couldn't preserve the Constitution if he allowed the nation to dissolve in order to preserve the institution of slavery. On that September afternoon, Abraham Lincoln issued a proclamation that in one hundred days all slaves within any state still in rebellion would become free, and that the military power of the United States would be used to assure their freedom.

The proclamation should have sent waves of enthusiasm through the North, but it didn't. In the Congressional elections that fall, the Democrats were swept into a majority, and they took control of state legislatures that had been considered safe Republican territory. Even Lincoln's home district went over to the other side. People began to wonder if the President might have a change of heart before his announced deadline for the Emancipation Proclamation to take effect. But they didn't know the kind of heart they were dealing with. He had promised freedom in states "still in rebellion," and exempted those which had elected representatives in Congress. He did what he could to encourage them to elect such people, even though he was surrounded by men who were far from willing to forgive and forget. But to Lincoln, the issue was bigger than any of them. He told Congress that they all would "be remembered in spite of ourselves." Emancipation was the only way to save the Union, he said. "We know how to save the Union. The world knows we know how to save it…. In giving freedom to the slave, we assure freedom to the free." On New Year's Day, 1863, saying "but anyway it is going to be done!," Abraham Lincoln signed the document.

Once it was done, not much changed. His authority didn't extend into the states affected, and he didn't free any slaves in the North or in Border States with representatives in Congress. The war ground on, and General Lee had brought it to the North. But by midsummer the Union Army controlled the Mississippi River, and after their victories at Gettysburg and Vicksburg they began to turn the tide. But the Rebels weren't beaten yet. And though the politicians had long since given up on Mr. Lincoln, the people were solidly behind him, and when the Republicans met to pick their candidate for the 1863 election, they picked the President to succeed himself, and he won easily.

The war finally came to an end a few weeks after his second inaugural, and though it had taken a dreadful toll on the man, he knew he still had a tough job ahead. The national mood was to take revenge on the states that had seceded. But he told the people that forgiveness was the only possible answer and promised to work to welcome them back. But he never had a chance to keep the promise. Five days after celebrating the end of the war, President Lincoln was gunned down and killed by an assassin.

He had already achieved a kind of immortality among the common people, and his martyrdom insured it. He had always been a man of the people and if the politicians were often frustrated by his leadership, the most cynical of them eventually came to understand what Lincoln had been showing them all along: that government of the people, by the people and for the people can not be allowed to perish from the earth.

The 17th President
ANDREW JOHNSON
(1865-1869)

Andrew Johnson's old tailor shop in Greenville, Tennessee. Humble beginnings have often been considered a presidential hopeful's greatest asset, but few can claim a more mundane pre-presidential career than former tailor Andrew Johnson.

Back in 1824, if you were to ask anyone in Raleigh, North Carolina, if anything good would ever become of sixteen-year-old Andrew Johnson, you'd probably have received a worried smile and a sad shake of the head for an answer. In those days, no one in town would have given a dime for the lad's chances. In fact, the local tailor, James Selby, ran an advertisement in the local paper offering a ten-dollar reward for information leading to the capture of a whole gang of teenagers, and ended by saying: " … or I will give the above reward for Andrew Johnson alone."

Andy's crime, as folks around Raleigh understood it, was that he had thrown rocks at the Widow Wells's windows. He and his pals said that all they were doing was trying to get the attention of her daughters, who they considered "right smart," and, besides, no windows were broken. But Mrs. Wells let them know

she was going to "persecute" them to the full extent of the law anyway.

By that time, Andy had his belly-full of persecution, and decided to run away from home. He had lost his father at the age of three, and as soon as he was old enough his mother had apprenticed him to the tailor Selby. And when Andy left town, he was careful to take his tailoring tools with him, which angered his master even more than the loss of a hired hand. Young Johnson hadn't been a model worker anyway. He was a trouble-maker who lured the other apprentices into doing all kinds of time-wasting things like swimming whenever they felt like it. He even had the effrontery to ask Selby to teach him to read during working hours.

When Andy left Raleigh, he planned to stop at Carthage, about sixty miles away. But when he got there, he thought he felt Mrs. Wells's breath on his neck, and he kept on going, supporting himself as an itinerant tailor as he went.

He decided to stop at Columbia, Tennessee, where he got a job in a tailor shop and spent his days listening to stories about Andrew Jackson, who lived a few miles down the road and was thought-of in those parts as part-man, part-god. Young Andy drank it all in, and based his political outlook on Jacksonian lines. He would eventually outdo Old Hickory as a populist.

Word eventually reached him in Columbia that his mother was destitute, so he went home again. His former employer was out of business by then, but all was not forgiven, so Andy loaded his mother, his stepfather and all their belongings into a cart and headed back across the mountains toward Tennessee. They stopped their trek at Greeneville, which happened to need a tailor at the time. Andrew Johnson announced that they had found the best in the business, and opened his own shop. Two months later, he married Eliza McArdle, a local girl he had met when he passed through town the previous year. He was eighteen years old, she was seventeen.

Of all the things Eliza was to give Andy during their life together, one of the most important could almost be considered her dowry. She knew how to read and write, and her new husband was an eager

student. He never quite mastered spelling, though. When he was President, he misspelled his own name, and when it was called to his attention, he thundered, "It is a man with a small imagination who can't spell his name more than one way."

Even though he could read and write, the idea of going on to college was out of the question, but Johnson did the next best thing. He joined the debating society at a local college and used it to cultivate his principles, his speaking voice and his skill as a debater. Meanwhile, his tailor shop had become the central gathering place for Greeneville's working people to exchange news and gossip and to grumble about the patrician Whigs who controlled the local political life. Almost every hour of every working day there was a lively conversation going on in the shop, and to make sure they all got their facts straight, the proprietor hired a man to read books and newspapers aloud for fifty cents a day. And when there was no one around to talk to, the tailor propped a book in front of him to read as he worked.

Finally, the boys decided to do more than just talk about politics. The town was governed by rich planters and merchants who never allowed any opposition in local elections, but in 1829 the gang from the tailor shop picked their own candidates and distributed ballots at the polls on election day. Their entire slate was elected to the town council, and Andrew Johnson was among them. They repeated their success in the next three elections, and then made Andy Johnson Mayor of Greenville. Needless to say, the Whigs were upset. But, for all their huffing and puffing, the tailor won the next two elections. He might have done it again in 1835, but he had another job by then. The people had elected him to the Tennessee Legislature.

He was like a fish out of water in state politics and lost his chance for a second term. But Andrew Johnson had a passion for learning, and two years later he had learned his lessons well enough to win a chance to redeem himself in the legislature. Through it all, his business flourished and he was able to send his four children to private schools. He got more than his money's worth because he spent part of each evening studying their lessons as part of his own self-education.

He was well-known as a stump speaker by then, and the Democratic party leaders relied on him to get their message to the farmers and working class people of East Tennessee. On the other hand, when he told them that he wanted to represent those people in Congress, they were horrified. But he didn't give the Democrats a choice. He ran as an independent and won.

Johnson didn't follow the party line as a Congressman, but though his record was respectable, he didn't take Washington by storm, either. Nor did he jump into the social scene, which is the way most officials play the game of Washington politics. His idea of fun was spending time in the Library of Congress, even though it was never a popular gathering place for his colleagues, past, present or future. When his term ended, he ran for a second and won in spite of lukewarm support from the Democrats.

And in his second term he was more independent than ever. Even his fellow-Tennessean, President James Polk, couldn't count on his support. But the people back home understood independence better than almost anything else, and in spite of a bitter mud-slinging campaign, Johnson was reelected to Congress for a third term. But only by a three-hundred vote majority.

Squeaking into Congress chastened him, and Johnson didn't oppose the President or his party when he went back to Washington. But even after the fence-mending, he decided not to run for a fourth term because the Whigs had gerrymandered his district to include counties solidly in their camp. He had another job in mind by then, anyway. In 1852 he became Governor of Tennessee.

His business had prospered during his ten years in Congress, and Eliza had taken good care of his money. They had bought property in Greenville and were said to be worth about $50,000, a tidy fortune at the time. But none of his neighbors was surprised that the tailor was rich. Andy Johnson squeezed all the value out of every nickel, and he was just as tight with the public purse. When he left Congress he was given a check for $768 in back pay, but returned $216 representing days he hadn't actually worked.

In spite of his wealth, he still considered himself a friend of the working man, and they loved him for it. When he ran for a second term as Governor, he won by a landslide – in spite of a stand defending Catholics and immigrants, of whom there were very few in Tennessee – against the Know-Nothings who were sweeping elections in other states. He also took a stand against prohibiting the sale of liquor, which gave rise to rumors that he was a drunk. He wasn't.

Johnson's impeachment trial became one of the most memorable events of his Administration, even if the charges themselves were questionable.

He didn't run for a third term, but in 1857, when he became a United States Senator, he said: "The people have never deserted me; and, God willing, I will never desert them."

As a Senator, his loyalty to the party that elected him was the same as it had been when he was a Representative, almost non-existent. Andy Johnson was his own man. But he kept the faith with the people. He was single-minded about a bill to give every householder his own homestead from public lands, and his battle to get it passed gave him national recognition. When the bill finally passed Congress, it was a tribute to Johnson's doggedness. He had worked against stiff opposition for fourteen years, first in the House and then in the Senate, for such a victory. But his jubilation was short-lived. President Buchanan vetoed the Homestead Bill, and Congress sustained it. But there were better days ahead for Senator Johnson.

After Abraham Lincoln was elected in 1860 and Southern States began holding conventions to consider secession, Congress was sharply divided along regional lines. But, true to his independent spirit, Andrew Johnson, nominally a Southern Senator, damned both sides, charging that both the secessionists and the abolitionists were trampling the Constitution, and went on to charge the South with nothing less than treason. It hardly constituted oil on troubled waters in the halls of Congress, but Johnson's stock with the people in every part of the country went up dramatically.

As the debate wore on, Johnson dug in his heels, and even his bitterest enemies had to admit that his speeches delayed the disunion that seemed inevitable to everyone except Andrew Johnson. When his own state began leaning toward secession, he went home to do what he did best, to make stump speeches. There were parts of the state he couldn't cover because passions were running too high against him. He was threatened with lynching more than once, and carried a pistol to defend himself against tough-minded secessionists. All of his audiences were filled with them. In the end, Tennessee seceded and Andrew Johnson was himself branded a traitor.

He narrowly escaped with his life and went back to Senate, even though the state he represented didn't consider him one of its officials any longer. He also called for an end to party politics in the interest of saving the Government. It was good news for President Lincoln, who needed bipartisan support more than ever. Within a few months, the President gave Johnson a new post. He was sent home to become Military Governor of Tennessee. It was risky business. There was still a price on his head back home. But the war there was going badly for the Confederates, and in a matter of weeks the Union Army was in control. It was a frustrating job, but Andrew Johnson was exactly the right man for it. During his tenure as Military Governor, more than seven hundred battles were fought in the state, and Johnson's sense of fairness to both sides was the only bright spot.

His efforts didn't go unnoticed. They brightened his political star in other parts of the country, too, and when the Republicans met to nominate Lincoln for a

The committee (right) that brought charges against Johnson was unanimously convinced they could remove him from office, but the Senate acquitted him by one vote when some members unexpectedly crossed party lines.

second term, the President quietly suggested that Johnson would make a good running mate. It was done. The man who had given up the safety of Washington to support the war effort went back to Washington in 1864 as the Vice President of the United States.

A few weeks later, Abraham Lincoln was dead and Andrew Johnson had become President. No President, possibly even Abraham Lincoln, ever faced such difficulties. The wounds of war were deep, and Johnson's heart was still with his people. And though he was President of all the people, his sense of loyalty and fairness made it more difficult for him to take the bold steps necessary to make reconstruction work. Congress was more divided than ever, but most of its members agreed that Andrew Johnson was their enemy. The Democrats among them felt that he had sold them out, and the Republicans thought he was still a Democrat at heart. Nearly all of them had served with him in Congress and thought they understood him perfectly. They certainly didn't consider him a man to be respected, and they set out to establish their own power without any fear of opposition from Andrew Johnson, President or not.

His problems came to a head in 1869 when he fired Secretary of War Edwin Stanton. Congress had recently passed a law, over Johnson's veto, forbidding the removal of Cabinet members without the consent of the Senate. It was high crime in the eyes of Congress, and impeachment proceedings were begun. In the end, seven Republican Senators broke ranks and voted with the Democrats against impeachment. The matter was dropped, but Johnson wasn't renominated the following year. His presidency had come to an end.

He went back to his tailor shop a greater hero among his neighbors than ever. Andy Johnson had spunk, they said, and they loved him for it. They proved it by electing him to represent them again in the Senate. The country was stunned, but few weren't impressed. A newspaper that had opposed him as President couldn't contain its admiration at the new turn of events, which it said was, "the most magnificent personal triumph which the history of American politics can show." Men who had voted to impeach him were his colleagues again. But if Andy Johnson held any animosity toward them, he didn't acknowledge it. "I have no wrongs to redress but my country's," he said, and launched into an attack on the corruption of the Grant Administration, characteristically laced with facts and figures that proved what he had to say. Congress was in no mood to listen, but the galleries were packed with people who were, the people Andrew Johnson wanted to reach anyway.

It was the last time he'd reach out to the people. At the end of the three-month session, Johnson went home to his family. But on his first day back he suffered a series of strokes and died. His was buried on a hillside overlooking Greeneville. A few years later a monument was built over the grave, its simple inscription summing up the career of the seventeenth President: "His Faith in The People Never Wavered."

THE PAROQUET OF THE WH—E HO—E.

The biggest national problem during the Johnson years was the reconstruction of the South. Cartoonists had a field day with his constant calls for strict interpretation of the Constitution, and pictured him as a beaten man once his term was over. Six years later, however, he became the only former president to serve as a U.S. senator and went back to Washington to sit side by side with the men who tried to impeach him.

61

The 18th President
ULYSSES SIMPSON GRANT
(1869-1877)

After General Robert E. Lee handed his sword to Ulysses S. Grant on April 9, 1865, the commander of the Union Army was on the receiving end of gifts nearly everywhere he went. His former nighbors in Galena, Illinois, took up a collection and gave him a sixteen-thousand-dollar house, furnished in the latest fashion. The citizens of Philadelphia gave him a house worth a good deal more, New York City gave him one hundred thousand dollars in cash, and Boston came up with five thousand dollars worth of books for his library. And he was pleased to accept nearly twenty prize horses, to his mind possibly the greatest gift of all, from individual admirers. Four years later, the citizens of the United States gave him the presidency.

But less than ten years before he moved into the White House, Ulysses Simpson Grant seemed to be doing all he could to live up to his boyhood nickname of "Useless." He had drifted to Galena with borrowed railway fare to take a job with his younger brothers as a clerk in their leather goods store. His brothers regarded him as an incompetent fool and the job as an act of charity. He had been cashiered from the army for drunkenness, he had tried selling real estate and failed in a booming market, and he had made a mess of trying to support his family by farming land that had been given to him. If anyone could be called a failure at forty, Ulysses S. Grant was that man.

It wasn't that he was a stranger to hard work. Grant was born in 1822 in backwoods Ohio, where survival depended on it. He began working when he was seven, and as soon as he was old enough to handle a plow he was put in charge of the family farm. His father had a tanning business to run and needed the help his oldest son could give. Young Ulysses was just as happy not to have to work in his father's shop because he detested the killing of animals, and couldn't stomach the idea of working with the skins of dead creatures. His love of animals, which was almost an obsession, made him one of the best horse-handlers for miles around, even as a small boy. But except for that, he didn't show much talent for anything else, least of all getting along with people.

His father was able to give him an education, and had bright hopes for his future. But when the boy was sixteen, he rejected an offer to follow in his father's footsteps and the elder Grant, who wasn't without influence, suggested that he might want to go the U.S. Military Academy at West Point instead. He didn't, but it was the lesser of two evils. Besides, it would get him out of Ohio, and give him a chance to see both Philadelphia and New York, something he had always wanted to do. But as for the trip up the Hudson to the Academy, Grant said later, "I would have been glad for a steamboat or a railroad collision by which I might have received a temporary injury sufficient to make me ineligible."

The authorities may have secretly wished the same. Cadet Grant was a misfit if ever there was one. His slouching posture may have been the worst ever seen at West Point, his marching style was better suited to a ploughman than a soldier, and in four years of trying, no one was ever able get across the idea that spit and polish was the hallmark of an officer and a gentleman. He seemed to find it offensive to brush his clothes, to button his jacket, to clean his gun or to get out of bed at the sound of a bugle call. He was marked immediately as "unsoldierly" and put into the special "awkward squad," where he stayed until it became awkward for his officers to leave him there.

He wasn't too interested in studying the arts of war, either, and spent as much time reading novels as accounts of the Napoleonic campaigns. But he wasn't a complete failure. At the end of his second year, he was promoted to sergeant, though it was whispered it was because he couldn't march in step and sergeants marched behind, not with, their men. But his career as a non-com ended in his last year and he became a private again. Still, he made it through the full four years. His class had been reduced from seventy-six to thirty nine, but Grant was still hanging on at graduation time. He ranked twenty-first in his class.

He went into the army as a second lieutenant after that, and was sent to a quiet post a few miles south of St. Louis. Not much happened there, except that he met Julia Dent, the sister of one of his former West Point classmates. He asked her to marry him, but before they could he was shipped off to Louisiana and didn't come back for four years. It was fine with him, he was too shy for courtship anyway. It was apparently fine with Julia, too, because when he finally did come back for her, she married him even though her father didn't approve.

But in the meantime, Lieutenant Grant got his first taste of a shooting war when he served as a quartermaster under Zachary Taylor, and later under Winfield Scott in the Mexican War. He was with the army when it reached Mexico City and served there for eight months in the army of occupation. It was during that time that he began drinking.

When he married Julia, and they were transferred to the shores of Lake Ontario, he took a temperance pledge, but it didn't stick. After he was made a captain and moved to the wilds of northern California, he went off the wagon with a thud, and his commanding officer finally asked for his resignation. On July 31, 1854, Captain Ulysses S. Grant became a private citizen without a job, without money and fifteen hundred miles from home.

He managed to get back to Ohio on borrowed money, and eventually reached Missouri, where his father-in-law gave him an eight-acre farm. When that failed, he tried to support his wife and four children in the real estate business and, failing at that, went to Illinois to accept the charity of his brothers.

Meanwhile, the country was heading pell mell into a civil war, and it seemed obvious that there would be a place in it for a West Point-trained army officer. After the attack on Fort Sumter, he joined Galena's volunteer militia company and turned the men into a presentable unit. But when they marched off to Springfield to join the state militia, he was the least presentable of all, and followed the company in his threadbare clothes several paces behind them.

He had hopes of becoming a militia officer, but the Governor couldn't seem to find anything for him to do. He put Grant in charge of creating forms for the adjutant-general and then turned his attention to handing out commissions to men with better political connections. Grant later said that he'd have been just as happy to sit out the war there, but he felt that since the government had given him an education, he had an obligation to use it in government service. But his letter to the War Department was never answered.

Eventually, he was made a drill master at a nearby militia camp. But though he did a good job of turning farm boys into soldiers, he still looked like a farmer himself. He couldn't afford a uniform. And when the volunteers moved out to fight the war, Grant went home. There was nothing more for him to do.

If the authorities didn't see any value in having Grant around, the men he had trained had acquired a grudging respect for him. And when it became obvious that the captain in charge of the Twenty-First Illinois was an incompetent, Captain Grant was recalled. They were an unruly lot and a lack of discipline had turned them into something more like a mob than a fighting unit. But within a month, Grant transformed them into a proud regiment. They even saluted the officers. But Grant, who had been made a colonel, still didn't look the part. He let junior officers lead his men in dress parades because he still didn't have a uniform

or a horse. A local businessman came to his rescue, and when his regiment moved into Missouri to chase down renegade rebels, he wasn't forced to walk and his clothes weren't threadbare.

Missouri wasn't the place for an officer to make a name for himself, but an odd bit of political maneuvering brought Grant's name up in Washington one day. Brigadier generals were created at the time by the President on the advice of political leaders, rather than on their military records. The Congressman from Galena was put out that no commissions had gone to any of his constituents, and he insisted on having at least one to his credit. He got what he wanted, and the ranking officer in his district read in a newspaper a few weeks later that he was now Brigadier General Grant.

The rest, as they say, is history. A few days after receiving his commission, he led an assault on Fort Donelson on the Cumberland River, and in an afternoon took not only the fort, but fifteen thousand troops. The people of the North, hungry for a victory, were ecstatic. Grant was promoted to major general and put in command of all the Union forces in Western Tennessee.

His record from there on made him even more of a public hero, and though there were disasters along the way, he earned a place in the hearts of the folks back home with an impressive victory at Vicksburg and at Chattanooga, cutting the Confederacy away from the Mississippi River and the West. But he got an even better reward than public acclaim. President Lincoln made him a member of the regular army rather than a general of the militia as he had been until then, and put him in command of all the Union forces.

General Grant with his wife, Julia, and one of his sons, Frederick Dent Grant.

Exactly thirteen months later, the Confederacy crumbled and General Grant was a national hero the like of which the country hadn't seen since George Washington himself. And America's enthusiasm never wavered, even through eight years of a disastrous presidency.

In a way, it was the adulation that brought disaster to the Grant Administration. He thought the presidency was a reward and not a responsibility, and he didn't have any feel for politics. That was just fine with the politicians. There was money to be made. A company had been formed to build a transcontinental railroad, and the Government was committed to help by donating public land and lending the builders $27 million or more to finance the project. It was like giving some Congressmen a key to the treasury.

They became stockholders in Credit Mobilier, the company that held mortgages on the unbuilt railroad, and sat back to watch the money pour in. After their scheming was revealed, the books were closed, and the Congressional investigation that followed didn't turn up any hard figures, nor any indictments. No one knows who made what, though the profits to the stockholders were estimated at $23 million, and most of them hadn't invested any of their own cash. It was conceded that Grant himself wasn't involved. He never seemed directly involved in any of the financial scandals of his eight years in office, in fact. But as

Grant was probably the most beloved war hero, Washington included, in the history of the country.

much as the people loved President Grant, he admired men who knew how to make money and was very good at looking the other way when they did.

He was indirectly involved in what was nearly a successful scheme by Jim Fisk and Jay Gould to corner the gold market by raiding the Federal supply. He smiled when Congress doubled his salary, and then said nothing when they raised their own and made the increase retroactive for the previous two years. He didn't raise an eyebrow when the Treasury Department hired an enthusiastic collector of back taxes and gave him half of all he found. And when his War Secretary resigned after being accused of peddling influence for profit, the President accepted it with "deep regret."

By the end of his eight years in the White House, Grant was weary with it all, and took his wife on a trip to Europe. They had no special plan, and said they'd come home when they ran out of money. They were gone more than two years and traveled around the world. When he came home, Grant's supporters were clamoring to send him back to the White House. He may not have liked the idea, but didn't discourage it. He needed the job. When he lost the nomination at the 1880 Republican Convention, he went to New York to find work.

He went into the investment business with a young man named Ferdinand Ward, who turned out to be swindler, and took Grant and his son for everything they had. By the time Ward went to jail to atone for his financial sins, the former President was left with less than two hundred dollars to his name. He had a small income from investments, but to all intents and purposes, the most popular man in America was broke.

No less a person that Samuel Clemens, better known as Mark Twain, came to the rescue with a contract for Grant to write magazine articles about the Civil War, and an advance of $25,000 on his memoirs. It would be enough to support him for the rest of his life, which it was now painfully apparent wouldn't be long. The former president had throat cancer. He worked as fast as he could on the book because he desperately wanted to provide for Julia after he was gone. And less than a month after the manuscript was finished, the great man died. The book realized $450,000 for his widow, more money than he had ever been able to give her in life.

His funeral was described by the London Times as the greatest assembly of distinguished Americans ever brought together. But it also represented an outpouring of affection by ordinary Americans. Grant was something more than just a war hero, he was one of them. A few years later, some ninety thousand ordinary people raised funds to build a marble tomb for the former president and his wife overlooking the Hudson River in New York. It became a more popular attraction than the Statue of Liberty for more than three decades. More than a quarter of a million people visited Grant's Tomb each year to remember the man who was possibly the most popular president who ever lived.

The 19th President
RUTHERFORD B. HAYES
(1877-1881)

When he moved into the White House, President Hayes banned smoking, cussing and drinking in the executive mansion. Most people put the blame on Mrs. Hayes, whom they called "Lemonade Lucy."

The advertising slogan, "I Got My Job Through The New York Times" could easily have been created for Rutherford Birchard Hayes, who may never have been President except for a bit of skulduggery that began in *The Times's* editorial office on election night, 1876.

The paper's first edition that night had said that first returns were inconclusive, but pointed out that the election seemed to be going to Hayes's Democratic opponent, Samuel J. Tilden of New York. It presented a dilemma to the editors. Tilden was a local boy, but *The Times* was a strong voice for the Republican Party in those days. As they met to decide what to say in their second edition, they received a message from the state's chief Democrat asking for their figures which, then as now, were considered unusually reliable. They also had an inquiry from the Democratic National Committee asking for their figures on the races in Florida, Louisiana and South Carolina.

Like good newspapermen, they read between the lines. If the Democrats weren't sure their man had carried those four states, why print the news that Tilden had won, as the rival Tribune had done? They proceeded to assume that Hayes had carried all the questionable states except Florida, and pointed out that if Hayes was a winner in the Sunshine State, he'd be President by one electoral vote.

It was heady stuff. What if he could? One of the editors went to the Republican National Headquarters and galvanized them into action. They sent wires to the party chairmen in all the doubtful states, telling them not to concede. Then a party official boarded a train for Florida to help nudge it out of the doubtful column. Meanwhile, each the other states involved claimed a Hayes victory, and the post-election final edition of *The Times* reported that the Republican candidate had won. But it wasn't over yet.

The Democrats didn't take it lying down. They raised technical questions about the legality of elections in a half-dozen states, and confusion reigned for more than a month. The law required that all returns should be validated by December 6, the day the electoral college was scheduled to meet, and Louisiana, the last state to report, waited until less than an hour before the deadline. By declaring for Hayes, it gave him the presidency by the one vote *The Times* had claimed back in November. And that's when the crisis really began.

The Democrats issued a challenge, and each state was required to resubmit its vote. In Oregon, one of the Republican electors turned out to be a Federal employee, which is illegal, and the Democratic Governor appointed one of his own fellow party members to replace him. It gave one of the state's three votes to Tilden, and changed the balance in the Democrat's favor.

At the same time, it was revealed that an Oregon

65

Republican elector had been "bought" by the other side for $10,000, and then it was reported that similarly "outrageously villainous" manipulations had taken place in other states as well. The Democrats countered with what they said was proof that the other side had paid even more and said that both sides had been offered Louisiana's votes for a million dollars. Neither side admitted to having paid anything, but one of the players pointed out that "the spirit of politics is different in Louisiana than it is with us."

As the charges and countercharges raged and boards of inquiry were established, inauguration day was coming fast, and no one knew for sure whose hand would be placed on the Bible come March 4. It was up to Congress to decide. But Congress has never been known for making speedy decisions, especially when politics are involved. Hayes proposed that the President of the Senate should make the decision, based on the certification of each state's election board, and his finding taken to the Supreme Court for final judgement. Tilden said that both houses of Congress should investigate which state canvasses were valid and leave the final decision up to the House of Representatives. It was only natural. The Democrats had a majority in the House. The President of the Senate, who had replaced the deceased Vice President, was possibly the most loyal Republican in the country.

While the country was waiting for a decision, passions ran high. There were threats of an armed uprising. Democratic war veterans banded together to pledge a hundred thousand soldiers to march on Oregon to claim its vote. Republicans promised half

again as many armed men to take Oregon and California, too. Tilden supporters pointed out that, as Governor of New York, he had the power to call up the National Guard in his state, and the influence to produce the militias of several neighboring states.

Tilden himself was more conciliatory, though far from willing to give up. He called for arbitration, which the politicians interpreted as an invitation to make deals. The Southern bloc was interested in ending occupation by Federal troops. They were also interested in a transcontinental railroad across the South, and called for the excommunication of carpetbaggers from the political process there. They found a willing partner in Mr. Hayes, who had been thinking along those lines anyway.

On the other hand, neither of the presidential hopefuls was sure of the complete loyalty of his party brethren. Both men had run campaigns dedicated to driving the rascals out, and as they were discovering, rascals don't go without a fight. There were politicians on both sides who would have been pleased to see their own candidate on the outside looking in. When Hayes seemed willing to make a deal with Southern Democrats, the Northern Republican bosses began to grumble, and cracks began appearing.

It was finally agreed that a special commission composed of members of both houses and the Supreme Court would iron out the mess, and that their decision would be binding unless it was rejected by both the Senate and the House. Both candidates were against the scheme, but both finally agreed to it.

The commission worked on a state by state basis, and in the end ruled that all of the Southern states in question, as well as Oregon, were committed to Hayes. But there was still plenty of counting and probing to do, and the Democrats in the House decided to stall the effort by talking it to death. A filibuster could keep the commission's decisions from coming to the floor for a vote and render them moot.

The talkathon finally came to an end, and voting began, after a marathon eighteen-hour session two days before inauguration day. At four in the morning, the President of the Senate announced that Rutherford B. Hayes had received 185 electoral votes and Samuel J. Tilden 184. "Wherefore, I do declare," he said, "that Rutherford B. Hayes of Ohio, having received a majority of the whole number of votes is duly elected President of the United States." It was over. But some newspapers couldn't resist referring to the President-elect as Rutherfraud B. Hayes.

Neither Hayes nor Tilden were the kind of men to involve themselves in a gutter-fighting political circus, although both were thoroughly experienced politicians. Hayes had engineered his own inauguration, but had emerged as an independent man, as William Cullen Bryant wrote, "whose very name is conclusive evidence of the most uncompromising determination of the American people to make this a pure government once more." Tilden had been involved in the downfall of the infamous Tweed Ring in New York City and was perceived as a dedicated enemy of corruption. The country had been rocked by scandals during the Grant Administration, but the President himself was still immensely popular. Both candidates in the 1876 election were selected on the basis of their high ideals and their admiration of Grant as a man. But, as was customary in those days, neither of them actually campaigned for the office. That was the job of the party leaders. And that was the problem. They were, by and large, the same men who had got Grant into trouble, and in spite of high-sounding rhetoric, they wanted to keep the good times rolling.

Like Andrew Jackson, Rutherford B. Hayes was born a few months after the death of his father. The elder Hayes, a descendant of a family that emigrated from Scotland to Connecticut in the 1680s, had made a respectable living in New England before moving on to Delaware, Ohio, where he built the town's first brick house and furnished it more elegantly than any house for miles around.

Ironically, one of the sources of his income was a distillery. As President, Hayes imposed a strict ban on alcohol at the White House, much to the chagrin of Washington partygoers, one of whom commented after a state dinner that "the water flowed like champagne." Hayes took all the credit for the ban along with a prohibition on smoking and cussing inside the White House gates. But most people put the blame at the door of Mrs. Hayes, the former Lucy Dare Webb, daughter of a prominent family from Virginia and Kentucky whom most Washingtonians called "Lemonade Lucy."

As a young man, Hayes hadn't suffered any of the usual hardships associated with fatherless boys in the 19th century. He was looked after by his mother's brother, Sardis Burchard, one of the richest men in Ohio. Burchard owned the biggest retail store in Cleveland and he had bought so much land in that part of Ohio that the Seneca Indians referred to him as "the man who owns all the land."

With money comes influence, and there was almost no one in Ohio who didn't owe at least one small favor to Sardis Burchard. He saw to it that his nephew had the best possible education, first at expensive private academies, then at Kenyon College. Hayes went on to study law at Harvard, and then opened a law practice in Lower Sandusky, moving quickly on to Cincinnati, where business was better.

From that point on, he didn't need Uncle Sardis's money any longer, though it was always available to him if he did. His law practice was a huge success and a sideline of land speculation more profitable still. By the time he married Lucy, he was able to buy the most elegant house in Cincinnati for her, and was starting to think in terms of a career in politics for himself.

His first elective office was as city solicitor, a job he gave up just before the outbreak of the Civil War when he joined the army as a captain. In the space of a few months, he became an adjutant general, and before much longer he had gone through the ranks, so to speak, to major general. It was a title he treasured for the rest of his life, and he swelled with pride at being called "General Hayes."

He became something of a war hero back in Ohio when he sustained a major wound in combat, and the local politicians took advantage of it by nominating the General as a candidate for Congress. Hayes was pleased to accept the honor, but pointed out that there was still a war to fight and that he'd neither campaign for the office nor serve until his country didn't need him any longer in the field of battle. They kept him on the ballot anyway, and he was elected. But true to his word, he didn't go to Washington until almost a year after the war had ended.

It is the kind of stuff American voters have always treasured, and they reelected Hayes to Congress in 1866. After that, they gave him two terms as Governor of Ohio. He turned down a bid for the U.S. Senate in 1872, but he was reelected Governor again four years later, and a year after that he became the Republican candidate for President.

The long road didn't end on inauguration day. There were death threats and Hayes was urged to go to Washington in secret, but he insisted on riding to the Capitol in an open carriage. Six special government agents were assigned to protect him, the first time the "Secret Service" took on the responsibility for a President's life. But their services weren't required. Hayes had taken the advice of his advisers and had secretly taken the oath of office two days earlier, but the public ceremony went off as scheduled without the threatened disruption. And then he proceeded to make a statement that changed the way America looks at itself.

Hayes did not campaign when he ran for his first political office. But later in life he was out there kissing babies with the best of them.

Like so many of the men who preceded him, the major thrust of his inaugural address was a search for solutions to the Southern problem. He said it was time for them to get back to self-government, and that the Federal occupation of the Southern states should end. He also said that the Government had an obligation to establish rights for the people it had emancipated. Then he told his audience that it was time for the United States to stop thinking of itself as a union of states, but as a nation. It was almost a year into the country's second century, but it was a new idea. And it was food for thought.

He began to put the idea to work by withdrawing Federal troops from the South and ending the era of Reconstruction. And then he took on the politicians who had grown fat over the years through the dispensing of Federal jobs with an executive order making it a rule that Federal employees could not be required or permitted to take part in political organizations. It didn't do much for his personal popularity, but it required that anyone on the Government payroll who also held a party post had to resign one or the other. He had made good on his promise to reform the civil service and, for a change, the rascals were beginning to be driven out. His own fellow Republicans were affected as well as Democrats, and neither side had much use for Rutherford B. Hayes.

In the middle of his Administration, Hayes's old adversary, Tilden, reopened the wounds of the election by calling for a Congressional investigation of new irregularities he said he had uncovered. But after more than six months of hearings, the committee concluded that Tilden's men were more guilty than Hayes's and the matter was quietly dropped. Hayes was exonerated and Tilden's political career ended.

Hayes had said that he didn't want a second term, and the party leaders, who weren't too enamored by the way he had hit their pocketbooks, took him at his word. But they ran on his record and won. He retired to the Ohio mansion his uncle had bequeathed to him and spent the rest of his life making it more magnificent than he had found it, just as he had done with the office of the presidency.

Hayes decided not to run for a second term, much to the relief of the job seekers he had left out in the cold. However, his successor ran on the Hayes record and won.

The 20th President

JAMES A. GARFIELD

(1881)

In 1872, a strange man who in his checkered career had been a street corner evangelist, a bill collector, a blackmailer and a storefront lawyer, decided to try his hand at politics. An ambassadorship would be nice way to begin, he thought, and eventually the road would surely lead to the presidency itself.

Charles Julius Guiteau took the first step by writing a speech supporting the candidacy of Horace Greeley in the '72 election and delivered it at every opportunity he could find. Greeley lost anyway, and Guiteau went back to preaching on street corners. But he believed God had singled him out for greater things, and when it seemed that former President Grant would be the Republican nominee in the 1880 campaign, he changed a few words in his Greeley speech and got ready to take to the hustings for Grant.

As it turned out, James A. Garfield was the Party's choice but that was no problem for Guiteau. All it took was a new paragraph and a new title, and after sending it off to the printer, the writer sat back and waited for invitations to deliver it from every available stump. None came, but when Garfield won the election, Guiteau was convinced it was his speech that did the trick. He had spent several months sitting in the lobby of New York's Fifth Avenue Hotel, the Republican Party headquarters, and developed a nodding acquaintance with all the important leaders who rushed past him each day. All of them had been handed copies of his speech, even though it is unlikely any of them read it, and they generally regarded him as an eccentric. Guiteau, on the other hand, regarded them as intimates, and after the Garfield inauguration he expected red carpet treatment at the White House.

To his credit, the new President didn't even smirk when the scruffy little man told him he expected an appointment as Minister to Austria. When the office-seeker was told the post had already been filled, he allowed that he'd settle for Paris instead. Garfield politely agreed to turn the request over to his new Secretary of State, James G. Blaine. Guiteau, who had often tipped his hat to Blaine back at the Fifth Avenue Hotel, was sure his old friend would take good care of him.

But Blaine was unimpressed, and Guiteau began haunting both the State Department and the White House, leaving behind notes signed only with his initials. As he was wearing out his welcome, his single suit was wearing out even faster. His shirt was frayed, his socks long since discarded, and it was obvious he was long overdue for a square meal. But Charles Guiteau was a determined man. After more than two months of daily visits, though, his confidence began to waver. A White House usher threatened to have him arrested if he ever showed his face there again, and on the same day, the Secretary of State told him never ever to mention the name Paris in his presence again.

It was the day Charles Julius Guiteau decided that "if the President was out of the way, everything would go better." He had a little bit of money left and invested ten dollars in a fancy pistol. He could have gotten a cheaper model, but his sense of destiny told him that his gun would eventually become a museum piece.

He began haunting the city jail with the same doggedness he had shown at the White House. If he was going to kill the President, he needed to be sure of being taken to a place that would be safe from lynch mobs. Once he was satisfied that the jail was safe and comfortable, he started stalking Garfield. He couldn't shoot him in the White House because he had worn out his welcome there, and he couldn't get him in a crowd because he didn't know how to handle a gun. But he knew his time would come.

His best opportunity came a full month after he began, and after he had made at least three attempts and lost his nerve each time before pulling the trigger. As Garfield was crossing the waiting room of Washington's Baltimore & Potomac railroad station on his way for a vacation, the assassin fired two shots into his back and rushed off in the direction of the nearest policeman who hustled him off to the safety of the jail.

The doctors who saw Garfield in the next few hours gave up all hope that he'd survive his wounds. But he lived through the night, and even seemed on the way to recovery the following day. He lived through eighty more days, in fact, with his personal popularity rising with each daily medical bulletin. By the time he died in mid-September, there wasn't a person in America who wasn't overtaken with genuine grief, except possibly Charles Julius Guiteau who was convinced all the way to the end of a hangman's rope that his act had been an act of God.

James Abram Garfield had considered himself a man of God all his life. He grew up on the Northern Ohio frontier, where religion bound people together. He had been "saved" by the Disciples of Christ at nineteen, and a year later enrolled in the sect's own school to continue his education in mathematics and science and in the ways of the world through the eyes of evangelical Christians. He took to it like a duck to water, and his zeal made him the school's best debater. It also put him in great demand as a preacher and it was a rare Sunday that young Garfield didn't appear in the pulpits of at least two churches.

He said he felt that the hand of the Lord was guiding him to some higher purpose, and in 1854 he ventured out of the wilderness to become a student at Williams College in Massachusetts. The hand that guided him there belonged to Mark Hopkins, the school's President, who became his mentor. Garfield's view of the world broadened under Hopkins's wing, but he stuck to his faith and spent weekends touring New England as an itinerant preacher. It seemed obvious that he had made a career choice, but at the end of his two years at Williams, he decided that it would be better to become a teacher because, "it is disagreeable to talk of money in connection with the Gospel, and yet I must."

He needed money because he wanted to marry

James A. Garfield had been a mule driver and a stevedore, a college president and a congressman, but in 1880, the image of a farmer seemed to suit him best.

PUBLISHED BY CURRIER & IVES. COPYRIGHT 1880, BY CURRIER & IVES, N.Y. 115 NASSAU ST. NEW YO

FARMER GARFIELD
Cutting a Swath to the White House.

Lucretia Rudolph, daughter of an influential member of the Disciples of Christ, and a trustee of Garfield's former school, the Eclectic Institute, back in Ohio. Garfield had earned the money to go to Williams by teaching at the Eclectic, and his old job was still open. He decided to take it, make Lucretia his wife and live happily ever after in the Ohio Western Reserve. But he had seen the outside world by then and things weren't quite the same back home as he remembered them. Even when they made him President of the school and he was able to liberalize its outlook, he felt he should operating on a bigger stage.

Garfield's big chance came when a state senator died, and he was chosen to succeed him. His well-developed skill as a speaker made him a star in Columbus, and in the national election of 1860 his speeches for the Lincoln-Hamlin ticket were credited with delivering the Ohio vote to the Republicans. When war broke out, he was one of the first to join up, but the Governor, who had the final say in such matters, rejected his request on the grounds that he was too valuable in the Legislature. Eventually, though, he was appointed Colonel of the 42nd Regiment, a sorry bunch of farm boys with nothing to recommend them but enthusiasm, and very little of that. Garfield had some experience in dealing with such lads back at the Eclectic Institute, and he turned them into soldiers in a few weeks, drilling and disciplining them by day and educating himself in the arts of war by night.

They gave a good account of themselves in Kentucky and Garfield became a hero back home. He was soon put in command of a brigade and his fame spread even wider. It didn't go unnoticed by the Republican leadership in Ohio, who were desperate for a congressional candidate. When they asked him, Garfield refused to volunteer. He had long since developed a personal policy of never taking an assignment that didn't come looking for him, and so the politicians went to work to draft him. He won the election by a three-to-one margin.

But in the meantime, he was still in the army, and in the period between the election and the convening of Congress he was made a general and sent to Tennessee as Chief of Staff of the Army of the Cumberland. And when Congress got down to business at the end of 1863, the thirty-two-year-old freshman Representative from Ohio took his seat in a brass-buttoned general's uniform. He would soon get rid of the uniform, but he kept the seat for the next seventeen years, during which time he would serve as Chairman of the powerful Appropriations Committee.

Almost from his first day in Congress, he was something of a curiosity because of his voice. He himself said that in all his years in the House, almost none of his colleagues could be heard in every part of the room as well as he could. And as an ex-preacher who had developed a florid, classical style of oratory, all of his colleagues listened to what he had to say. He became known as a radical, who not only viewed all Democrats as agents of Satan, but didn't think all Republicans were saints, either. Among the

Republicans he despised was Abraham Lincoln, who he described as a "second-rate Illinois lawyer." But in the interest of party harmony, he did agree to support the President for a second term.

He didn't get along very well with Andrew Johnson, either, saying that Lincoln's successor was nothing more than a back-sliding Democrat and, as he delighted in pointing out during Johnson's campaign for reelection, so was Lincoln's assassin, John Wilkes Booth. But if he had made enemies of some Republican Presidents, his loyalty to the Party itself verged on fanaticism, and he became one of its acknowledged leaders. Typically, though, he found it hard to respect its other leaders, and he joined with others to form a wing of their own. But just as typically, when they proposed that he should run for the Senate, he refused unless the nomination first came to him. It didn't, and he stayed in the House of Representatives.

Some of the mud hurled at members of Congress who bought railroad stock during the Grant Administration stuck to Garfield, who had been approached by the stock peddlers and had invested in the scheme. But he had also seen the error of his ways and got out long before the scandal broke. Yet it didn't help his political career, and for the first time he had to work for reelection. It shook his faith in politics, but not enough to be counted out.

He was the senior Republican in the House by then, and in line to become Speaker, which he often said was the highest office he ever really wanted. He was made a member of the bipartisan committee formed to make a final decision on the contested election of Rutherford B. Hayes, and he found himself in a position to change the fortunes of his beloved Party. And in the midst of it all, his own fortunes changed when the Ohio leadership made him a United States Senator.

It was then that serious rumors around Washington had it that Garfield was on the verge of becoming President. Garfield himself, characteristically, put down the rumors and accepted an offer from presidential hopeful John Sherman to represent him as a delegate to the 1880 Republican National Convention. It was one of the stormiest conventions of all time, with former President Grant trying to make a comeback and a half-dozen others, including Garfield's friend, Sherman, trying to stop him. After twenty-eight ballots, almost none of the delegates had changed their votes, and none of the contenders had enough to win the nomination. The activity in the smoke-filled back rooms went on around the clock, and when it was reported to Garfield that he was being considered to break the deadlock, he said "I won't permit it."

They surprised him with the announcement that he had received sixteen Wisconsin votes on the thirty-fourth ballot. When he rose to his feet to protest, the chairman ruled him out of order and the bandwagon started rolling.

It meant that each of the state delegations had the right to alter their own votes before balloting could be considered closed. Before the poll was over, Garfield had been nominated by acclamation. It meant that he'd have to give up the Senate seat he had just won without ever filling it, but in spite of his protestations the candidate was a happy man. He retired to the front porch of his home in Mentor, Ohio, to keep an eye on the campaign and wait for the voters to have their say. It was a close election as it turned out, the closest in American history in fact, with the margin of victory at less than one-tenth of one percent. When the votes were counted the Democrats talked of contesting it, but backed down when they remembered the trauma of the Hayes-Tilden election. The outcome gave Garfield something more than a lease on the White House. It breathed new life into a tottering Republican Party and now he had a chance to rebuild it in his own image.

In the early days of his Administration, Garfield was able to calm the troubled political waters, and showed signs of becoming one of the great presidents. He was even, in his short term, able to reduce the national debt, saved the taxpayers some $10 million a year and produced enough confidence in the Government that it was able to sell its own bonds without consorting to middlemen. The people, who had been hungry for presidential leadership, felt they had found their man, and many were saying that he was the greatest President since Andrew Jackson. In terms of popularity, they may have been right. But no President before him, Jackson included, had as much political savvy as James A. Garfield. And by the beginning of his first summer in office, when he was finally able to put his knowledge to work, the future looked very bright, both for the President and the country. It was then he decided he could could take an extended vacation on the New Jersey shore. But a man with a gun changed everything.

In spite of the availability of modern devices to locate the bullets that had been fired at him from an assassin's gun, medical science wasn't able to extend James Garfield's presidency past its 199th day.

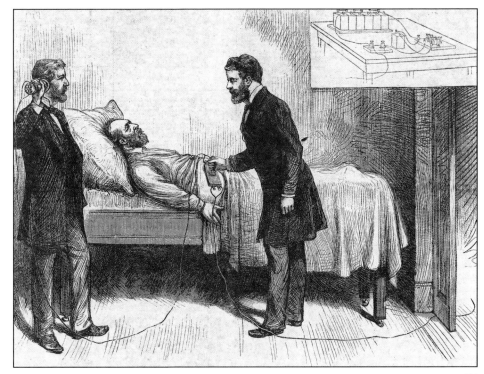

The 21st President
CHESTER A. ARTHUR
(1881-1885)

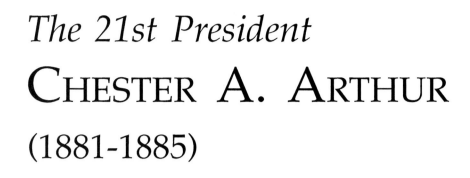

"Chet Arthur President of The United States? Good God!"

It doesn't rank as one of the great political slogans of American history. But during the weeks President James A. Garfield was fighting for his life after having been struck down by an assassin, it was the most commonly-heard comment about his possible successor, Chester A. Arthur. As *The New York Times* said of the Vice President, "no holder of that office has ever made it so plainly subordinate to his self-interest as a politician and his narrowness as a partisan." But no one was nearly as nervous about the succession as Mr. Arthur himself. When word reached him that the President had died, he wept openly, not for the dead President, but for the new one, and said, "I hope ... my God, I do hope, it's a mistake."

Though he was the most urbane of all the presidents, Chester Arthur enjoyed an occasional picnic in the country.

During the Grant Administration, a wing of the Republican Party known as the Stalwarts had amassed a huge amount of power following their philosophy that every job in government had a price tag, and every official owed time and loyalty as well as money to the party boss. Chief among the bosses was Senator Roscoe Conkling of New York, and Chet Arthur was his chief henchman. It was only natural that when the job of Collector of the Port of New York became open, President Grant gave the nod to Arthur in return for his hard work and unswerving loyalty to Republicans in general and Stalwarts in particular.

Of all the jobs in the Federal Government, the Collector at the New York Custom House was easily at the top of the heap in those days. The $50,000 annual salary, the same amount the President earned, made it a plum all by itself. Members of Congress and Supreme Court Justices earned only $7,500. But more important, the Custom House payroll was close to $2 million, which was worth employee kickbacks to the Party of nearly $40,000 a year. And the Collector was the man who decided who got jobs and who kept them.

Chester Arthur was easily the right man for the job. He earned his stripes as the head of the New York Quartermaster office with the rank of Brigadier General during the Civil War. Responsible for all the army's food and equipment purchases in New York State, he became a very important man to the local business community. He earned their respect through what they saw as a sense of fairness, and he earned their friendship with his personal style and flair for the good life. By the time he got the Collector's job, he had established himself among the important businessmen in New York by joining all the right clubs, and was more like one of them than the political hacks who had been Collector in years before. Even though they knew he was Conkling's boy, they also knew they could trust him and he became their conduit to the White House. He didn't let them down. He also won the confidence of his employees by using his influence to save some from proposed job cuts, and to save all from projected salary cuts. And the Republican politicians loved him from the beginning. Everyone who knew him knew they could count on him for favors big and small; to find jobs, to rush shipments through customs. Whatever needed to be done, he gave them service with a smile.

They all agreed Chet Arthur was the hardest-working Collector any of them could remember. But that could have been just a matter of who they compared him to. He did improve efficiency to a remarkable degree, but he almost never showed up for work himself until early afternoon. Chester A. Arthur was a *bon vivant* during an age still remembered for its lavish life style. He enjoyed nights out with the boys, and almost never arrived home before the small hours of the morning. But his nights on the town, much as he enjoyed them, were another facet of the job. They cemented friendships and extended his influence, which helped make Roscoe Conkling and the Stalwarts all the more powerful.

After years of agitation to reform the civil service, all hope was abandoned during Grant's second term, and men like Chester Arthur were free to dispense favors on a grand scale. And because he did it well, he became the first man in a generation to keep the job of Collector for the full four-year term. When Grant nominated him for an unprecedented second term, the Senate confirmed it without debate and without a dissenting vote.

But when Rutherford Hayes became President, the issue of civil service reform came back with a vengeance, and a special commission was established to investigate the operation of a half-dozen custom houses, beginning with the one in New York. For six long weeks, the spotlight was on Chester A. Arthur, and he apparently had reason to squirm. The Commission concluded that his New York operation was overstaffed, inefficient and corrupt. Few employees earned less than $500 a year in bribes, and many admitted to collected twice as much. As for Arthur himself, he said that as far as he was concerned there was no way to improve the efficiency of the New York Custom House, and that he had never hired anyone who wasn't qualified to do the work.

The Commission was unimpressed. It asked for a twenty percent staff cut and longer hours for the people who kept their jobs. President Hayes responded by saying that the best way to change things and restore confidence was to start at the top, and Arthur was asked to resign. The Collector was given the option of accepting an ambassadorship, which would have allowed him to leave New York with his head high and his personal reputation intact. But Arthur was still a loyal Conkling man and rejected the offer as the Senator got ready to do battle with the President over his fiefdom at the edge of New York harbor. Hayes nominated businessman Theodore Roosevelt, father of the future President, to replace Arthur, but he needed the approval of the Senate. And as Chester Arthur sat tight, Conkling began manipulating his colleagues in Washington. After more than a month of debate, Hayes's nomination was rejected.

But Hayes didn't give up. Four months later, a Government investigator reported that an employee of the New York Custom House had pocketed more

than $40,000 of Uncle Sam's money and then had been promoted. It led to two separate investigations, and in mid-summer, when Congress wasn't in session, Hayes suspended Arthur and, because Roosevelt had died, gave the job to Edwin Merritt. He knew he'd have a problem with confirmation when the Senate convened again, but he was sure Merritt could bring about enough change in the meantime to make it hard for them to object. Arthur, meanwhile, refused to resign and in December he went to Washington to save his job. But after two months of stormy testimony, the Administration won and Chester A. Arthur was out of a job.

He wasn't without resources, though. After Merritt began sharing his office, he went back to his old law practice. he didn't lack opportunities for clients, thanks to the contacts he had developed at the Custom House. And he used his time to strengthen the Stalwarts' political fences. As far as he was concerned, things would get better when the do-gooders were voted out along with Hayes in the next election, and he was willing to wait.

Arthur and his fellow Stalwarts went to Chicago for the 1880 Republican Convention firmly committed to renominating former President Grant and making the country safe for the New York machine again. But for all their manipulative skill, the Stalwarts couldn't muster enough votes for their man. And when the deadlocked convention settled on James A. Garfield, the boys in the smoke-filled rooms decided that the ticket headed by an Ohioan needed to be balanced with a running mate from New York, which delivered the most electoral votes.

Arthur was a Stalwart Republican, in the days when just being a Republican wasn't good enough. The party was divided and the job of keeping each faction running in the same direction was more challenging than running the country.

Chet Arthur was what they called a dandy back in the 1880s. He was always well turned out and preferred the company of men who shared his sartorial sensibilities.

Senate and taking his fellow Senator, Thomas Platt, with him. Their letters of resignation, ironically, accused the President of wrongfully rewarding political cronies with lucrative jobs. It went against their principles, they said.

When they went back to New York, the Vice President followed them, making it dramatically clear that, though he was a member of the President's team, his loyalty was still with the former Senator. In fact, they were in Albany together, manipulating New York's divided Republicans on July 2 when President Garfield was shot. And to make matters worse, the assassin, Charles Guiteau, announced to the police officer who arrested him, "I am a Stalwart, and now Arthur will be President." The most common interpretation of that remark among Washington gossips was that Conkling and Arthur had engineered the assassination.

With all that as background, it isn't surprising that most Americans were in a state of panic that this man, Chester Alan Arthur, was suddenly so close to becoming President of The United States.

But Mr. Arthur wasn't what he seemed to be. It was true that his political career had centered on New York and was further narrowed by his loyalty to a political machine. He had developed a genius for politics in his years at the public trough, but he had never developed any illusions about how much he could accomplish, as politicians often do. During the months Garfield lay dying, Arthur's activities were held up to close scrutiny, and he came up a winner. *The New York Sun*, which had never said many good things about him, told its readers, "He is a gentleman in his manners ... his bearing is manly and such as to prepossess his favor on all whom he meets. Truth in speech and fidelity to his friends and his engagements form a part of his character. he has tact and common sense." By the time he took the oath of office, the people were ready to give him the benefit of the doubt.

Roscoe Conkling had no doubts that he'd be named Secretary of State, and was no doubt surprised when the new President passed him by. General Grant made other suggestions for Cabinet posts, and his choices were passed over, too. Then Arthur confounded everyone by ignoring New Yorkers as completely as Garfield had when he was dispensing patronage, and he confounded Conkling further by refusing to replace William Robertson as Collector of the Port of New York. Eventually, the President offered Conkling a seat on the Supreme Court, but the Boss gruffly turned him down. It was a great honor, to be sure. But the salary was only $7,500 a year.

No one called him Chet any more, but though Arthur's political outlook had changed, his outlook ion life stayed the same. He refused to move into the White House until it was redecorated, and he sent to New York for Louis Comfort Tiffany to do the job. When the work was done, the widower President installed his sister as "Mistress of the House," and began entertaining on a scale that no president before him had ever dreamed of. It was to be expected. None

Roscoe Conkling was shocked when he heard that the likely candidate would be Chester A. Arthur, and advised his lieutenant not to accept. But Arthur, in a rare show of independence, decided to go for it. He was able to deliver the New York delegation, even though Conkling boycotted the caucus, and took the nomination on the first ballot. Conkling sat out most of the election and there seemed to be a rift between him and his friend the candidate. But after the inauguration all was forgiven ,and the two men were a team again.

When Garfield passed over New York hopefuls in his Cabinet appointments, Conkling began a war against the Administration, and his most loyal supporter was one of its key members, the Vice President himself. But Garfield was tough and responded to Conkling's threats by withdrawing his nominations of New York Stalwarts to lesser Government jobs, leaving the Senator swinging in the wind without any patronage at all. And to add insult to the injury, he nominated William Robertson, a Conkling enemy, to take over the New York Custom House. Conkling responded by resigning from the of his predecessors was as urbane as Chester A. Arthur.

His work habits were about the same as they had been back in New York, too. He showed up for work late and left his office early. As one president-watcher reported, "Great questions of public policy bore him. No President was ever so much given to procrastination as he is." But he picked good men to help him do the job and fought hard for civil service reform. He had a calming effect on the country that had been traumatized by scandals on every level of the Federal Government, and the second presidential assassination in less than twenty years. And for all his perceived weaknesses, he surprised nearly everyone by bringing a new dignity to the presidency. He may have been a party hack in another life, but President Arthur was clearly a changed man. The Republicans were among the first to notice, and by the time they met to pick their candidate in 1884, a poll of his former cronies back in New York indicated that more than half of them wouldn't support him for dog catcher. It may have been the ultimate compliment.

If the politicians deserted him, the people gave him high marks, and as his Administration came to an end, they were nodding in agreement with *The New York Times's* assessment that Arthur's presidency "has unquestionably been more satisfactory than was expected." Mark Twain added, "I am but one of 55 million; still, in the opinion of this one-fifty-five-millionth of the country's population, it would be hard indeed to better President Arthur's Administration."

No one knew that Arthur was fatally ill and had no intention of running for a second term. He went through the motions to stop rumors about his health, but he had known from the beginning that after 1885 he'd "go into the country and raise big pumpkins." He had been born in rural Vermont, but Chester Arthur wasn't a country boy. When he retired, he went back to New York to pick up the pieces of his law practice. He died less than a year later. At his funeral, the man who had become a master of machine politics early in his career was eulogized not as the man he had been, but the man he became. "Good causes found in him a friend and bad measures met in him an unyielding opponent," said one. And even men who had opposed him said among themselves, "Chet Arthur President of The United States? Good man!"

Arthur may not have been an outdoorsman, but he much preferred being out in the fresh air to being cooped up in his White House office.

The 22nd and 24th President
GROVER CLEVELAND
(1885-1889 & 1893-1897)

Grover Cleveland was the first Democrat to become President in 24 years, and there couldn't have been a more unlikely candidate for the job. When he took the oath of office in Washington, it was the second time in his life he had ever been to the capital. The audience he addressed that day was the largest he had ever seen, and almost no one in the crowd had ever seen him before. The only elective offices he had ever held were as Mayor of Buffalo, New York, and Governor of the State of New York, and he hadn't served a full term in either job.

Yet here he was, all 280 pounds of him, double chins hanging below a walrus moustache, looking for all the world like "the hangman of Buffalo," which was what the Republicans had called him in the recent campaign. The slur stemmed from the fact that once, while Cleveland was a county sheriff, he stepped in to hang a man when the official executioner lost his nerve.

There had been seven different candidates for the presidency in 1884, including one championing women's rights and another advocating temperance. The Republican candidate, James G. Blaine, was much better-known than Cleveland, and a much more experienced politician. But he also had a record of his own to defend, and it was less than honorable. After it had been revealed that he had used his influence as Speaker of the House of Representatives to help a railroad in return for the right to sell its bonds at an inflated commission rate, *The New York Times* switched its support to Cleveland. It must have broken *The Times's* editorial board's heart to support a Democrat, but it announced it could no longer recommend a man like Blaine who had revealed himself as "a prostitutor of the public trusts, a scheming jobber and a reckless falsifier."

All in all, it was a nasty campaign. None of the candidates spent as much time attacking the issues as they did attacking each other. There wasn't much in Cleveland's public record to attract negative attention, so the Republicans began looking into his private life.

Ten years before, a local widow, Maria Halpin, had "bestowed her favors" on several Buffalo men, including Mr. Cleveland. She became pregnant and claimed that the father of her son was the rising young lawyer. Cleveland accepted the responsibility and arranged for the boy's adoption. Maria, meanwhile, turned to alcohol and eventually suffered a mental breakdown. Cleveland arranged to have her institutionalized and forgot about the whole thing until one day, in the midst of the presidential campaign, demonstrators appeared at his door shouting, "Ma, Ma, where's my Pa? Gone to the White House. Ha ha ha."

If there was anyone in America who hadn't heard of Grover Cleveland by then, they couldn't read or they didn't go to church. It was exactly the kind of issue that could sell newspapers and could help preachers hold the attention of their parishioners. Before long, lurid stories were circulating that Cleveland had kept a harem in his bachelor apartment and had spent much of his time prowling the streets of Buffalo looking for innocent women who could satisfy his lust for a few hours before being spirited away to some dark insane asylum. It was a terrific issue for the women's rights candidate, who worried in her speeches about what effect Cleveland's debauches would have on otherwise pure, but impressionable, young men; not to mention the impact a Cleveland presidency would have on the mother, daughters and sisters of every American man.

It was all very titillating until the real father was tracked down. His name was shrouded in secrecy because he was a prominent married man. But in exchange for anonymity, he told the press that Cleveland, who was single at the time, took the responsibility both for him and for the poor fallen woman. Short of marrying her, he had "done the right thing," he said. The tide turned dramatically in Cleveland's favor and, fortunately, the election was still four months away, more than enough time for the voters to forget the scandal. Cleveland, on the other hand, didn't forget, and even though newspaper reports ultimately cleared his name, he never forgave the press for bringing it up in the first place, and he steadfastly refused to grant interviews for the rest of his life. It was a policy that eventually made his life as a public man more difficult than it should have been. He may have had good reason to be angry, though, because the affair may have contributed to an unusually close election. When it was over, Cleveland carried his home state by slightly more than a thousand votes and the national election by less than 24,000.

The Republicans said that Grover Cleveland had been elected by accident, but if that was the case, it may have been the happiest accident that ever happened to America.

After all those years of one-party rule, the republicans were living off the fat of the land. And after winning the 1884 election, the Democrats got the idea that they could begin doing the same thing. But Grover Cleveland wasn't the man to help them do it. In his first term, he vetoed more bills than all twenty-one of his predecessors combined. He also set a new record for replacing office holders, and not one of the firings was based on anything more or less than a careful look at the man's record. Who did the looking? No less a person than the President himself. He was a demon for work. During his first few months in office, he didn't even have a secretary. It never occurred to him that he needed one. He wrote his own letters in longhand, and since there was only one telephone in the White House, he was perfectly capable of answering it himself.

Words like "industrious," "honest," "fair," usually come to mind in connection with Grover Cleveland. A newspaper that supported him in the campaign ran a short editorial under the headline, "Four Good Reasons For Electing Cleveland." It said, "1. He is honest. 2. He is honest. 3. He is honest. 4. He is honest."

He seems to have come by it honestly. He was born Stephen Grover Cleveland, the fifth of nine children of a Presbyterian minister and his wife, in Caldwell, New Jersey. He was fifteen when his father died and he took on the responsibility of supporting the family. He was never out of a job after that. When he was eighteen, he set off for the greener pastures of Cleveland, Ohio, an on the way stopped off in Buffalo to visit his uncle, Lewis Allen, a successful local farmer. It happened that Uncle Lewis was writing a book on the pedigrees of American short-horn cattle, and persuaded his nephew to stay and help him with it. Before the project was over, he convinced the boy to stay and used his influence to get him a job in a local law office where he could learn enough to become a lawyer himself.

Once he passed the bar, he became well-known for his thoroughness. No one ever accused Grover Cleveland of brilliance, even during his presidency, but he seemed to love hard work and spent long hours in the library before ever appearing in court, then memorized all the facts so he wouldn't let his client down. His attention to detail confounded the competition, who almost never did their homework as thoroughly. At one point early in his career, he turned down a chance to become a highly-paid corporation lawyer because he said he didn't need the money, and he was having too much fun with what he was doing.

He felt the same about politics. All he knew about partisanship was that he was against the gang currently in power, but he didn't care enough to do anything about it. But in 1863, as a favor to a sick friend, he accepted an appointment as Assistant District Attorney of Erie County, and unwittingly entered the world of politics as a Democrat. Six years later they put him on the ballot for the office of Sheriff. He told them he didn't want the job, and they told him not to worry. He was nominated to strengthen the candidacy of their congressional hopeful, and they said there was no way a Democrat could be elected to a local office. They were wrong.

He was possibly the most unlikely man ever to run for any office. He weighed about 280 pounds. He had thinning hair and watery eyes hidden under heavy lids. His moustache drooped like a limp dishrag, his double chin looked somewhat like the underbelly of a frog. His voice was slightly high-pitched but flat at the same time. And his complexion was almost dead white. But in those pre-television days, looks couldn't kill a candidate, and 19th-century voters liked men they could trust, probably because they were such a novelty.

"Big Steve" Cleveland was what they used to call "a man's man." When he wasn't burning the midnight oil in his law library, he could usually be found in a hunting or a fishing camp sipping whiskey, playing

Grover Cleveland was the first president to be married in the White House when, at the age of forty-nine, he made twenty-two-year-old Frances Folsom his bride. His family, he said, made life "one grand sweet song."

During his two years in the White House as a bachelor, Cleveland shared the space with a good old friend (right). Cleveland had said that he never had "the slightest particle of ambition" to become president, but after his first inaugural (below), it didn't take much prodding to get him to run for a second term. When he lost that election, it took even less effort to convince him to try again four years later.

poker and swapping off-color stories with the boys. Except for work, it was all he really wanted to do. Women interested him, but he wasn't interested in being married to one.

Culture didn't interest him much, either. The only books he enjoyed were law books, and an occasional sing-along satisfied any need he may have had for listening to music. He did love good food, the more the better, but he was a classic meat-and-potatoes man and proud of it.

But if he loved the good life, he had enough of his Puritan ancestors' blood in his veins to temper it with unbelievably high moral standards. And when he ran for Mayor of Buffalo in 1881, he won by a landslide even though he was a Democrat in solid Republican territory.

But if he was the candidate of the Democrats, Cleveland was about as non-partisan in his outlook as any politician America has ever produced. His wrath against extravagance and inefficiency was legendary, and it didn't matter to him what party label the extravagant and inefficient wore. In his mayoral campaign, he told the voters that he believed public officials were nothing more or less than "the trustees

of the people." A newspaper rewrote the phrase and it came out: "A public office is a public trust," and it became Cleveland's job description for the rest of his life.

He had been Mayor for less than a year when his successes in cleaning up Buffalo propelled him to the candidacy for Governor of New York. He said he didn't want the job, but accepted it as inevitable, and began to root out corruption in Albany as he had done on the shores of Lake Erie. It was a big job, but he took on the Tammany machine, nominally connected with his own Party, and his generally successful effort attracted the notice of important Democrats outside the state. When they met to pick their presidential candidate in 1884, the boys in the back room were excited about this man with the Mr. Clean image. But he didn't have much more to recommend him. He had told them that he had "not the slightest particle of ambition" to be President. His combined service as Buffalo's Mayor and New York's Governor added up to slightly more than two years. On the other hand, he had done more in that short space of time to prove that the words "honest" and "politician" weren't a contradiction in terms than any other man at the convention.

He was at work at his desk in Albany when word reached him that he had been nominated but, characteristically, he barely skipped a beat and went right on working.

Cleveland had been President for two years when, at the age of 49, he decided it was time to get married. It made him the first Chief Executive to be married in the White House, and his twenty-two-year-old bride was the perfect choice to brighten the place up. The former Frances Folson, who had just graduated from college, more than made up for what her husband lacked in personal charm. She charmed him, too. He once told a reporter that life in the White House was "one grand sweet song," a remarkable departure from the attitude of most of his predecessors, most of whom agreed with President Lincoln that, rather than glory, the office brought nothing but "ashes and blood."

Cleveland easily took the nomination for a second term, and won the election by nearly 96,000 votes. But the votes were in the wrong places. He lost the presidency by 70 electoral votes. Among the states that went for his opponent, Benjamin Harrison, was New York, Cleveland's own political base, where the machine politicians had worked against him on principle or, rather, their lack of principles.

Because of his showing in '88, the Democrats renominated him again in 1892, and his victory made him the 24th as well as the 22nd President. He won the popular vote for the third consecutive time, which only Andrew Jackson had done before, and the democrats had found a new lease on life. But their candidate wasn't a loyal party man, and before the second Cleveland Administration was over the Party was divided and thinking of Grover Cleveland as more of a liability than an asset.

His second term wasn't the same "grand sweet song." It was marked from the beginning by a depression, which led to mass unemployment, labor union troubles and distress in the West, where they had never particularly liked Cleveland anyway. He handled the problems the same way he always had, one at a time. But the country was changing. He managed to keep it from changing for the worse, which a lesser man might not have done, but when he retired to his classic Georgian house in Princeton, New Jersey, he was a broken man. When he died there eleven years later, his last words were, "I tried hard to do right."

He had left Washington one of the most unpopular of all the Presidents. He had refused to let party loyalty come ahead of what he perceived as best for the people. In return, congressional leaders on both sides of the aisle regarded him as their enemy. He distrusted the press and didn't care who knew it. But time heals all wounds, and eventually his efforts to do right vindicated him. In the world of politics, it's a rare man who can earn his place in history by placing pure honesty above everything else. But Cleveland always had been a political maverick. His honesty was his downfall as President, but in the end, the truth didn't hurt Grover Cleveland.

By the time his second term as President was over, Cleveland's popularity had plummeted but, as the cartoonists liked to point out, he, at least, thought another four years would be welcome.

The 23rd President

BENJAMIN HARRISON

(1889-1893)

A sure winner in any game of presidential trivia would be to name the man who was the son of a President as well as the father of one. His name was John Scott Harrison, son of William Henry Harrison, the ninth President, and father of Benjamin Harrison, the twenty-third.

He missed his place in history because of his father rather than in spite of him. He began his career as a partner in one of the most prestigious law firms in the State of Ohio, and was well on his way to political fame and financial security when he was forced to give it all up to run his father's estate. William Henry Harrison had inherited an impressive estate, and had built an even grander one of his own. But financial setbacks made keeping it all together a full-time job, and the job fell on his son's shoulders. John Scott did, however, manage to find time to serve as justice of the peace for two decades, to serve in the Congress of the United States, and to father twelve children.

Benjamin Harrison was born at the home his grandfather had built at North Bend, Ohio. Like his brothers and sisters, he was educated on the 600-acre family farm, and when he was fourteen he was sent to a private school to help him get ready for college. His father had hoped to be able to send him to one of the prestigious New England collages, but financial pressures made it necessary for him to enrol at the nearby Miami University of Ohio instead. He studied law in Cincinnati and was admitted to the bar at the age of twenty-one.

By the time his law career began, Ben Harrison was already married to the former Carrie Scott, and when their first child was born they moved to Indianapolis, Indiana, where he was able to establish himself as one of the city's leading attorneys. When the Civil War began, he sued his influence to recruit more than a thousand young men to form the 70th Indiana Volunteer Infantry, and led them off to war as a lieutenant. They gave a good account of themselves in Kentucky, Tennessee and Alabama and when General Sherman led his march to the sea across Georgia, the 70th was in the van, and Lieutenant Ben Harrison received a battlefield promotion to Brigadier General.

When he went back to Indianapolis to pick up the pieces after the war, he was welcomed home as a hero, and was certain he could keep the promise he had made to Carrie that their lives from then on would be filled with "quiet usefulness." Like all returning veterans, he was faced with a debt that had been accumulating while he was away. But, unlike most of them, he had a thriving business to go home to, and even before he hung up his uniform he had been given a profitable sideline as Supreme Court Reporter. In return for collecting and organizing all the decisions of the state's high court, he was able to sell the resulting books to lawyers and keep the profits. He added a new wrinkle by offering to pay express costs for out-of-town customers, and sold out the first edition of the 1864 report in a few weeks. His profit was $1,500, far above anything his predecessors had ever dreamed of earning.

It was only natural that such success would raise eyebrows around town, and eventually Harrison's activities caught the eye of the local collector for the Bureau of Internal revenue. He said that Harrison was a book publisher and that made him subject to taxes on his income. Harrison replied that he was an official of the State of Indiana and as such exempt from Federal taxation. The tax man wouldn't back down and the case went to court. The judge agreed with the tax collector. A circuit court reversed the decision on appeal, and Harrison got his money back. All wasn't forgiven, though. Even in his White House years he regarded tax collectors as a necessary evil, but an evil nonetheless.

As editor of the court reports, Harrison became an authority on legal precedents, which made him a more effective lawyer. And his reputation extended beyond the legal profession and into the world of politics. he had also become a spokesman for the veterans he led off to war. His speeches let them know he understood their problems, and let the politicians know that he could be a vote-getter. His status as the grandson of a President was the icing on the cake, and he proved his value to the Republican Party campaigning for General Grant in 1868.

Between Grant's election and his inauguration, Ben Harrison represented the State in a sensational murder trial and won not only his case, but a new reputation in every part of Indiana. It was time, many

Republicans agreed, to make him their candidate for governor. They tried and failed in 1872, but charges that "plunderers" had engineered the convention to keep a good man man down pushed his political star even higher. Meanwhile, he himself seemed inclined to give up politics in favor of his law practice, which had by then become the most successful and best-known in the State of Indiana.

When party leaders approached him to run for governor again in 1875, he politely refused, saying he was much too busy even to think about it. But before the convention was over, newspapers in both his native Ohio and his adopted Indiana began saying that General Harrison was a front-runner for the 1876 presidential nomination. He wasn't, of course, but the talk, combined with serious splits within the party, resulted in his nomination for governor as "the most popular man in Indiana." It was all done without the candidate's knowledge and over his objections. At first he refused to accept the honor, but after two suspenseful days he finally accepted. The men who nominated him considered themselves independents, but Ben Harrison was the most independent of them all.

Until four days before the election, it looked like Harrison would win in a landslide. The veterans were foursquare behind him, and he looked for all the world like Indiana's most popular man, as his supporters had claimed. But then a third party candidate suddenly withdrew from the race. The Democrats charged that the Republicans had bought him off. Harrison brushed off the charges and kept on campaigning. But when the votes were counted on Friday, the thirteenth of October, the former General had lost the election to democrat "Blue Jeans" Williams. It was a "triumph of blue jeans over blue blood," said a local newspaper. And the message that Benjamin Harrison was one of the local elite wasn't lost on the national Republican leadership.

The presidential election was still a few weeks away, and Harrison took to the hustings for James A. Garfield. His speeches in a half-dozen states gave him even wider national attention, and when he went home to Indianapolis, he was not only the Party's leader in an important state, but the recognized spokesman for young Republicans everywhere in the country.

There was pressure on the new President to represent Indiana in his Cabinet, and the natural choice seemed to be his old friend, Benjamin Harrison. He had delivered his state's electoral votes to Garfield, and had answered the call to take to the stump in other states as well. In fact, Garfield had let it be known that Harrison was the only Hoosier he'd consider for his Cabinet. But Ben Harrison had other ideas.

During the campaign he had quietly planted the thought that he'd like to represent Indiana in the U.S. Senate, and when the republicans took control of the Legislature, his wish came true. As a freshman Senator, he was foursquare on the side of the republican Administration, but soon an assassin's bullet changed everything. Benjamin Harrison didn't have the new President's ear, and without it his influence for patronage to dispense among the Party faithful back home evaporated. But it forced him to rely on his own instincts and political talents, and he soon had the respect and close friendship of most of the important congressional leaders.

By 1884, talk was revived that Benjamin Harrison was the perfect choice as the Republican presidential candidate. But this time the talk was coming from dozens of state delegations to the upcoming convention.

Harrison busied himself with Senate matters and refused to confirm that he'd like the candidacy, and when the Republicans met in Chicago that summer, Senator Harrison was back home in Indiana. He worked hard for the Republican ticket that fall, but candidate James G. Blaine lost the election and Indiana's electoral votes. And when Benjamin Harrison went back to the Senate, it was about to be presided over by a Democrat.

He decided to turn the loss of power to his advantage, and became a leader in the inevitable battle between President Cleveland and the opposition. Hardly a day went by that he didn't take to the floor to speak out against Cleveland, and all the while he was carefully collecting the grievances of former office-holders in both parties which he used in a heart-wrenching speech claiming that the president had wronged widows and orphans in his patronage fight. By the time he was finished, there was hardly a dry eye in the place, and Benjamin Harrison had established himself as a champion of the little people hurt by the juggernaut of politics.

He lost his Senate seat in a bitter fight in 1887, but he had predicted it and said, "I shall shed no tears, for life here is not to me enjoyable." And, free of the Washington scene, he was able to work on reforming the national Republican Party, a job he took on with enthusiasm. When the Party met to pick a candidate in 1888, he was a serious contender, and finally the competition faded, leaving Harrison the convention's choice on the eighth ballot. A few months later he was

Though Benjamin Harrison lost the popular vote by some 90,000, he carried the day with the majority of electoral votes, and even a downpour on inauguration day couldn't dampen the enthusiasm of his fellow Republicans.

President by sixty-five electoral votes, but he wasn't exactly the people's choice. Benjamin Harrison's total of the popular vote was some 90,000 less than Grover Cleveland's.

Even before his inauguration, Harrison sent a message, in the form of his Cabinet selections, to the Republican bosses that he intended to be his own boss. He gave James G. Blaine his old job as Secretary of State, but not until after Blaine had been forced to beg for it, and then he proceeded to name men he trusted to the other seven posts, without once consulting the bosses. And for the next several months he filled other jobs the same way. He claimed to be beholden to no one, but patronage was a way of life in nineteenth-century politics, and when Benjamin Harrison broke the rules, he also broke important ties to the Party and, oddly enough, to the people.

But not all of the people. During his entire political career, the former general was outspoken in his support of Civil War veterans, and had had introduced legislation in the Senate on two different occasions to provide them with liberal pensions. As President, he was able to get a pension program passed. It provided help not only for G.A.R. veterans, but for their children, parents and widows as well. By the end of the Harrison Administration, the yearly cost of the help came to more than $135 million. And its passage pushed the Federal budget over the billion dollar mark for the first time in the history of the Republic.

There were reminders that it had been a long history. Benjamin Harrison was known as the Centennial President because his inauguration fell near the hundredth anniversary of George Washington's. As a descendant of a signer of the Declaration of Independence, he had been the star of centennial celebrations since '76 when he went to Philadelphia to sound the keynote for the country's hundredth birthday. But none of the ceremonials was as impressive as Harrison's visit to New York in 1889. Before he left, he began a campaign to give greater importance to the American flag by issuing an order to have the Stars and Strips flown over every schoolhouse in the country, not to mention the Capitol and the White House in Washington. In a hundred years, no other president had ever thought of such a thing.

His Administration is often relegated to the back pages of history. But during Benjamin Harrison's four years in the White House, he led an expansion of trade with Latin America, he welcomed six new states into the Union, he signed the Sherman Anti-Trust Act into a law that still stands and he succeeded in establishing a protective tariff, an issue that had plagued the country for generations. But politics came back to haunt him in 1890 when the Democrats took control of Congress. It forced Harrison to look outward and to concentrate his attention on foreign affairs. And because his Secretary of States, he took on the job himself.

He took on all comers, from Great Britain to Chile, and let the world know that the United States had come of age and wouldn't stand still for any of them. But in the end, if the great powers of the world were impressed, the folks back home apparently were not, and in the 1892 election Grover Cleveland retook the presidency by more than 375,000 votes, the biggest majority since Lincoln was elected for the second time.

Every time Benjamin Harrison appeared in public over the next two years, he was met with speculation that he might be a presidential candidate again. But he was determined not to be. "The repugnance to further public service," he said, "deepens with me every day." He was active in the nomination and election of William McKinley in 1897, and then he started a whole new career.

He had reestablished himself as a lawyer, and when Venezuela became involved in a border dispute with British Guyana, Harrison was hired as its chief counsel. When the hearings opened in Paris, the British Attorney General spoke for fifty-two hours, and Harrison's rebuttal lasted twenty-five. In the end, the tribunal favored the English, but neither side could claim a real victory. And Benjamin Harrison's status as a lawyer suddenly became more important than his position as a former president. But he clearly enjoyed both roles, and before he died suddenly of pneumonia in 1901, he was arguing cases in the Supreme Court by day and dispensing political advice by night on an increasingly frequent basis. In the eulogies that followed, it was generally agreed that Benjamin Harrison had died at the moment of his greatest usefulness. History has taken a different view. During his four White House years, the Centennial President had set the stage for the United States to accept the challenges of the next century.

When he was President, Benjamin Harrison and his wife, Caroline, shared the White House with their son and daughter-in-law, their daughter and son-in-law, and three grandchildren, as well as with Caroline's father and her niece.

The 25th President
WILLIAM MCKINLEY
(1897-1901)

Though he could look unapproachable, William McKinley was called "sunny" when he was a boy, and as an adult, even his political enemies enjoyed his company.

We all accept as an article of faith that George Washington was first in the hearts of his countrymen, but no president, not even Washington, touched the hearts of people who knew him quite as warmly as did William McKinley. We tend to become cynical about nice guys a century later, but even in the glare of history he remains beloved. No other word suits him quite as well.

Even as a kid growing up in Niles, Ohio, people called him "sunny." He was unusually close to his mother, whose fondest dream for her son was that he would become a Methodist preacher. Both his parents were determined that their children should have the benefits of a good education, and when William was nine they moved to Poland, Ohio, which had a high school. The boy was an eager student, and when he graduated from Poland Academy he went off to college in Pennsylvania, but was forced to drop out when his father's business failed. He went to work as a teacher to help support the family and was saving to go back to school when fate stepped in in the form of the Civil War.

He was among the first to join up and was sent to help fight the war in Virginia with the Twenty-Third Ohio, a regiment commanded by future president Rutherford B. Hayes. Like everyone else, Hayes liked the young soldier, and when the outfit became part of the Army of the Potomac and marched off to the Maryland campaign, he promoted him to sergeant and put him in charge of supplies. It wasn't exactly a job that required heroics, but McKinley took it seriously, and during the Battle of Antietam he calmly delivered hot food to the front line troops. In return, Hayes promoted him again, making him a lieutenant on his own staff, and later said that he was "one of the bravest and finest officers in the army." That was before the day McKinley received a battlefield promotion to major for riding under fire to warn a regiment they were about to be surrounded.

By the time he went back to Ohio he had developed a deep hatred of war, and though he later became a frequent speaker at veteran's encampments, he made it a point never to mention the fighting that had brought them together. He had also decided during the war years that he didn't want to be a preacher after all, and decided instead to get into politics. His mentor, General Hayes, had gone to Congress by then, and when he heard that McKinley had enroled in the law school at Albany, New York, he was horrified. His former aide was too good for politics, he said, and dashed off a letter advising him to get into railroading instead. "A man with half your wit ought to be independent at forty," he said. But William McKinley's mind was made up. Major McKinley was already independent.

After he passed the bar he moved to Canton, Ohio, where he joined every organization in sight, from the Masons to the Knights of Pythias. He became superintendent of the Methodist Sunday school, and he joined the Republican Party. He made a name for himself as an attorney by defending striking coal

miners who had been thrown in jail for starting a riot, and he earned their loyalty be refusing to accept any payment for securing their acquittal. He cut his political teeth campaigning for Hayes in his 1867 bid to become Ohio's Governor, and surprised everyone in a traditionally Democratic corner of the state by being elected himself to the office of prosecuting attorney.

He also found love in Canton the day he met Ida Saxton, the daughter of a local banker. She gave him a new dimension. She had been raised and educated for a cultured life, and had taken the traditional grand tour of Europe before she met her future husband. She gave him a taste for good wine and fine clothes, and generally knocked away the rough edges of his frontier upbringing. Their love never diminished, but she also brought him a difficult life. Their second child died in infancy, and not long afterward Ida began developing convulsions, which left her an invalid for the rest of her life. Then, at the age of three, a daughter they both adored died, just as her father was campaigning for a seat in Congress. He won the election and he and Ida went to Washington the same year Rutherford Hayes went to the White House. Mrs. McKinley wasn't able to attend state functions and the Congressman chose to stay home to attend to her. But their close friendship with the President gave them a social life of sorts that helped them forget their troubles.

McKinley was also a close friend of James Garfield, and he and Ida were frequent guests at the White House during the short Garfield presidency, but neither of them was invited there very often after Garfield's assassination, and they became relative recluses during the rest of McKinley's congressional years. He spent all his free time with his wife, often sitting through entire evenings in the dark because the light bothered her eyes.

But if William was completely attentive to Ida's

needs, he never neglected his career, which was important to both of them. During the day, when he was taking care of business, she busied herself with handicrafts. It was said that she crocheted more than five thousand pairs of bedroom slippers, more than enough for all of Washington's officialdom. And she also enjoyed making satin neckties, which became a kind of presidential trademark. But she was never as happy as when her beloved William was at her side. As she was fond of saying, "He is a dear good man, and I love him." When he was away, he never let a day go by without writing a letter to his wife. And when any well-meaning associates inquired about her health, he usually just smiled and said that she was "improving."

McKinley was away from home a good deal during his years in Congress. He was nearly as devoted to the Republican Party as he was to Ida, and he was always available to spread its gospel. Like so many of his predecessors, he had developed a talent for debating during his growing-up years. But he had the added advantage of a clear and easy voice. He had also cultivated a simple style. And though his speeches often ran on for an hour or more, he never seemed to waste words. He became a kind of matinee idol, and his appearance at a political rally was a sure guarantee of a large and interested audience.

Beyond that, he was very much in demand simply for his company, even among his political opponents. His Methodist upbringing meant drink was anathema to him, and he was offended by off-color stories. But he had developed a taste for cigars, and in the company of his cronies was rarely without one. And, in deference to Ida, who couldn't deal with cigar smoke, he also chewed tobacco, usually a cigar half, and his accuracy in hitting a spitoon was legendary.

The most notable accomplishment of his congressional career was the 1890 tariff that bore his name. It gave newly emerging American industry and the country's farmers the protection they had been demanding. But it also contained a series of compromises that made it more political than practical, and the Democrats not only attacked it, but avenged themselves on the bill's author by redistricting the State of Ohio, and when McKinley ran for reelection he was overwhelmed by a Democratic landslide. He lost by 300 votes in a new district that had an opposition majority ten times that big, but a near miss is a miss all the same, and after fourteen years in Washington the McKinleys moved back to Ohio.

He was an important Republican in a key state, and talk of a run for the presidency had already begun. But first there was another job to tackle. William McKinley became Governor of Ohio. He used his tenure to solidify the labor vote, and he even gave women the right to vote in school elections. It was obvious from the beginning that he like the sound of the presidential rumors and was working hard to make them come true. But he had always made it a point to reveal as little as possible about himself, and as the 1892 election approached, he kept quiet as to whether he'd accept the nomination if it were offered.

McKinley's whistle-stop campaign for the presidency was a joy for both candidate and voters. But it was the children, who couldn't vote, who had the best time of all.

President Harrison, who wanted a second term, saw to it that McKinley was made chairman of the convention, a job that would take too much of his time to leave any left over for politicking. The ploy worked, but it put McKinley in the spotlight, and when he adjourned the convention, he was carried out of the hall on the shoulders of admiring delegates, who seemed intent on ignoring the man they had made their standard-bearer.

During the campaign that followed, the Ohio Governor was asked to speak in every state in the Union, and when it was all over, even though the Republicans had lost, William McKinley was stronger than ever. Before he had a chance to get on with his life, a close friend he had helped with business loans over many years went bankrupt, leaving McKinley responsible for his debts, amounting to close to $100,000. After considering leaving politics to pay the debt, he finally turned his affairs over to a group of trustees. But the publicity was potentially bad for the image of a man who hoped to managed the country's financial affairs. On the other hand, the man was William McKinley. Ordinary people began sending him nickels and dimes and a fund was begun. He disclaimed it, but the money kept coming. Then old debts were repaid, and people of means began donating larger amounts. Once he made it clear that no promises would be made or kept in return for the contributions, his Scottish pride was soothed, and eventually he was out of debt. Before it was over, the entire debt was paid through contributions from more than 5,000 individuals, and he was reelected Governor of Ohio by the largest margin in the state's history.

He retired from local politics at the end of his second term, but though he and Ida settled down to a life of relative ease, and celebrated their twenty-fifth wedding anniversary "like newly-married people," William McKinley was a busy man. He felt he had been pre-ordained to be president, but he also knew that destiny needed a little boost here and there, and dedicated himself to strengthening alliances and building an organization. Before it was done, his routine included sending more than three-hundred letters a day, making use of the new long-distance telephone lines and making speeches to enthusiastic crowds in every part of the country.

By 1893, as the country was emerging from a depression, the press began to call him the "Advance Agent of Prosperity," claiming that the protection of his formerly-discredited tariff was the answer to everyone's prayer. He had cultivated labor support all his life, and businessmen joined the workers in their enthusiasm. McKinley looked unstoppable, but the next presidential election was still three years away. And there were some people in America who didn't care for the idea of a McKinley presidency. They tried to find skeletons in his closet, but except for his financial troubles, which had long-since been forgiven, there were none. In desperation, one group began a whispering campaign that McKinley was an agent of the Pope because he had appointed Roman Catholics to some state jobs.

But when the Republicans met to pick their candidate in 1896, McKinley was the odds-on favorite. The big state bosses tried hard to stop him, but their opposition only served to make him seem more honest. And from the convention's opening gavel, his nomination was never seriously in doubt. In November he won a comfortable victory over Democrat William Jennings Bryan.

In its early days the McKinley Administration seemed like a dream come true. Members of Congress from both parties agreed there had never been a president like him. One, who had opposed his candidacy, said it was "because of his great wisdom and tact and his delightful individual quality," and no one denied it. But all is never sweetness and light in Washington, and McKinley had his share of problems. And the biggest of them had a name: Cuba. He had developed a passionate hatred of war, and was determined not to intervene in Cuba's cry for liberation from Spain, which had already resulted in fighting as far back as 1868. McKinley preferred diplomacy, but over the years a strong attachment to the Cuban cause in Congress, in the press, and even among the people, made neutrality a nearly impossible course. He was quietly successful in a year of negotiation, but on February 15, 1898, the U.S. battleship *Maine* was blown up in Havana Harbor, and two months later the President, convinced that further diplomacy was useless, asked Congress for a declaration of war against Spain.

Huge numbers of people turned out wherever McKinley was scheduled to appear for a speech, and when he went to Buffalo, New York, in 1901, the turnout was the biggest of his career.

It was often called "a splendid little war." It was over relatively quickly with minimum cost in men and material. And in the end, as one observer pointed out, it pushed America "forward in the estimation of the world than we would have done in fifty years of peace." It also united the country as a nation for the first time in its history. When it was over, North and South were closer than they had ever been, and Americans began thinking of themselves as "number one" in the world for the first time.

It gave the President new responsibilities as the administrator of a world power, but the country was prosperous and Mr. McKinley more highly thought-of than ever. He was nominated for a second term with no opposition. And by popular demand, a hero of the late war, New York's Governor Theodore Roosevelt, took the second spot on the ticket. It was a fateful choice.

On September 6, 1901, during a visit to the Pan-American Exposition at Buffalo, New York, thousands turned out for a glimpse at the President and possibly a chance to experience his famous handshake. Among them was a man named Leon Czolgosz. His mission was to kill the President, not because he had anything against McKinley, but because he hated all government and by inference hated the man at the top. He may have been the only man in America who hated William McKinley, in fact. But he had a gun. As they carried the President off to a makeshift hospital with two bullets in his body, he wondered aloud about who had done this to him. "Must be some misguided fellow," he said.

McKinley's audience at the 1901 Pan-American Exposition included one Leon Czologosz, whose handgun brought the McKinley Presidency to a premature end.

The 26th President
THEODORE ROOSEVELT
(1901-1909)

Any youngster who has never had a teddy bear could probably be considered underprivileged in modern America. And it's hard to imagine how the country itself could have grown up without the privilege of having experienced the bear of a man who became its twenty-sixth president.

The stuffed bears were named for him, according to the legend, because he once adopted a bear cub whose mother had died. If it's true, it's also highly likely that Theodore Roosevelt shot her. He was not a simple man to understand. He knew more about birds than most professional ornithologists and more about animals than men who make zoology their life's work. And though he loved them, he took delight in killing the best specimens. He was a historian, whose major works on the Naval War of 1812 and his four-volume *Winning of The West* are still considered the most authoritative books on those subjects. And among his other twenty three published books, he is also revealed as an authority on natural history and science as well as political philosophy. Even at the height of his presidency, he never read less than one book a day, and most often two or three. And he never read a book, whether it was a current novel or the biography of an obscure Roman, from which he couldn't quote long passages, from memory, even years later.

The man who Mark Twain said was "clearly insane … and insanest upon war and its supreme glories," managed to keep his country out of war in an era when the whole world seemed intent on destroying itself, and moved the United States to the status of a world power with his own incredible diplomatic powers. And if he gloried in war, Theodore Roosevelt was the first American to receive the Nobel Peace Prize.

The same man who climbed trees on the White House lawn, swam naked in the Potomac in the dead of winter, and loved to shock passing strangers with outrageous facial contortions was also one our most dignified chief executives. His manners were courtly and correct, and he didn't save them for diplomatic functions. Whenever a woman entered a room, for instance, the President was instantly on his feet, no matter what he was doing, often to the surprise of others in the room, including the honored woman. Theodore Roosevelt was the man who led us into the 20th century, but for all his boisterous informality, he was a 19th century patrician with all the graces intact.

Possibly because of all those teddy bears, and surely because of the image of him that has come down through the years, it's only natural to refer to him as "Teddy." It was what people called him in his own time. But he considered the name vulgar, and called it an "outrageous impertinence" if anyone used it in conversation with him. When he was growing up, he was known as Teedie, often shortened to just plain Tee. But as an adult, he was Theodore to his family and friends and that was the way he wanted it. It had been the name of the only man he ever really sincerely admired – his father.

The elder Theodore Roosevelt was the son of Cornelius Van Schaack Roosevelt, one of the richest men in America, and a sixth-generation New Yorker. He was a junior partner in the importing firm of Roosevelt & Son. He was also a pillar of the Madison Avenue Presbyterian Church, a member of all of New York's most important clubs and a tireless fundraiser for dozens of charities.

The youngest of his four children was what they called "sickly" back then. From the age of three Teedie was subject to severe asthma attacks compounded by stomach trouble and pounding headaches. His attacks were frightening, and the family never knew when they would spend the night pacing the floor with the boy in a desperate attempt to restore his breathing, or when a family outing would be ruined because of his problem. But it was a close-knit family, and the troubles seemed to bring them closer together.

When he was ten, his father took Teedie aside, put his arm on the frail boy's shoulder and told him, "You have the mind, but you have not the body, and without the help of the body, the mind cannot go as far as it should …. You must make your body." He didn't waste a day. At first he went to a local gymnasium and began lifting weights, hoisting himself on parallel bars and pounding a punching bag. It was a painfully slow process that continued for the rest of his life. His father soon installed a gym in

Theodore Roosevelt became a national hero by leading a cavalry charge of his hand-picked regiment, the Rough Riders, up Havana's San Juan Hill during the Spanish-American War.

have had, and went west to become a rancher and experience a "vigorous open-air existence" in the Dakota Territory.

He had already become a partner in an outfit called the Maltese Cross Ranch, and in 1884 he got out his pearl-handled six-shooter, his tailor-made buckskin jacket, his alligator boots and his belt with the silver-plated buckle, and went out to the open range, no longer a silent partner. He lived on the ranch in a rather luxurious log cabin surrounded by books, comfortable furniture, fine clothes and other trappings that gave a whole new meaning to the word "dude." He had built his body into a magnificent machine by then, and a professional boxer who had taken him on found that he was "a strong, tough man; hard to hurt and harder to stop." But he surely didn't look it. Especially in those tailor-made clothes. Naturally, he became fair game for the cowpokes, but one night in a Montana bar he let them know he wasn't your average dude.

A drifter wandered into a crowded bar where Roosevelt was drinking and began making unkind remarks about lily-livered Easterners, especially the four-eyed kind. When he'd had enough, T.R. calmly took off his glasses and flattened him with a single punch. His image changed on the spot, and the story of what they called "the saloon incident," spread like a prairie fire. Nobody ever mentioned Roosevelt's glasses again, and nobody even thought of him as a misplaced Easterner. Modesty was never one of Roosevelt's qualities, but in this case he made an exception. Whenever the subject came up, he brushed it off as a lucky punch. "He was standing too close to me," he said, "and his feet were too close together." It may the only time in the history of the West that anyone ever offered a scientific analysis of a bar-room brawl. Meanwhile word had gone out that Mr. Roosevelt didn't have patience with bullies. It was true. He much preferred using the word as an adjective.

After two years of making himself at home on the range, he went back to New York to run for Mayor. He lost the election, but a month later became a bridegroom again when he married the former Edith Carow, who eventually bore him four sons and a daughter. His firstborn, Alice, the only child of his first marriage, was three years old when her brother, Theodore, was born. And by then the family was ensconced in a new house on Long Island, which he named Sagamore Hill.

The house became his political base, and was as well-known as the White House itself during the Roosevelt presidency. But when they settled there and began to raise a family, T.R. had decided against politics as a career. The Democrats were firmly in control both in Washington and New York State, and he didn't have the patience to wait for the voters to drive them out. He was twenty-nine years old and very much a man in a hurry.

Men of influence in the Republican Party thought he was wrong, and a group of them asked President Harrison to appoint him to some kind of job. Harrison responded by making Roosevelt Civil Service

their Manhattan townhouse, and after that no Roosevelt home was ever without the equipment required to keep the master of the house in shape.

When he was fourteen, he was given a gun and a pair of glasses. He had already developed a love of small animals and birds, stuffed. But until that moment he had never realized that his eyes were as weak as his body. The glasses helped him stalk bigger and better specimens, the gun helped him acquire them for his collection, and every house he lived in was filled with stuffed birds and animals, trophies of T.R.'s hunting instinct, many of which were expertly mounted by the amateur taxidermist who would eventually become President of the United States. By then he would be well- known as a conservationist, and the avowed enemy of "swinish game butchers," but still a man who took pleasure in killing the best specimens he could find.

When he was a teenager the family moved from the house near Madison Square, where Teedie was born, into the less congested part of Manhattan close to the string of Fifth Avenue mansions built for the Vanderbilt family. But they didn't move to acquire better neighbors. They wanted to be closer to Central Park, where they felt the air might be better for the still-frail young man.

After his graduation from Harvard University and a year at the Columbia University Law School, he married Alice Lee and took her home to the house near Central Park. Four years later, on Valentine's Day, eleven hours after the death of his mother, Alice died. Young Roosevelt, who had already served two terms in the New York State Legislature, gave up New York, as well as any political dreams he may

Commissioner. After years of wrangling over reform, it was easily the most thankless job in all of Washington and it had a salary to match. But Roosevelt took it on and handled it with an enthusiasm the commission had never seen before. He made sure that the press knew his every move, which didn't sit well with politicians who would rather have kept some of their moves hidden. But as he himself said, "all we are doing is enforcing the law." And building a reputation for Commissioner Roosevelt.

He held the job for six years and became a kind of fixture on the Washington scene, something roughly comparable to a windmill. He said he enjoyed dealing with "big interests and big men," but when New York City reformed its police department, he asked for and got an appointment to become one its four commissioners. Though there were three other men sharing the responsibility and their jobs didn't have real power, he took charge in his usual fashion, allowing his colleagues high-sounding responsibilities and putting himself in charge of press relations. Before long the national press was taking notice, too, and to this day many Americans think that T.R. was the one and only Police Commissioner in New York, and a powerful, crusading one at that.

Even crusaders get weary, though, and when William McKinley became President, T.R. put on his meekest look and suggested "I should like to be Assistant Secretary of the Navy." It seemed like a modest request, and though McKinley didn't want him in his Administration, he finally made the appointment and Roosevelt went back to Washington.

He landed running, of course, and began an intensive campaign to expand the country's defenses in general and its navy in particular. He managed to talk the Secretary into a summer-long vacation, and by the time the weather began to turn cool, he had visited a dozen important navy bases, cruised on its big ships and, most important, gained the ear of the President. By the end of the year, he was one of the most influential men in the Federal Government, not to mention the most entertaining, as the press so often mentioned.

Then, at the beginning of 1898, the battleship *Maine* was blown up in Havana Harbor, and the war with Spain Roosevelt had been predicting gave him a new place on the national stage. He had done all he could to get the navy into fighting shape, and decided he could do more in the army. Sending off a wire to Brooks Brothers in New York for a lieutenant colonel's cavalry uniform, he resigned his job and left for Texas to round up a troop of "harum-scarum rough-riders." He also went to New York to recruit some "gentleman rankers" to help keep them in line, and after a few

T.R.'s enthusiasm was legendary, but of all the things he loved, his family was first in his heart. The Roosevelt children, shown here with the President and his wife, Edith, are (from left to right) Quentin, Theodore, Jr, Archie, Alice, Kermit and Ethel.

months of training they were on their way to Cuba, and the charge up San Juan Hill that made heroes of them all.

When they arrived back home, Colonel Roosevelt was the best-known hero of the war and a shoo-in when he ran for Governor of New York. It was a foregone conclusion by then that he'd eventually be president. But there was plenty of time for that. He supported McKinley's renomination at the 1900 Republican Convention, and modestly accepted the second place on the ticket. He didn't relish the job, but he expected it would keep his name in the papers until the 1904 election. He felt that the Vice President had nothing to do, and in the case of his own vice presidency, he was right. Four days after his inauguration, Congress adjourned and his duties as president of the Senate were over for nine months. T.R. decided to take a vacation. Six months later, William McKinley was gunned down and Theodore Roosevelt was President of the United States.

He was renominated again in 1904, and elected by the biggest majority any president had ever received. And through his second term the people, who admired and adored him, expected he'd run for a third and planned to vote for him when he did. But he said that "the strong executive should not be the perpetual executive," and stepped aside in favor of William Howard Taft. But once he gave up the presidency, he clearly missed it. Four years later, disappointed in the Taft presidency, he formed the Bull Moose Party from the Republican's progressive wing and ran again. He expected to be beaten and he was, but his spirits never flagged for an instant. He spent the rest of his life working for progressive Republicans, and keeping his own opinions on America's place in the world in America's consciousness. The Republicans tried hard to convince him to run for New York State Governor again, and then offered him another presidential nomination, but he refused. Being president had been a great adventure for Theodore Roosevelt, but life itself was a great adventure for him, too.

In his years of retirement at Sagamore Hill, he welcomed a steady stream of visitors with the same word that had become his trademark at the White House. "Dee-lighted!" he would say. And no one ever got the idea he didn't mean every rolling syllable of it.

Roosevelt said he found the presidency "a bully pulpit," and he never missed an opportunity either to shake a few hands, say a few words or at least tip his hat in the direction of an undecided voter.

The 27th President
WILLIAM HOWARD TAFT
(1909-1913)

When he was thirty-two years old, William Howard Taft offered himself in contention for an appointment to the Supreme Court of the United States. A number of his fellow judges in Cincinnati, Ohio, engaged, as he put it, in "the innocent fun of pushing me." The Governor of Ohio pushed for the appointment, too, and when the President visited Cincinnati Taft worked hard at pushing himself. But he allowed that it was "very good fun and that is all. My chances of going to the moon and donning a silk gown at the hands of President Harrison are about equal." Harrison was not unimpressed, though, and gave the young man a sort of consolation prize by appointing him solicitor general.

It is a post any lawyer would envy. In practical terms the solicitor general is the attorney general's attorney. He would be asked to write legal opinions for the President himself, and though he would not appear at the Supreme Court in a silk robe, Will Taft would be the man who would represent the Government in cases that came before the Court. More important still, to any man with political ambitions it meant an opportunity to rub elbows with all the important movers and shakers in Washington. But young Mr. Taft didn't have any political ambitions at all. He took the job as a stepping stone toward an eventual appointment to the nation's highest court.

After all, he had been rubbing elbows with movers and shakers most of his life. His father, Alfonso Taft, had served as both secretary of war and attorney general in President Grant's Cabinet and President Arthur had made him minister to Austria and then to Russia. He was a leading attorney in the important city of Cincinnati and had served as a Superior Court Judge. Will himself had been a judge of the Superior Court, and when he was tapped to fill a new post as United States circuit judge, he resigned as solicitor general and went home to Cincinnati to become a big fish in a smaller pond.

He also found time to become dean of the Cincinnati Law School, where he had been a student, and devoted several hours a week lecturing to future lawyers. And all the while, he kept a close eye on the Supreme Court. A very lustful eye.

But during his eight years as a circuit-riding judge, Taft was also quite content with his life. His wife, Nellie, and their three children made him supremely happy and he sincerely loved his job. He was a devoted Republican, but doggedly followed a policy of staying out of politics, even though he often said privately that the Grand Old Party was in desperate need of reforming. He was especially vexed when his fellow Ohioan, William McKinley, was nominated for the presidency, and he was sure his judgement had been sound when President McKinley passed him over for an appointment to the Supreme Court. But then one day in January, 1900, McKinley approached Taft with an entirely different idea that would change his life, even his consuming ambition. The President wanted him to go to the Philippines as president of a new commission to bring order to the island group the U.S. had recently purchased. It looked like a thankless job. There was strong opposition in the islands to American control. Taft pointed out that he was personally opposed to American expansion and, besides, he didn't even speak Spanish. The President "might as well have told me that he wanted me to take a flying machine," said Taft. It took him more than a month to make up his mind, but in the middle of May, Taft was on a boat headed for Manila. Fortunately for his peace of mind, the Wright Brothers wouldn't prove that flying machines were practical for another three years.

Even if there had been an airplane service across the Pacific in those days, they'd probably have tried to talk him out of it if William Howard Taft had tried to buy a ticket. He weighed about 325 pounds at the time. During a stopover in Japan, he was given a ricksha tour of Nagasaki. "I had one 'pusher' in addition to the jinrikisha man when I began," he wrote, "another joined when we were halfway up a steep hill, and it seemed to me that when we struck the last hill the whole village was engaged in the push." He added that wherever he went, the naturally small Japanese "gathered in crowds around me, smiling and enjoying the prospect of so much flesh and size." They may have been sizing him up to become a sumo wrestler, but he had other things to grapple with.

He had no doubt that the Filipinos should

When Taft decided to accept the presidential nomination, he admitted he was a poor politician, but went home to Cincinnati to put together a team of advisors. Unfortunately, he did not include his mentor, Theodore Roosevelt, in his plans and the former friends became enemies.

eventually have their own self-government, but he knew that a lot of things had to be done before they could. Among those things was clipping the wings of a rather authoritarian military government that was currently running things. It should have been easy, it was an American military government. But it was headed by General Arthur MacArthur, who had strong opinions about everything, especially the idea of being replaced by a former judge who smiled a lot and didn't seem to have what he considered proper respect for the military.

Taft kept on smiling, even though MacArthur refused to move from the presidential palace and relegated him to a rundown house in the suburbs. Eventually Taft wore the General down, and when he was replaced the civilian commission went to work in earnest, and Taft's powers were expanded when he was made Governor of the Islands. It was a job he took very seriously. No less a person than Vice President Theodore Roosevelt said in a magazine article that the only man he knew who combined the qualities that would make a first-class President of the United States and a first-class Chief Justice of the United States was Judge William H. Taft of Ohio.

Less than two months later, Mr. Roosevelt was President himself. He and Taft were very close friends and it seemed likely that, if there were a vacancy in the Supreme Court, the friendship and open admiration of the new President would make Taft's dreams come true. But he had acquired a new sense of mission in the Philippines, and when an appointment was finally offered, Governor Taft turned it down.

Chief among his problems at Manila was the Catholic priests who had acquired vast estates under Spanish rule. They had lost their lands in the revolution that drove the Spanish out, but now, with the Americans in control, they were asking to have their

estates restored. The Filipinos themselves were opposed to the idea because the tyranny of those same priests had been what their revolution was all about in the first place. But there were larger political questions at stake, not least of which was the attitude of Catholic voters in the United States. It was one of those problems that politicians go to great lengths to avoid. But Taft was a judge, not a politician. His solution was to buy the land the priests claimed as theirs and then have them replaced by new clerics, preferably Americans.

It was easier said than done. The scheme needed Vatican cooperation, but the United States had traditionally avoided diplomatic contacts with the Pope. Governor Taft was the President's choice to open the door, but it needed to be done tactfully so that anti-Catholic voters wouldn't turn on the Administration. Rome, on the other hand, was interested in exploiting the mission as a foot in the door for later, more formal, contacts. It was a delicate assignment, but Taft was equal to the task, eventually lowering the Vatican's asking price of $10.7 million in gold for the nearly 400,000 acres to less than $7.5 million. His horse trading impressed the folks back home as well as his constituents in the Pacific, and William Howard Taft's political star was in the ascendency.

After having turned down the Supreme Court post on the grounds that he was needed in the Philippines, President Roosevelt ordered him home anyway. He wanted Taft in his Cabinet, and made him secretary of war. It was a job that required some attitude adjustment. Mr. Taft was a dedicated pacifist. It also altered his attitude toward the world of politics. His successes in Rome and in the Philippines had made him a highly-regarded figure among influential Republicans who were talking seriously of making him their candidate for President. Taft himself began taking the idea seriously, and when he was offered another appointment to the Supreme Court, he turned it down again.

But, in the meantime, there was the incumbent President to think about, and Theodore Roosevelt didn't have a more loyal man in his Cabinet than William Howard Taft. About the only thing he didn't do was run the War Department. Taft had become Roosevelt's trouble-shooter. On one occasion when the President decided to take a vacation, he announced that he wasn't too worried about what might happen while he was away because, as he put it, "I've left Taft sitting on the lid."

When he announced that he wouldn't run for reelection in 1908, Roosevelt let the party leaders know that the man he preferred to succeed him was the man who had been so good at keeping the lid on the opposition. And when his choice was confirmed, he let the voters know that a vote for Taft was a vote of confidence in his own Administration. But between the convention and the election, Roosevelt's enthusiasm began to cool. The two men still strongly admired each other, but Taft's campaign style wasn't nearly pugnacious enough for the old Rough Rider, who began to realize that it wasn't his fight after all. But their friendship survived the campaign, and so did candidate Taft. As President, though, Taft represented something quite different from his predecessor and friend. The rift between them opened wide even before Taft's inauguration when he replaced most of the men who had served in the Roosevelt Cabinet. By the end of four years, President Taft and former President Roosevelt had become bitter enemies. The Republican Party itself was divided, and as it girded its loins for the 1912 campaign, Roosevelt's name was heard as often as Taft's when the talk turn to the people's choice. In the end Taft prevailed, even though it was apparent that the people themselves preferred Roosevelt. T.R. responded by bolting from the party and running as an independent, and both he and Taft were assured the permanent status of private citizen.

Much of Roosevelt's pique at his successor came from the discomfort of being sidelined. Ex-President Taft, on the other hand, was delighted to go back to his real love, the law. But before he could arrange the move home to Cincinnati, he was offered a professorship at Yale University, his Alma Mater, and he accepted the job without any of his characteristic soul-searching. His Administration had been a disappointment, and he admitted that he was overjoyed at the prospect of leaving Washington, no matter what the destination. "Being a dead politician, I have become a statesman … with a sense of freedom that I have never had before," he said.

He spent the next eight years at New Haven, dividing his time between giving the young men at the Yale Law School "the proper sense of proportion as to the actualities of life," and fulfilling the role of statesman through a heavy schedule of lecturing and writing. Though he had said he was a dead politician, he was still an ardent Republican, and energetically opposed the policies of his successor, Woodrow Wilson. But it was loyal opposition. When war began in Europe in 1914, he sided with the President, and against former President Roosevelt, in a policy of neutrality. But when America finally became involved in the war, Taft drifted away from his support of Wilson, so far away, in fact, that he joined forces with the despised Roosevelt to elect Republicans to Congress in 1918. Two months after they had won their joint fight, T.R. was dead, and Taft was quick to say that, "Had he died in a hostile state of mind toward me, I would have mourned the fact all my life. I loved him always and cherish his memory." They were sincere words from a man who never learned the meaning of the word "hate."

When the war ended, Taft devoted himself to the battle to establish a League of Nations. He had been involved since 1915 in a movement to create what he called the League to Enforce Peace, and though Wilson's idea for international peace-keeping was slightly different, Taft toured the country drumming up bipartisan support for the Democratic President's ideas. When they were defeated in the Senate, Taft was furious and turned his wrath on Wilson, who he said had deliberately sabotaged his own plan.

As a Republican, he was happy to work for the election of Warren G. Harding in 1920. As an avowed enemy of Woodrow Wilson, he was overjoyed. But the greatest joy of all was still ahead. In 1921, President Harding appointed him Chief Justice of the United States Supreme Court. When the power to make such appointments was in his hands, Taft had made a rule that he wouldn't appoint any man over the age of sixty to any court, and now he himself was sixty-three.

But there was no really serious objection, and after he put on that long-coveted silk robe, Chief Justice Taft said that "In my present life I don't remember that I ever was President." Now that the chief ambition of his life had been realized, he acquired a new one, to serve ten years on the bench, then retire and enjoy the fruits of his success. He almost reached his goal, but poor health caught up with him, and he was forced to retire in February, 1930. A month later he was dead. But if his presidency had been less than successful, his years as Chief Justice were a triumph. He streamlined the Federal court system, using some of the political tricks he had picked up in the executive department to reform the judicial. He enhanced its prestige, too. Before Taft's appointment, the Court had always deliberated in the Capitol Building. But Taft lobbied for a separate Supreme Court Building, and convinced Congress to appropriate the money for it. His name doesn't appear on the pediment, but his spirit is there, and it is his monument. Of all the institutions of Government, William Howard Taft loved the Supreme Court more than any other. When he retired, his colleagues told him, "We will call you Chief Justice still, for we cannot give up the title … which you have made dear to us." For Mr. Taft, it was an honor much finer than being addressed as "Mr. President."

Taft and his wife, Helen, had a daughter and two sons, Charles and Robert. Robert (on the right) ultimately became a powerful U. S. senator from Ohio.

The 28th President
WOODROW WILSON
(1913-1921)

In September, 1910, a huge crowd gathered in Jersey City, N.J., to hear the retiring President of Princeton University make his first speech in a political campaign. He had been expressing his views for some time, and most people had a good idea where Woodrow Wilson stood on the philosophy of government. It was well known that he would probably be the candidate for President in two more years. But now he was their candidate for Governor, and most New Jerseyites wondered if an academic was equal to the job of stooping to deal with ordinary politicians. He had been speaking from an ivory tower all those years, but now the professor had thrown his silk hat into the ring, and people couldn't help wondering if he himself hadn't been thrown to the wolves.

He surprised everyone. At the end of his speech he surprised the wolves most of all. After having frankly told the voters that it made him uncomfortable to make a speech asking for something, he said, "I feel I am before a great jury. I don't want the judge to butt in. I am content to leave the decision in your hands." In subsequent speeches he kept on surprising the voters of New Jersey. Not only did this PhD speak in a language everyone could understand, he was sincere and honest as well, a very unusual quality in a political candidate.

Even before his inauguration, he fought and won a battle with the established party bosses over a senate seat one of them had thought he had earned, and by the time he took the oath of office it was quite clear that Governor Wilson did not intend to be bossed. A local newspaper reported that "this long-haired bookworm of a professor who had just laid his spectacles on his dictionary came down to the Trenton State House and licked the gang to a frazzle."

Strangely, the gang came to like the Governor's style. It was a new experience for them to vote with their conscience and not for special interests. Woodrow Wilson the bookworm had been transformed into a master politician in what seemed like the twinkling of an eye. But he had been preparing himself for public service all his life. It was in his genes.

When James Wilson arrived in Philadelphia from Northern Ireland in 1807, it seemed predictable that he carried with him the seed of a future President of the United States. His first act was to take over the Philadelphia Aurora, one of the most influential newspapers in the country, where he had taken a job as a printer. His second was to join the movement to the West. He migrated to Ohio where he build a tidy fortune speculating in real estate, became a bank executive and got himself elected to the state legislature. He published a newspaper in Steubenville, built the first bridge across the Ohio River, and even though he didn't have a law degree he served as a judge of the Court of Common Pleas. When it was suggested that he should run for Governor of Ohio, party leaders rejected the idea because they said James Wilson was too outspoken.

Woodrow Wilson's other grandfather, Thomas Woodrow, was outspoken, too, but he's more often characterized as scholarly. All of his family back in Scotland had been writers or clergymen for generations, and he himself came to America as a missionary, bringing the Gospel and the morals of the Highlands to the heathen in the wilds of Ohio.

The combination of James Wilson's brash Irish ways and Thomas Woodrow's conservative Scottish conscience created one of the most unlikely figures ever to emerge on the American political scene, and the most high-minded of all the American Presidents.

James Wilson had seven sons, all of whom were as driven to succeed as their father had been. The youngest was given a different challenge from the others. It was decided that Joseph Wilson should follow an academic life, and he was as successful at that calling as his brothers became in theirs. He was valedictorian of his class at Jefferson College and established an enviable record in post-graduate work at Princeton University. He became a college professor after that, and in 1855 answered the call to become pastor of the First Presbyterian Church in Staunton, Virginia. The following year his wife presented him with his first son, their third child, three days after Christmas. They named the child Thomas Woodrow Wilson.

During his tenure at Staunton, Dr. Wilson expanded the parish by some 30 members and earned a reputation for miles around as the best preacher

Virginia had ever seen. But his talent was lost to Virginia in 1858 when he was asked to take over a larger and more prosperous church in Augusta, Georgia. Young Tommy spent his boyhood years there, and was influenced by his father's work as a chaplain in the Confederate Army and his mother's dedication to the wounded troops that were housed in their church after it was converted to a hospital. The experience of those years molded the boy into a classic Southern gentleman, a quality he never lost.

In 1870, the family moved again, this time to Columbia, South Carolina, when Reverend Wilson became a professor at Columbia Theological Seminary, and three years later young Tommy, who by then was beginning to prefer being called Woodrow, went to Davidson, North Carolina, to begin college in preparation for a career as a Presbyterian minister. He left within a year because of poor health, but by 1875 he was ready for school again and enroled at Princeton, where he expanded his interests and changed his goal. Instead of becoming a minister, he now wanted to be a lawyer. And everyone who knew him agreed it was a wise choice. He was one of the University's best debaters, and had developed a remarkable skill as a writer.

He went from there to law school at the University of Virginia, and though he didn't graduate he was admitted to the bar in Georgia and practiced law for a time in Atlanta. It was there he met Ellen Louise Axson, also the offspring of a Presbyterian minister, whom he married two years later. In the meantime, he had decided against law as a career and went to Johns Hopkins University in Baltimore, where as a student he published his first book, *Congressional Government*. Soon after, armed with a Doctor of Philosophy degree, he became professor of history at Bryn Mawr College.

In 1890, he went back to Princeton again as professor of jurisprudence and political economy. Twelve years later he was made president of the University and had published a five-volume *History of the American People*. By that point, six different universities had offered him their presidency, including the University of Virginia, which had made the offer three times.

His eight-year tenure at Princeton was marked especially by the liberalization of time-honored, but restrictive, traditions and earned him national recognition, which didn't go unnoticed by the bosses who controlled the Democratic Party in New Jersey. He seemed like the perfect man to clean up their reputation, and they were sure that, once elected, they could hide behind him and conduct business as usual. But Woodrow Wilson had a different vision. He saw himself as a reformer. Among his first acts was to change the state election laws and clip the wings of the bosses.

Two years later, the Democrats nominated him to run for President. He won easily because the Republicans in the person of President Taft and the Bull Moose Party in the person of former President Theodore Roosevelt were busier fighting each other than the real opposition. When the counting was over and Taft discovered he had gathered only eight

Electoral Votes compared to Wilson's 435, he said that more people had voted for him to become an ex-President than for any man in the history of the United States.

Wilson's own sense of history was colored a great deal by his Southern roots and his Presbyterian background with its strong belief in predestination. Even before his election, he reminded the leadership of his party that he wasn't at all interested in repaying political favors. They were stunned when he told then that "God ordained that I should be President of the United States," and that they would be fools to go against His wishes. He let members of Congress know that if he needed their help he'd ask for it, but that they shouldn't bother keeping their phone lines open.

After his inauguration he was single-minded about what he perceived as God's mandate that the United States, through him, should work to achieve peace in the world once and for all. The world seems to have had other ideas. Within a year, war broke out in Europe, and he was inclined to stay out of it and to take on the role of peacemaker. But opinion began to run against him with the sinking of the British ship *Lusitania* in 1915 with the loss of 128 American lives. Still, he managed to delay what many thought was inevitable, and successfully ran for a second term in 1916 with the slogan "He kept us out of the war."

Meanwhile, his beloved wife, Ellen, died, leaving him grief-stricken. And his grief was increased when he was finally forced to ask Congress for a declaration of war against Germany. His speech resulted in a standing ovation to which he responded: "My message today was a message of death for your young men.

The 19th Amendment to the Constitution, which gave women the right to vote, was proposed and ratified during the Wilson Administration.

How strange it is to applaud that." He also made it a point never to refer to men in uniform as anything but "boys," a term we still use, because he remembered the young people who had been his students for so many years.

But life goes on, and within eighteen months of his wife's death he remarried. The new Mrs. Wilson, the former Edith Bolling Gault, became the most controversial First Lady in the history of the presidency when President Wilson suffered a crippling illness in 1919. The disaster struck in the midst of a debate with the Senate over the treaty that would end World War I. The President was fighting for the formation of a League of Nations, but the opposition, led by Senator Henry Cabot Lodge, was formidable. Wilson took his case to the people on a cross-country speaking trip, but before it ended, his left side became paralyzed by what was later diagnosed as thrombosis. The First Lady decided to shield him from the public eye in hopes of keeping Senator Lodge's forces at bay. In the process, she kept the whole country in the dark. But it was never revealed why the President couldn't be seen or visited even by members of his Cabinet.

The Secretary of State, Robert Lansing, tried to convene Cabinet meetings, and suggested that the President should follow the letter of the Constitution and turn the Government over to the Vice President. But the letter of the Constitution says that such a thing depended on the President's inability to discharge his duties. It seemed obvious to everyone that Wilson wasn't able to do all that was required of him, but in the end it was really just a matter of opinion, and the President's doctor refused to certify that the man was incapacitated. Vice President Thomas Marshall was just as happy about that. He didn't want the job, didn't feel qualified for it and, quite simply, didn't want to be bothered. Earlier in his term, when Wilson was in Europe negotiating the peace treaty that was so important to him, Marshall had refused to accept any

Wilson was the first president to cross the Atlantic while in office. His 1918 journey to participate in the peace talks also included attending ceremonial banquets with the heroes of the First World War.

37962

presidential responsibility. When asked to attend Cabinet meetings, he had said, "If I can't have the President's $75,000 salary, I'm not going to do any of the President's work."

In the midst of the secrecy, rumors spread like wildfire across Washington. At best, they said the President had gone mad; at worst, they said he was dead. And everyone agreed that the First Lady had taken over the reins of the Government. More than likely she hadn't. The business of the Executive Branch went undone for several months. On rare occasions a bill would be signed, but no one except handwriting experts believed the signature was the President's. Diplomats weren't able to present their credentials in person at the White House. Officials weren't able to resign because their formal letters were unopened. Appointees weren't able to assume their duties because the President had neglected to formalize their appointments.

Little by little his health returned, but by the time he was able to appear in public again, very few people recognized the frail, partially paralyzed man who had fought so hard for his peace plan and lost. He began holding Cabinet meetings again, he received visitors in his wheelchair, and even began talking of running for a third term in the 1920 election. But though the nominating convention included an outpouring of affection for the fallen President, the Democrats opted for a ticket that included Ohio's Governor James Cox for President and New York's Governor Franklin D. Roosevelt as his running mate. They were defeated in November, and when the new President, Warren G. Harding, presented himself in Washington for the inauguration, former President Wilson was too frail to climb the steps to be at his side as he took the oath of office.

Wilson retired to a mansion on S Street in Washington, an almost forgotten man. But only the politicians had forgotten him. He became a symbol to the people who remembered what he had done, what he had tried to do. In the midst of the roaring Twenties, he became a link with a gentler past and the people loved him for it. When he was invited to appear at the burial of the World War's Unknown Soldier in 1921, many Americans got their first glimpse of him, and suddenly all the rumors that were still circulating were swept away. He was the hero of the day, hailed by the crowd as the greatest soldier of them all. The experience revived him, and revived his hope that one day his dream of a League of Nations would come true. He received visitors after that day, took long drives in the country and occasionally appeared in public, confident that he would get well and could continue his fight for world peace. But his health never returned, and he would never fight again. Woodrow Wilson died on February 3, 1924, more than five years after he had become an invalid and hidden from public view. A few days earlier, he had quoted another President when he was asked how he felt. "John Quincy Adams is all right, but the house he lives in is dilapidated, and it looks as if he will soon have to move out."

The 29th President
WARREN G. HARDING
(1921-1923)

If you don't blow your own horn, who will? Joining the band back home in Marion, Ohio, may not have been pivotal to Warren Harding's presidential election, but it did it no harm, either.

When he was beginning his rise in politics in the State of Ohio, one of the party leaders said to Warren Gamaliel Harding, "You know, you'd make a dandy-looking president." The young newspaper editor from Marion smiled his best "Aw, shucks!" smile and went back to the poker game.

It wasn't an idle statement. Beyond his dandy looks, Warren G. Harding was a Republican, a native Ohioan and a self-made man. It was a formidable combination. Since the Civil War, half the Presidents had been Ohioans, and among the Republicans who became President between 1869 and 1920, the only two who weren't from Ohio were Theodore Roosevelt and Chester A. Arthur, both of whom moved up from the Vice Presidency. And at the turn of the century, the mood of the whole country was very much Republican.

But at the time the observation was made, Harding didn't seem to want much more out of life than he already had. He was one of those people who "gets things done." His newspaper, the Marion *Star*, was the most influential in the Ohio heartland, and even if he had won it in a game of cards, he built it from a nonentity to double the circulation of its two competitors combined. He was a booster of small town values, too, unabashed in his enthusiasm for giving the rich every opportunity to get richer and his belief that the poor could get rich, too, if they weren't lazy and shiftless. He was tireless in his support of the Marion Chamber of Commerce, which kept him in close touch with potential advertisers for his newspaper. But even without a business to build, Warren Harding probably would have been a booster anyway. He was a 33-degree Mason, an Elk and a Rotarian among other things. If there was a hand to be shaken or a back to be slapped, Warren G. Harding was usually first in line. He was a man who liked people, and those who mattered, as well as those who didn't, liked him even more.

He was one of them, after all. He was born the son of a doctor in nearby Blooming Grove. As a young man he was known all over the county as a man who knew how to have a good time. Fathers were usually pleased to see him in the company of their sons. Mothers were pleased to see him on the front porch with their daughters, even though they couldn't help worrying just a little.

He had been to college, had worked as a grade school teacher, was a great cornet player and was manager of the town's baseball team, for which he played a respectable first base. He had read some law and earned a few dollars as a country lawyer, and he kept himself in better-than-average style by selling life insurance.

One of the very few people in Marion who had no use for young Harding also happened to be the richest man in town. But Harding married his daughter anyway. He was 25 years old at the time. Florence was 30. Many say it was the turning point in his life, in spite of the fact that Amos Kling, his new father-in-law, swore that his life would end very soon if he had anything to say about it. Among other things, Warren put an end, or at least a curb, to his former wicked ways; and his bride, whom he began calling "the Duchess," rolled up her sleeves and went to work to mold his talent into something resembling success.

By many standards, Warren G. Harding already was a success. He had made some good investments and even though he was only 25 years old, he had the means to build a stylish two-story frame house, complete with stained glass windows and solid oak trim, for his bride and her young son by a previous marriage.

But Florence wanted more and she was willing to work to get it. She talked him into changing the *Star* from a weekly to a daily paper, and then appointed herself circulation manager and advertising salesman. Harding embellished the idea by making the daily politically independent, but publishing a weekly edition supporting the Republican cause. Eventually, with Florence's help, he was able to buy out his competition and had the only game, or rather games, in a fast-growing town. Meanwhile, Florence was helping him in other ways. He was a natural social animal, but she showed him how to get more than just pleasure from his talent.

He became a public speaker, and a very good one at that. His voice was probably his best asset; its pitch made him easy to hear even in large spaces without ever becoming strained or grating. He had the appearance to go with it, too. He was just over six feet tall with impeccable posture. He knew how to wear clothes, and looked perfect for every occasion. His teeth were even and pearly white, his hair neat and richly black. His skin had a dark, healthy glow and he had a smile that inspired confidence in men and made

women weak at the knees. Before very long, the audiences for his speeches were bigger than those for his newspaper, in spite of Florence's impressive efforts to build the latter. It was all very strange, because Warren Gamaliel Harding had almost nothing to say.

He thought he had a way with words, but the fact was he didn't. He did invent a few words during his career, the most fascinating of which described his own speaking style. He called it "bloviating," which is taken to mean the ability to speak for any length of time on any subject without actually saying anything. He loved to use alliteration, and in one speech he pushed the idea to its limits by saying, "Progression is not proclamation nor palaver. It is not pretense nor play on prejudice. It is not personal pronouns, not perennial pronouncement. It is not the the perturbation of a people, passion-wrought, nor a promise proposed." What, then, is progression? Don't ask.

Apart from the purple parade of P's, the statement contained a clue to the Harding style. He was looking for support from the Progressive wing of the party, but he didn't to alienate the other side. Those who chose to, heard "progressive" when he began bloviating about progression, but that wasn't what he said at all, and he could prove it to anyone who had the patience to read the speech.

H.L. Mencken, who had a way with words himself, said that the Harding speechmaking style was "rumble and bumble, flap and doodle, balder and dash." A leading Democrat said that it was "the big bow-wow

When he was President, Harding kept the White House doors open, a little too wide some said, but the first meeting of his Cabinet actually took place outdoors in the Rose Garden.

FIRST MEETING OF THE HARDING CABINET AT THE WHITE HOUSE WASHINGTON, D.C. MARCH, 8, 1921.

style of oratory," and added, "His speeches leave the impression of an army of pompous phrases moving over the landscape in search of an idea." And a candidate who had the misfortune of running against him complained that he felt "not unlike a duelist whose opponent has chosen to settle the dispute by a quiet game of solitaire."

Yet, as the man said, Harding had all the qualities of a dandy-looking president. And if his speeches weren't very illuminating, very few could resist giving rapt attention to the tall, well-dressed man and his incredible sincerity. He offered the voters a kind of old-fashioned grandeur with a common touch that made people think he had placed a comforting arm on their shoulder and let them know he understood the inner turmoil they were feeling in a fast-changing world. He said it best himself when he ran for the presidency on a promise to return the country to "normalcy."

It was inevitable that he should get into politics. When he was only 22 he served as a delegate to the Republican state convention. At 26, he was president of the local Young Republican Club and a few years later was sent to the Ohio State Senate, at which time he added an elegant front porch to his home in Marion. After all, William McKinley had started on the road to the White House by making speeches from his front porch over in Canton. And though he denied it to the very end, young Harding had made up his mind that he was going to be President. His journey there began in 1903 when he was elected lieutenant governor, and he took a serious turn in the right direction in 1914 when he became the first United States Senator elected directly by the people of Ohio.

It was in the Senate that he attracted the attention of the powers that be in the national Republican Party, and he was hand picked to serve as chairman of their 1916 convention with the specific assignment of keeping Theodore Roosevelt and his Progressives from taking over. He won the battle for them in June, but they lost the war in November. Four years later, the Republicans met again very much divided, but eager to get back into power. It was then that the famous "smoke-filled room" entered the annals of American politics. Four months before the convention, one of the party's leading lights said, " ... At about eleven minutes after two o'clock on Friday morning at the convention when fifteen or twenty men, somewhat weary, are sitting around a table, one of them will say 'Who will we nominate?' At that decisive time, friends of senator Harding will suggest him. In fact, I think I might suggest him myself."

Harding got the nomination on the tenth ballot on Saturday morning.

The Democrats nominated an Ohioan, too. James Cox was a millionaire newspaper publisher who had become Governor of Ohio, but the voters, even in the Buckeye State, couldn't think of a good reason to cast their ballot for him, or for Harding, for that matter. As one observer pointed out, "The people, indeed, do not know what ideas Harding or Cox represents; neither do Harding or Cox. Great is democracy." In the end

For years before anyone seriously thought he might be elected president, everyone who knew Warren G. Harding agreed that he looked "presidential."

they decided to vote against one or the other rather than for either one, and more than half the voters didn't bother to show up at the polls. But those who did elected Harding in a landslide.

He wasn't in the White House very long when the country was plunged into a severe economic depression. He attacked the problem by working to reduce government influence over business, a policy J. P. Morgan hailed as "extremely courageous." When it was pointed out that a million-and-a-half were out of work, he said "this parasitic percentage is always with us." And when labor leaders appeared at the White House, he dismissed them with the accusation that "labor men are not advising workmen to accept necessary reductions in wages and give an opportunity for a revival of industry." When farmers complained that they were on the verge of starvation without Government help, he said that such paternalism would "stifle ambition, impair efficiency, lessen production and make us a nation of dependent incompetents."

But through it all, the President's popularity with the people never wavered. He had a genius for public relations and, as a former newspaperman, enviable relations with the press. His relations with the Senate were quite another matter. As the gulf between the President and Congress widened over a multitude of issues, the politicians on the Hill began attacking not the popular President himself, but the men he associated with, the ones they called "The Ohio Gang." The war started with revelations that Harding's cronies exerted influence over him through late-night poker games where hard liquor was served, even though a Constitution Amendment specifically prohibited drinking. But it came to an ugly head with a scandal that carried the cute name of "Teapot Dome."

Three huge reserves of oil on Government land had been set aside for the use of the Navy, but in 1922 Harding's Secretary of the Interior, Albert Fall, had leased one of them at Teapot Dome, Wyoming, to oil man Harry Sinclair. When the Senate began investigating, they found that the other two oil fields had also become the private preserve of Sinclair and another oil man, Edward Doheny, who had paid $100,000 to Fall for the privilege. Sinclair had won the right to drill on public lands by offering Fall a piece of the action in the form of stock in his company. Even after the scheme was exposed, Harding stood by his Interior Secretary, calling the private leases "rational, natural and becoming development." He was so solidly committed to Fall's policy, in fact, that when another developer moved in to drill oil on public land, he called out the Marines to drive him off, saying that he was protecting the people's interests because the oil reserves had been leased to Sinclair and Doheny "at the best possible advantage to the Government." In the end Fall was forced to resign, but Sinclair gave him a new job, just before he and Doheny went off to jail.

President Harding didn't live to see it happen. In 1923, he set off on a speaking tour that took him all the way to Alaska. But at every stop along the way he seemed older than at the stop before it. On the way back, he suddenly became violently ill and died quickly. Just as quickly, rumors began circulating that he had been poisoned, some said by the Ohio Gang who were afraid of what might happen to them in the 1924 campaign. Others saw a conspiracy between Mrs. Harding and the presidential doctor. Florence refused an autopsy and ordered an immediate burial. The conspiracy theory grew a year later when the doctor died suddenly on a visit to Mrs. Harding. And it came to a head when Florence herself died within another six months. In death, Warren G. Harding became even more fascinating than he had been in life. He was branded a philanderer, and a woman who claimed to have been his mistress sued his estate for support of her daughter. His cronies charged that he had manipulated them and they had been been nothing more than pawns in the scandals of his Administration. Members of the White House household staff rushed to print with books suggesting that Mrs. Harding was the real villain, the evil influence that turned an honest man of the people into a reluctant crook.

But by then, neither President nor Mrs. Harding were alive to defend themselves. Eventually the talk of conspiracies turned from titillation to boredom and historians began to take a kinder view of this man whose greatest weakness was a desire to please all the people all the time and to make them see the Great Light of conservative Republicanism. They began to agree with an observation made by *The New York Times* that Warren Gamaliel Harding was "a very natural human being with the frailties mixed with the virtues of humanity."

In spite of the scandals that rocked his Administration, Harding never lost the affection of the people. He walked among them as one of them, and if there was a cloud over his head, no one seemed to notice.

The 30th President
CALVIN COOLIDGE
(1923-1929)

Once, during a White House dinner party, a Washington matron confided to Calvin Coolidge that she had made a bet with some friends that she could get him to say more than two words. "You lose," said the President.

He once told a frustrated reporter that he thought it was best not to say much. "If you don't say anything, no one can call on you to repeat it," he explained. But by keeping his thoughts to himself and never bothering to call attention to his accomplishments, Silent Cal proved one of the great axioms of human relations. No one knows how good you are unless you yourself tell them.

On August 23, 1923, when he was told that President Harding had died and that he was about to become the chief executive, he said, "I think I need a drink." The drink he chose was a popular soft drink of the day known as Moxie. Though the name is also a slang word for courage, Mr. Coolidge was not making an editorial comment. He avoided that like the plague.

But even though he never bothered to tell anyone, Calvin Coolidge was a man of unusual courage and perseverance. When he moved into the White House, he found himself surrounded by party hacks and hangers-on in the midst of one of the greatest scandals ever to involve the presidency. He didn't call any press conferences nor clear air time to reassure the people that he was going to begin a heroic housecleaning. He simply rolled up his sleeves, cleaned up the mess and let the courts take care of the rascals. Without comment.

It wasn't as though Coolidge kept the press in the dark about what he was up to. He established a policy of regular press conferences, and at the end of his first one he was given a standing ovation. In an era when politicians routinely blame "the media" for the country's problems, it's difficult to picture a president who actually seemed to like the press. Especially when that president is remembered as a man of few words. What made Coolidge different was, as he himself explained it, " ... I have tried to refrain from abusing other people." He also said that "The words of the President have enormous weight and ought not to be used indiscriminately." But his relationship with the Washington press corps wasn't a love feast.

Plenty of newspapers opposed him, but he was philosophical about it. "There is no cause for feeling disturbed about being misrepresented in the press," he said. "It would be only when they begin to say things detrimental to me which were true that I should feel alarm."

He pointed out that the highest tribute to his Administration was that the opposition based so little of their criticism on things he said. But he said so little it was frustrating to his friends as well as his enemies. He hadn't been President long before word got around that he wouldn't amount to much. Nothing could have been further from the truth. Where his predecessor had promised a return to "normalcy," Coolidge in his quiet way reminded the country that it needed old-fashioned honesty. If he had been a man of words, stability would be one he'd have used often.

He was a hard man to understand in the context of the America of the Roaring '20s. But those who knew their history knew him well as a representative of the kind of stock that had made the country work in the first place. He was a Vermonter through and through. He was hard-working, thrifty, unmoveable, practical, very much in the mold of the people he grew up among. He said their lives were "hard but wholesome," and that they "suffered many privations and enjoyed many advantages, without any clear realization of the existence of either one of them." He was proud to be descended from people who had what he called exemplary habits. "Their speech was clean and their lives were above reproach," he said. They had no mortgages on their farms. If any debts were contracted they were promptly paid. Credit was good and there was money in the savings bank. The break of day saw them stirring and their industry continued until twilight .... They cherished the teachings of the Bible and sought to live in accordance with its precepts." Calvin Coolidge did all he could to be just like them.

He had a bit of the maverick in him, but that was normal, too. The first Coolidge to arrive in America was a Massachusetts Puritan who came from England in 1630. Some of his descendants found the Bay Colony less than free and liberated themselves by migrating to the mountains of Vermont. It was this branch that produced the future President, who was born on the Fourth of July in 1872 in the living quarters behind his father's general store at Plymouth Notch.

The elder Coolidge was a pillar of the community. He was elected to the State Legislature three times, and served all his adult life as the town Constable. He was also a Justice of the Peace and the only Notary Public for miles around. He was the only man in Plymouth Notch who wore a suit with a white shirt and tie every day of the week and not just on Sundays. It gave young Calvin a lot to live up to, and he took the responsibility very seriously.

After graduating from Amherst, he went to Northampton, Massachusetts, to work in a law office whose partners were active in local politics. One served as District Attorney and the other Mayor of the city. Through them, he received a well-grounded education in both criminal law and local government, and when he was admitted to the bar less than two years later, he landed running. He became a member of the Northampton Common Council and soon after was appointed City Solicitor. Eventually he was elected to the State House of Representatives, a job he left to become Mayor of Northampton. His basic interest was in his law career, not politics, and when he saw an opportunity to go the Massachusetts Senate, he gave up the Mayor's job in hopes that serving there would be helpful to his practice. He had planned to retire after two terms as a Senator, but he couldn't pass up an opportunity to become President of the Senate, and stayed on, growing more influential in Massachusetts politics with each passing year. In 1915, he became Lieutenant Governor, and three years later he was elected Governor.

He became a national figure during a dispute over whether the Boston police had a right to make their

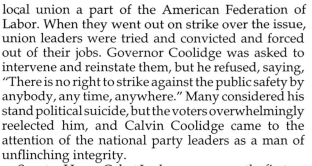

Calvin Coolidge was the only president to be sworn in by his father, who was a Justice of the Peace in Plymouth Notch, New Hampshire. Coolidge was visiting there when President Harding died, and as the Vice President, he assumed the office.

local union a part of the American Federation of Labor. When they went out on strike over the issue, union leaders were tried and convicted and forced out of their jobs. Governor Coolidge was asked to intervene and reinstate them, but he refused, saying, "There is no right to strike against the public safety by anybody, any time, anywhere." Many considered his stand political suicide, but the voters overwhelmingly reelected him, and Calvin Coolidge came to the attention of the national party leaders as a man of unflinching integrity.

Senator Henry Cabot Lodge was among the first on the bandwagon, and proposed placing Coolidge's name in contention for the presidency in 1920. By the time of the convention his enthusiasm had cooled, but Coolidge entered the lists as a Massachusetts favorite son. In the end, Warren G. Harding took the nomination, but the delegates, sensing that their choice had been dictated by powerful Senators, took matters into their own hands and made Coolidge his running mate.

When the Coolidges arrived in Washington, the new Vice President didn't turn talkative, but in his own way he became something of a social butterfly. He willing accepted any and all dinner invitations because the idea appealed to the frugal side of his nature and, as he pointed out to his wife, Grace: "Got to eat somewhere." After they moved into the White House, Grace became one of the most popular First Ladies in the history of the presidency. She entertained heads of state and other important people as though they were guests in her home back in Northampton, and the only change she made in her life was that she began wearing more expensive clothes. She wore clothes well and dressed tastefully, but back home she was more likely to wear dresses she had made herself. As First Lady, she continued to sew, but her husband's greatest pleasure in life seemed to be to help her select formal gowns, and even though he was a notorious penny-pincher, he never stinted on clothes for Grace. In fact, if she seemed to be planning to wear the same gown twice, he refused to allow her to do it.

It was something he had done all their married life. The presidency changed very little about the habits and lifestyle of Grace and Calvin Coolidge. On August 2, 1923, when President Harding died, the Vice President was back home in Plymouth Notch, Vermont, and when word reached him that his life was about to change dramatically at nine-thirty that night, Mr. Coolidge was fast asleep. He was tired because he had spent the afternoon helping a neighbor with his haying, but even if he had frittered away the afternoon on the front porch with one his favorite Havana cigars, he'd have been asleep by that late hour anyway. He was awakened by a telegraph messenger carrying the sad news, because there was no telephone in the house. There weren't any in all of Plymouth Notch, for that matter.

The elder Coolidge, as Justice of the Peace, administered the oath of office that made his son the 30th President of the United States. The oath was taken on an old family Bible by the light of a kerosene lamp. Electric lights hadn't come to Plymouth Notch, either. President Coolidge was pleased to be the only President sworn in by his father, and when he was reelected in 1924, he became the only one sworn in by a former President, when William Howard Taft, the Chief Justice of the Supreme Court, administered the oath.

Coolidge would probably have been just as happy if he had followed his original plan of becoming a successful country lawyer rather than a politician. His heart never seemed to be in it when the time came to stage a photo opportunity, as Presidents had begun doing almost as soon as cameras were invented. The Summer White House in 1927 was the State Game Lodge in the Black Hills of South Dakota. Coolidge would have preferred to be in the granite hills of Vermont, but he did all he could to look like one of the boys in a role that would have been better suited to President Theodore Roosevelt. He dressed like a cowboy, proving once again that it takes more than clothes to make an image. He had learned to fish as a boy and claimed he enjoyed the sport, but to the chagrin of photographers, he insisted on wearing white kid gloves while he was doing it. He never developed a stomach for baiting hooks, either, and that job became one of the duties of the Secret Service. The National Parks Service got into the act, too, by stocking streams to make sure there would be an occasional fish at the end of the line where the worm had been.

It was after one of his fishing expeditions in South Dakota that he surprised everyone, including his wife, by issuing one of the strangest statements ever delivered by a President.

He didn't say anything, actually, but had it written on little slips of paper that might have come from fortune cookies. Each reporter following him was handed one, and each carried exactly the same message: "I do not choose to run in 1928." It was the fourth anniversary of his presidency, but still a full ten months before the Republicans would meet to pick a candidate. Coolidge had won by a landslide in 1924 and could easily have repeated the triumph for another term. But what was odd about the statement was that it didn't say he wouldn't be a candidate. Other hopefuls needed to tread softly, lest the popular incumbent should decide to let someone else make his choice for him. State delegations stayed under the President's control, and Coolidge kept them there until the following June with his twelve-word statement.

When it was all over, he said he was surprised that anyone had considered his message cryptic. He never intended to run again, he claimed, because "it is difficult for men in high office to avoid the malady of self-delusion. They are always surrounded by worshippers. They are constantly, and for the most part sincerely, assured of their greatness." He said that he felt a statement that he would refuse the nomination was not within his concept of the requirements of the office, but in the end, in his quiet way he told the party leaders that "We draw our Presidents from the People. It is a wholesome thing for them to return to the people. I came from them. I wish to be one of them again."

He was happy to go home again to the rented house in Northampton that had been their home since he made Grace Goodhue his wife. Without a budget for entertaining, they did very little, and the former President drifted back to his old habit of staying in bed every morning until nine. Those who did visit them never seemed to notice that the silverware and linen carried the monogram of a local hotel that had gone out of business and liquidated the furnishings at bargain prices. Calvin Coolidge was a man who loved a bargain more than appearances. This was the same man who, when asked by a local bank to become a depositor to enhance its prestige, suggested that he could be made an "honorary" depositor.

The house in Plymouth Notch where he had grown up and taken the oath of office still didn't have a telephone or electric lights. A phone had been installed when he used it as a summer retreat in 1924, but he had it removed when he went back to Washington. The former President spent vacations there in his retirement, and enjoyed sitting in a rocker on the front porch enveloped in cigar smoke. A friend who once shared the pleasure with him mentioned that he must be proud to see so many cars passing by just to have a look at the presidential birthplace. "It's not as good as yesterday," said Cal, "there were 60 of 'em then." The place attracts more than 50,000 people every year these days. It would make Calvin Coolidge proud.

Before moving on to Washington, Coolidge was Governor of Massachusetts, where his ceremonial duties included welcoming the doughboys back from World War I.

The 31st President
HERBERT HOOVER
(1929-1933)

Herbert Hoover was one of the first presidents to use the medium of radio to communicate. But there were times when family secrets, at least, needed to be kept private. At such times, the President and his wife carried on their conversations in Chinese.

When he became Food Administrator in the Wilson Administration, Herbert Clark Hoover made a decision that seemed unimportant, if not a bit odd, but changed the way history would record his own Administration and provided a graphic clue to the secret of his success as well as one of his consuming passions. He dropped his middle initial.

He reasoned that as a public figure he would be required to sign his name hundreds of times a day, and that by eliminating the capital C, he'd save perhaps as much as half an hour a week for more important things. In everything he did, Herbert Hoover was a model of efficiency.

America at large got its first taste of the Hoover style in the early days of World War I. He was in London when the shooting started, and was overwhelmed with reports from the managers of companies he owned in Russia, in Australia, Burma and South Africa that banks were closing and payrolls couldn't be met. In Russia, his workers were being mobilized as soldiers, and the mining empire he had built seemed to be crashing around him. But he wasn't the only one with problems.

The American Consul, an old friend, called Hoover with an even bigger one. About a thousand American citizens had descended on the Consulate when they found that their dollars were being refused at local banks and hotels. It left them without a place to sleep or cash to arrange transportation home, and the Consul had no funds to bail them out. Hoover went right to work. He took all the gold and currency from his office and set up shop to exchange dollars for pounds to allow his fellow countrymen to check back into their hotels, and possibly find passage home. But the next day, the problem grew worse when thousands more began arriving from the Continent. Hoover galvanized the local American community and established an office to help the refugees. Then he mobilized Americans in other parts of Europe to funnel even more stranded tourists through London. In less than two months, they had helped more than 120,000 Americans escape the war and had loaned them more than $1.5 million to help them get home. Every loan was repaid.

As Hoover and his wife were getting ready to board a ship headed for home themselves, another friend presented him with a new challenge. Twenty-five hundred tons of food destined for the starving population of Brussels were bottled up behind a British blockade. Hoover intervened, and got permission to let the shipment go through, but the British were afraid that the Germans would intercept the food, and ruled that no other shipments would be allowed. In the meantime, reports from other Belgian cities indicated that the whole country was on the brink of starvation and that the French were suffering, too. Herbert Hoover cancelled his trip and began working on the problem of where he'd find enough food to supply ten million people, and then, having found it, how he'd get it to them.

He set up a committee of American executives and went to work. They used their connections to raise private funds from all parts of the world and recruited young people to help with the work. The first supplies arrived in Belgium less than a week after the committee

was formed, and within another week Hoover had secured a signed agreement from the Germans that the effort wouldn't be stopped. He had also convinced the British to let his relief ships through their blockade.

Hoover personally directed the effort until the U.S. entered the war, and then he went to Washington to organize the food supply for America and her allies. When the war was over he went back to Europe to organize the recovery, never once accepting any fees or reimbursement of expenses. By the fall of 1919, when he got home again, he had decided against public service as a career. But he had been transformed into a public hero, and he had developed some strong ideas on how he could help America. When President Harding asked him to take on the job of Secretary of Commerce, he made a decision to join the Government. It wasn't as though he didn't have an option. An international mining company had offered him a partnership with a minimum guarantee of a half-million dollars a year.

Offers like that weren't unusual in Herbert Hoover's life, but if you were to have met him as a boy, you probably wouldn't have taken any bets on it. He had been born to a pioneer Quaker family in West Branch, Iowa. His father died when he was six and his mother two years later. Herbie's seven-year-old sister went to live with their grandmother; and his twelve-year-old brother and he joined the families of two different uncles. Eventually he went to Oregon to live with yet another uncle, John Minthorn, whom he had never met, but who had promised to see to his education.

When Bert was fifteen his uncle went into the lumber business and offered the boy a job in the office. It meant he had to leave school, but the pay was fifteen dollars a month, and that added up to a kind of independence. It also gave him a chance to learn bookkeeping and typing, not to mention how to run a business. He went to night school to learn mathematics and in the process developed a love for reading as well. And in the midst of it all, through the influence of an engineer in his uncle's office, he decided that he would become a mining engineer.

His dream came closer to reality when Stanford University was established and he was accepted in its engineering program with the promise that he could earn his way to a degree. He was part of Stanford's first graduation class in 1895, and he was fired with ambition, not just because it came naturally to him, but because he had met a blue-eyed girl with a charming grin. Her name was Lou Henry. He knew that as soon as he could afford it he would marry her. But when he left Palo Alto in search of a job, his net worth was forty dollars.

When the money was gone, he settled for a job as a laborer in a silver mine. The other men at the bottom of the shaft weren't too pleased to have a college graduate among them, but when they found him eager to learn from them, they were just as eager to show him tricks of the trade that ordinary engineers could never know. But the pay was terrible, and after drifting from one outfit to another, Bert finally went to the West Coast's leading engineer and offered himself for any job at all just for the chance to work with him. He was made a clerk, but he made a name for himself in the office when a survey was needed of a shaft he had become familiar with as a laborer. It got him a promotion, but it also landed him in the New Mexican desert where there was more work to be done.

His big break came when his boss offered him a consulting job in the Australian gold fields at the astounding salary of $600 a month. He hadn't been there long when he discovered a rich lode, and recommended that his employers invest in it. They were so impressed that they raised his salary to $10,000 a year and gave him stock in the operation. The entire industry was impressed, in fact. Not only had Hoover sniffed out a rich strike, but in running it he had accomplished the seemingly impossible by completely eliminating the labor troubles that had become traditional in the gold fields by picking good men, paying them what they were worth, and cutting costs with new, American-made machinery. Less than a year later he had an offer to go to China at double the salary. He agreed immediately he had cabled Lou Henry and she had agreed to marry him and go along.

His job in China was to modernize the coal and cement industries, and he encouraged his hosts to develop their iron, zinc and copper deposits, but the Dowager Empress was single minded about finding new gold deposits, and young Hoover was sent all over the country in elaborate caravans on the fruitless search. He found the experience frustrating, but in his travels, he became unusually well informed about the Chinese people. The Hoovers were in Tientsin during the Boxer Rebellion, and survived it largely because of Bert's efforts to organize food supplies for the Western community during the siege. When it was all over, they moved on to London, where he became a partner in one of the world's oldest and best-respected

Though he was a self-made millionaire, candidate Hoover knew how to use the common touch to his advantage in his 1928 election campaign.

105

mining firms. But no sooner had he begun his new job when it was revealed that one of his new partners had embezzled a million dollars from the firm. Lawyers reassured them that the other partners weren't liable for the loss, but Hoover insisted that they should repay the money, which he argued really belonged to their clients. He ultimately convinced all of them, and himself, of course, to make up the loss from their own pockets. It took every cent he had managed to save in Australia and China.

It made Hoover a legend in the London business community, but he didn't spend much time in England basking in the glory. His travels took him around the world five times. When he went to South Africa to look over some coal mines, he discovered gold under one of them. He seemed to have a nose for knowing where to look for such things. On another trip to Australia, he developed a new process for removing zinc from the waste gathered in silver mines, and bought five millions tons of the seemingly worthless stuff to prove his theory. The silver mine became the world's richest source of lead and zinc, and the waste became more valuable than the silver. In less than seven years he built the company to three times the size it had reached in the previous hundred and fifty years, and he was the best known, and most envied, mining engineer in the world. He was thirty-eight years old and a multi-millionaire and in 1908, Herbert Hoover decided to retire.

He moved his family to a house on the campus of Stanford University and became a consultant. Before long, he had offices in a half-dozen cities around the world and all of them were busy. He had an interest in a lead mine in Burma, and it was busy, too. Five years after he had turned it into a profitable operation, a new shaft became the biggest producer of lead, zinc and silver in the world. By the beginning of World War I, when he suddenly became a public figure, Herbert Hoover was one of the most successful businessmen in the world.

When he and Lou moved into the White House in 1929, business was booming and the Twenties were roaring at full tilt. Prosperity was the watchword, and if anybody in the United States wasn't happy, the future was almost certain to get better. Best of all, the new President was a man who understood high finance.

Then, on October 30, the whole thing came apart. The stock market collapsed and the country was dropped into the biggest depression it had ever seen. Hoover couldn't have prevented it, and seemed helpless to find a way out of it. Even Calvin Coolidge, who never had a lot to say, noted "The country is not in good condition." A story about Hoover that was repeated time and again was that he was walking down the street with a banker friend and asked to borrow a nickel to call a friend. "Here's a dime," said the banker, "call both of them."

Hoover's wife, Lou, had traveled around the world with him on his various business ventures, and by 1928 a swing around the country in a campaign train seemed like a weekend jaunt compared with their earlier trips.

But Herbert Hoover wasn't friendless at all, of course. And he had a very good instinct for survival. During their years in Washington, which began during the Wilson Administration, the Hoovers were among the city's most important entertainers. Lou Hoover had plenty of experience. During their 44 years together, they had lived in 17 different homes in all parts of the world. During the siege at Tientsin, no less than five artillery shells landed in their yard. They had survived London bombing raids, often taking shelter in the basement of their house. And they managed to escape with their lives from a three-alarm fire in the White House on Christmas Eve in 1929.

His friends in the Republican Party had enough confidence in him to give him their nomination again in 1932, but unfortunately he couldn't muster enough friends to get reelected.

After his defeat, he and Lou went back to California, but eventually moved to New York, where they rented a $32,000-a-year suite in the Waldorf Towers, which would be home for the next thirty years. In 1946, two years after Lou died, Hoover joined the Truman Administration as a special consultant to help find ways to avert a postwar famine. The following year, and again in 1953, he headed commissions to study ways to reorganize the Government's Executive Branch.

After formally retiring in 1955, Herbert Hoover became an elder statesman in his 31st-floor tower suite. He had four desks there, one for each book he was simultaneously writing, and five secretaries who transcribed his penciled manuscripts. When he was eighty-five years old, he traveled 14,000 miles and made an average of two speeches a month. He worked hard for the Boys Clubs of America and for the Hoover Institution at Stanford University. He personally answered an average of 20,000 letters a year, saying that anyone thoughtful enough to write to him deserved an answer.

He had always led an active life, and never understood anyone who didn't. But he did have one daily activity that his neighbor, Cole Porter, must have applauded. Every afternoon at five, he indulged himself with exactly one and a half (no more, no less) Gibson cocktails, a drink he had invented some years earlier when he decided he didn't really like olives in martinis. He called it "the pause between the errors and trials of the day and the hopes of the night." But he knew that very few people would ever really understand the pace he chose. When someone once asked him how former presidents spend their days, he answered, "We spend all our time taking pills and dedicating libraries."

On a more serious note, on his ninetieth birthday, not long before he died, a reporter asked him how he had survived the long years of ostracism after his defeat for the presidency in 1932. Hoover's answer was simple. "I outlived the bastards," he said.

Hoover understood that lack of privacy goes with the territory when you are president. But he did rule that a man should never be disturbed while he was either praying or fishing. There were days when he wished he had done more of both.

The 32nd President

FRANKLIN DELANO ROOSEVELT (1933-1945)

O nce, when he was a young man, and before he became a politician, Franklin D. Roosevelt described himself as a "Hudson River Gentleman, yachtsman, philatelist and naval historian." Modesty was never, ever, anything anyone accused F.D.R. of, but he was much more than that, even then.

The problem was that he had never bothered to earn a living, and never did anything that didn't interest him. The term "Hudson River Gentleman" summed it all up.

The Roosevelt family had been squires in the Hudson Valley for generations. Isaac Roosevelt, the future President's great-great grandfather, started it all with a successful sugar refining business. His son, as future Roosevelt generations would do, married well and went into the banking business. It was he who established the family estate on the banks of the Hudson in New York's Duchess County, a comfortable distance from New York City. His son, James, studied medicine, but never so much as mended a broken leg. He used his talents to improve the livestock and the landscaping of the Hyde Park estate. His son, F.D.R's father, did the same thing, but he also devoted a lot of

attention to investing, an activity he had an exceptional talent for.

The future President was born at Springwood, as the estate was called, on January 30, 1882, the son of Sarah Delano Roosevelt, one of the wealthiest young women of her day, with a family background and social connections that may well have been among the most impressive in American history. The Delanos, like the Roosevelts, traced their American ancestry back to the earliest Colonial times. Though the first American among them didn't arrive on the Mayflower, he arrived in the Plymouth colony on the very next ship. His descendants were all shipowners, some operating as whaling captains, others as privateers, and Sarah's father made an impressive fortune on his own in the China trade when he was still in his twenties. After he lost it all in a financial panic, he went to Hong Kong and recovered his losses, and then some, in the opium trade. Young Sarah spent her early years in China, but went home at the age of ten to begin her education, and over the next decade spent about half her time in Paris. When she married James Roosevelt, a widower whose son was the same age she was, it represented the combining of two great patrician families, and the new Mrs. Roosevelt never let anyone forget it. Her stepson was already married, to the daughter of *the* Mrs. Astor, no less, and when she moved into Springwood, the big house seemed empty. She remedied that two years later when she brought young Franklin into the world.

Sarah's son was the apple of her eye and was given every advantage imaginable: trips abroad every year, a private tutor so he wouldn't have to associate with children his mother considered beneath him, and a summer home on Campobello Island in Canada, where he could enjoy the good life among his peers. He was her only child, after all.

He was educated at the exclusive Groton School and then at Harvard University. He went on to the Columbia University Law School after that, but dropped out when he was offered a job with a Wall Street law firm that was willing to to take a chance on him even though he didn't have a law degree. At about the same time, he married his cousin, Anna Eleanor Roosevelt, a niece of former President

Before becoming involved in politics, Franklin Roosevelt described himself as a "Hudson River Gentleman." At their Hyde Park estate, the squire, his mother, Sarah, and his wife, Eleanor, could easily have lived a long life of ease and relative obscurity.

Theodore Roosevelt, who gave the bride away at the wedding. T.R. was the head of what was known as the Oyster Bay branch of the family, separated from the Hyde Park branch by an accident of politics as well as distance. Teddy was a Republican, James a Democrat.

Franklin had no problem getting time off from his new job for their extended wedding trip to Europe. He never bothered to ask for a few days to move his bride into the townhouse that his mother had built for them on Manhattan's East 65th Street, connected to an identical house of her own next door. The fact was, Franklin Roosevelt's employers didn't care if he showed up for work at all. His social connections were what they were paying for, and in that regard he earned his salary hundreds of times over.

A lot of men with his background would have become insufferable playboys, but Franklin D. Roosevelt wasn't like a lot of men. He enjoyed a good time, to be sure, but his greatest joy, as he would prove years later in the White House, was dealing with people. It was inevitable that he would go into politics and, once having decided to do it, that the political establishment would welcome him with open arms. He planned his political career carefully, following the example of Theodore Roosevelt. Before anyone knew that he would even think of running for office, he had decided to begin with a term in the New York State Legislature, move on to Washington as Assistant Secretary of the Navy and then go back to Albany as Governor of New York, after which, with any luck, he would run for President of the United States. It was exactly the route T.R. had taken, and his cousin eventually did all of that. But even without such an illustrious role model, F.D.R. would probably have found his way to the White House on his own.

He took his first step with election to the New York Senate in 1910, and even before he went to Albany he became the most-watched politician in the state. The press was eager to find out more about this new Roosevelt in their midst; Tammany Hall politicians were just as eager to see if they could manipulate him. He hadn't been there long when he satisfied the former by positioning himself as a leader in a fight against the latter. The party bosses tried to dismiss him as just another "college kid," but they underestimated him. As he warmed up to the fight, he said "I have never had as much fun in my life as I'm having right now." He had grabbed the Tammany Tiger by the tail and the sounds of battle were heard all over the country. Unlike most state legislators who, even with the aid of graft, never lived in grand style in Albany, Senator Roosevelt had bought a town house there. It became a social center, especially for reporters who were pleased to respond to his hospitality and never failed to pick up good copy on every visit.

The battle was over the naming of a United States Senator, which was one of the prerogatives of the State Senate. Roosevelt succeeded in blocking the Tammany choice, but in the end their second choice, the man the bosses had really preferred all along, went to Washington. Senator Roosevelt learned his first important lesson in politics. But he had only entered the game six months before, and he already had a reputation as the man who stood up to Tammany Hall. Among the people who sat up and took notice was Governor Woodrow Wilson of New Jersey, who had taken on the party bosses in his own state and was being groomed to become the Democratic Presidential candidate in 1912.

Roosevelt jumped on the Wilson bandwagon right away. His own plan called for an appointment as Assistant Secretary of the Navy, but the timing was accelerated when he realized that Tammany would move heaven and earth to nip his career in the bud. Apart from the fact that he admired Wilson, he knew that he had to make a name for himself in Washington if there was any chance of political survival. When Wilson was elected, he got what he wanted.

Never in the history of the United States has there been a more enthusiastic Assistant Secretary of the Navy than young Franklin D. Roosevelt. He personally inspected nearly all the ships in the fleet, and when

Once he became President, obscurity couldn't have been further from Roosevelt's mind, and one can only guess the subject of this conversation with Gutzon Borglum, the sculptor of the Mount Rushmore Memorial in South Dakota.

the Navy went to war in 1917 he took it on himself to make sure it was properly mobilized. He was only the Assistant Secretary, but Roosevelt managed to outrun his boss on every front. When the war was over, he distanced himself from his boss when the Navy Department became involved in a Congressional investigation, and became involved in a personal crusade to make the Federal Government more efficient. In 1920, the Democrats made him their vice presidential candidate.

After losing the election, he became a vice president of a a surety bonding company, in charge of its New York office. It was largely a ceremonial job, and he had plenty of time left over for his private law practice, and for keeping his name alive by lending it to charitable and political causes. But then, in July 1921,

During World War II, President Roosevelt adopted Winston Churchill's famous trademark (right), a signal of "V" for victory. He was also known to tap out on a telegraph key (below) the well-known three dots and a dash that stood for the "V" in Morse code.

it began to look as though his career had come to an end. He contracted polio and lost the use of both legs. He was bedridden and near death until the following March, when he was finally able to stand up with the help of steel braces. He never did recover the use of his legs, but eventually his spirit came back. He didn't believe he could run for office again. How could a man who couldn't walk even think of running? But he thought he could still be involved behind the scenes and got aboard the bandwagon leading Al Smith toward the presidential nomination. His wife, Eleanor, took to the campaign trail and helped him in his election as Governor of New York while Franklin sat smiling in the background. The election put F.D.R. back in the limelight, and by 1924 he was ready to place Smith's name in nomination for the presidency. It was his first political speech since contracting polio, and many said it was the most important one he had ever made. Al Smith lost his bid, but the Democratic Party knew that Franklin D. Roosevelt was the one to watch. It was a valuable lesson for F.D.R., who began to understand that the ability to walk had absolutely nothing to do with running for office. In fact, after he died, a close associate said that his suffering made him all the more effective. "The patience necessary to the democratic process was built into his own condition," he said. "It is the same kind of patience he demonstrated in such small daily tasks as getting from place to place."

Smith took the presidential nomination in 1928, and Roosevelt was still in his corner. As a kind of reward for his services, he was given the nomination to succeed Smith as Governor of New York. On election day, Al Smith lost miserably, but Roosevelt managed to win by a small margin. He was one of the few Democrats to win anything in 1928, and as a result became a symbol of the Party's hopes for the future.

As Governor, he was able to keep the Legislature in a cooperative mood and the opposition on the defensive through his mastery at reaching the people through the radio. When the Great Depression began, he used the new medium to deride the Hoover Administration, and that kept his star shining among Democrats who could deliver the presidential nomination in 1932. He gave them an added incentive by winning the 1930 gubernatorial election by 750,001 votes. "I cast that one vote," said the Governor.

Even before then he was hard at work lining up support for the '32 nomination. And after the victory his supporters began working on securing it on the first ballot. Among the predictions from leaders in other states, the Chairman of the Nevada Committee wired Roosevelt headquarters that "There are five million people in the West who don't know T.R. is dead and will vote for your Governor." In the end it took four ballots to nominate Roosevelt, and he was elected in November by more than seven million votes. It was a new lease on life for the Democrats, whose leaders predicted they'd keep control of the White House for twenty-five years. It turned out to be thirty-six years, twelve of them with Mr. Roosevelt himself.

The new President's physical handicap was never mentioned, and there were many Americans who were never aware of it. The only time F.D.R. ever referred to his struggle was in an interview when a reporter asked him how he coped with the difficulties of his presidency. "If you had spent two years in bed trying to move your toes," he said, "you'd understand how easy the rest has been."

Roosevelt's White House years were far from easy. He went to Washington in the midst of the Great Depression and immediately began breaking every rule in the book to get it behind him. The country had never seen anything like his New Deal before, and getting his ideas translated to the law of the land, made him as many enemies as friends. In the process, he gave the country its first experience of such things as unemployment insurance, retirement programs, wage and hour laws, housing for the poor, jobs for the needy – all as the responsibility of the Federal Government. He completely transformed the country and the way the Government functions. Even though the term "big Government" has become fighting talk in some circles, he made the Government big enough to ensure that it could never again be controlled either by big business or by a powerful labor movement. He made the Government a servant of the people, and if

he made enemies in the process enough people loved him for it to make him the first President in history to run for a third term, and he made history again in 1944 by running for, and winning, a fourth.

His performance as an administrator and morale-builder was even more impressive after the United States entered World War II in 1941, and his personal style with other world leaders established the pattern for the peace that followed it. But he didn't live to see the peace he helped design. In April 1945, less than a month before the German surrender and five months before the end of the war with Japan, Franklin D. Roosevelt died at the Little White House in Warm Springs, Georgia.

Of all the epitaphs, the one that F.D.R himself would probably have liked best came from a Southern taxi driver who told an Administration official on his way back to Washington that in the years before the Roosevelt presidency he had been a factory worker. "They didn't even treat us like humans," he remembered. "We were paid sixteen cents an hour, and if you asked to get off on Sunday, the foreman would say 'All right, you stay away Sunday and when you come back on Monday, someone else will have your job.' – No sir, I'll never forget what President Roosevelt done for us."

From his earliest days as President, Roosevelt kept his programs in the public eye through the radio broadcasts he called "fireside chats."

The 33rd President
HARRY S. TRUMAN
(1945-1953)

Of all the American Presidents, none knew more about his predecessors than Harry Truman. He had a wonderful sense of history, but little understanding of his own place in it. When he retired in 1953, he told an interviewer: "I wasn't one of the great presidents, but I had a hell of a time trying to be one." Oh, if he could hear them now! Even the Republicans can't think of enough good things to say about Harry S. Truman.

He never really wanted the job in the first place. When Franklin Roosevelt suggested his name as vice presidential candidate on the 1944 ticket, he told F.D.R. to go to hell. It took a great deal of arm twisting and reminders of party loyalty to get him to change his mind. Eighty-two days after Roosevelt's fourth term began, Harry S. Truman became the 33rd President of the United States.

His vice presidency had been a compromise in the first place, and when the Trumans moved into the White House, the Democrats weren't too sure they had made such a smart move. They spent the next three years plotting to dump Harry before the 1948

In his early days in Kansas City, Harry Truman tried his luck at running a haberdashery store, which failed.

election, and they were chagrined when he said in a speech: "There's going to be a Democrat in the White House in 1949 – and you're lookin' at him." Almost none of the party leadership agreed. They had their eye on General Dwight D. Eisenhower, who had all the earmarks of a winner. The General had never voted and nobody knew if he was a Republican or a Democrat, but they were willing to give him the benefit of the doubt. As convention time approached with no word from Eisenhower, it began to look like they'd have to settle for the President after all. But they couldn't resist humiliating him.

The 1948 conventions were the first to be broadcast on television, and the Democrats decided to take advantage of the exposure, even though limited, to boom the possible candidacy of Senate Majority Leader Alben Barkley of Kentucky. They also used up prime air time with a fight over the platform's stand on civil rights, a very new issue back then. By the time they got around to giving their nomination to Truman, it was two o'clock in the morning. But for those who stayed up to hear him, he delivered a political masterstroke by announcing that he was going to call the "do-nothing Congress" into session in the middle of their summer vacation and would keep them sweating until they paid off their campaign promises. They had no choice but to appear, and when they accomplished nothing, as he had predicted, he had a perfect issue. It set the stage for a campaign full of surprises that ended with the biggest surprise of all, Harry S. Truman's reelection.

In his whistlestop campaign that year, Truman picked up the nickname of "Give 'em Hell Harry" as he toured the country hitting hard against Republicans in general and the Republican-dominated Congress in particular. The opposition called it "cheap politics," but Truman knew instinctively it was the very best kind of politics. He was candid, sometimes to a fault. In an era when the political pros were beginning to think that the way to win an election was to learn how to "use" television, President Truman stuck to his belief that meeting voters face to face was still the best policy. "When you get on the television," he said, "you're wearing a lot of powder and paint that somebody else has put on your face. And you haven't

By the Potsdam Conference in 1945, Truman had become, along with Josef Stalin (left) and Winston Churchill (right), one of the three most important men in the world.

even combed your own hair. But when you're standing right in front of them … the people can tell whether you're telling them the facts or not." He estimated that he stood in front of about twenty million people in '48. When he went to Dallas, Texas, he told his audience that he believed black citizens had the same rights as whites, and later the same day he shook hands with a black woman in Waco. Party professionals winced and the crowds hissed. But Harry had a secret none of them quite understood. He wanted to win, of course, but not deceitfully. "Win, lose or draw," he said, "people will know where I stand and a record will be made for future action by the Democratic Party."

There was never any doubt about where Harry Truman stood, and if people didn't like it, he never lost any sleep worrying about it. He was a man who believed in the simple values of the 19th-century Midwest. He had grown up in Independence, Missouri, where such things as hard work and uncompromising honesty were a way of life.

He said that by the time he was eleven he had read the entire Bible twice, and then he read it twice more before finishing grade school. He also said that he had read every book in the Independence Library before the end of his high school career. No one in town argued the point, but the cynics among them said he'd have had to have read a book a day to have accomplished such a feat. And those who allowed it was possible wondered where, then, he found time read all the books in his father's house, a collection

that included all of Shakespeare's works, Plutarch's Lives and every book written up until that time by Mark Twain. But if there were people who couldn't believe young Harry read every book at his disposal, others wondered if he hadn't been sneaking off to St. Louis in search of a bigger library. His head was filled with facts, trivial and otherwise, and as an adult, few men he met could match his understanding of world history.

He also found time during his school days for serious study of the piano, but he fit it into his day by starting at 5:30 in the morning. He found romance, too, in his fashion, through almost single-minded devotion to Bess Wallace from the day he met her in fifth grade. Whether Bess herself ever noticed is completely unknown, but she finally succumbed by marrying Harry in 1919. The wedding date had been postponed by World War I, but the long engagement that preceded it had been postponed, everyone said, by Bess's doubts that he'd be able to support her. There was never any doubt that he was willing to try, but he seemed to be on a collision course with failure, and when she turned down his first proposal of marriage, he pleaded in a letter to her, "Say, Bessie, you'll at least let me keep on being good friends, won't you?"

When he graduated from high school, his heart was set on entering West Point, but when he tested his eligibility to serve in the military and was rejected because of poor eyesight, he set his sights on a career in business. He enrolled in a business college, but was forced to drop out when his father's livestock business failed and he took a job in the mailroom at the Kansas City Star. From there he went to work as a timekeeper for a railroad, and eventually became a bank clerk. He made $100 a month, which he recalled was "a magnificent salary in Kansas City in 1905." At about the same time he joined a newly-forming National Guard unit. It satisfied part of his overall plan to get some military training, and it also put him in contact with the Pendergast brothers, who controlled the local Democratic Party.

He left the bank, and Kansas City, when his father leased a farm nearby, and he became enthusiastic about scientific farming as well as livestock breeding. But even though the work was hard and the hours long, he managed to make a name for himself in political circles and became the local postmaster, though he turned the job, and the salary, over to the widow who held the post before him. He also became Road Overseer, an important job that put him in personal contact with every voter in the district, all of whom were required either to pay a tax or work for the improvement of local roads. And he became a member of the town's school board. At the same time, he became an active Freemason, which put him in close contact with the business community and gave him a new spiritual outlook which he took very seriously all his life.

Through it all, the farm thrived, and it looked like Harry's future was assured. But when his grandmother died in 1909, leaving a contested will, the family lost the farm and acquired a staggering debt in the bargain. Harry did what he could, trying to make money by

selling real estate, moving on to a soon-to-fail mining scheme and finally as treasurer of a company selling dubious oil leases. By the time World War I began, he was sick of the people he had been forced to associate with, but now he had an opportunity to break the cycle.

His National Guard outfit was mobilized early in the war, and Harry was elected a first lieutenant. After his training, he was selected to be part of an advance party headed for France ahead of his regiment. He was promoted to captain soon after and saw action as commander of artillery Battery D, which had lost four commanders before him. Harry not only survived, but was credited with transforming an unruly bunch of soldiers, who had earned the name of "Dizzy D," into what was regarded as the best battery in the regiment.

He was thirty-five years old when he went back to Independence, and more than ready to start a new life. He began by marrying Bess Wallace, and then he invested in a St. Louis haberdashery store. The business failed in two years and Harry, as they say, lost his shirt. But he had cultivated his former political connections and the blow of the failure was softened when the Pendergasts made him a candidate for judge of the county court. He lost his bid for a second term on the bench, and took a job with the Kansas City Automobile Association, which tided him over until 1926 when he became presiding judge of the county court, a post he held for the next eight years. He became a United States Senator in 1934, a job he seemed to enjoy more than any other in his entire life.

During his ten years in the Senate, he earned some notoriety as chairman of a special committee to investigate war contracts. He uncovered billions of dollars worth of fraud and in one instance found enough olive drab paint in Government warehouses to cover every mailbox in the United States for the next thirty years, not to mention the Army's equipment during the Second World War.

As President, Harry Truman never flinched over tough decisions. He said that his political career was centered around a bit of advice from Mark Twain, "Always do right. This will gratify some people and astonish the rest." He had a sign on his desk that read "The buck stops here," and another nearby that stated "If you can't stand the heat, get out of the kitchen." And there were plenty of people in Washington who wished Harry Truman would get out of the kitchen. He had taken plenty of heat over his decision to drop the first atomic bombs on Japan in 1945, and there were many who never forgave him for bringing us into the nuclear age, even though the development of the bomb was already accomplished by the time he became President. But it wasn't until 1950 that the heat was turned up full blast. It was the result of what Truman called the most important decision he ever made.

At the end of World War II, the Japanese surrendered simultaneously to the Americans and the Russians, with the latter retaining its influence north of the 38th parallel in Korea. Five years later,

In the 1948 presidential campaign, Truman won the affection of the people and confounded the pundits by giving the Republicans hell from the back of a train.

communist troops began moving south of that line, and Harry Truman said that it was time to "stop the sons of bitches no matter what." The result was a United Nations action to stop them, and when American troops were sent to Korea, President Truman was accused of starting an illegal war.

He was still weathering that storm when he started another by firing the commander in the field, General Douglas MacArthur, for insubordination. It was possibly the most unpopular thing any president has ever done. The General came home and made a speech before a joint session of Congress and then began a tour of the country drumming up sympathy and, many thought, support to run for the presidency. Except to note that it had been inappropriate for a five star general to visit Washington without reporting to his Commander-in-Chief, Truman said nothing. He predicted that everybody would forget MacArthur in six weeks. He was right, almost exactly to the day. MacArthur himself had unwittingly predicted it when he told Congress that "Old soldiers never die, they just fade away."

When Truman retired and went home to Independence, he said that he wanted to live just like everyone else there. It was frustrating that he couldn't, and his neighbors decided it wasn't because he had changed, but because Independence had. They may

have been right. A story about him you still hear among old-timers is of the day he was out on the highway and spotted a woman struggling to recover a herd of loose hogs. He stopped his car and helped her round them up, and when he was asked later if that had been a dignified thing for a former president to do, he said, "I was a farmer long before I got to be President." And he didn't want any special treatment, either. When fax machines came into use in the late '50s, the local manager of Western Union thought it would be a nice gesture to install one in Truman's office. But the ex-President wasn't impressed. "Please come and take this crazy receiver you have set up in my office," he wrote. "It is nothing but a nuisance. When messages are sent to me they are supposed to be delivered by you. I am not your delivery agent. I have other things to do."

He lived to see his decisions as President exonerated and even praised by former critics. Toward the end of his life a newspaper columnist sent him an apology for having underrated him, to which Mr. Truman replied: "It is true that I did not always react pleasantly to criticism – or derisive comments – but I never for a moment questioned the right of anyone to do so. But I warmly welcome your reassessment of 'the period' and dare hope that it might be sustained by the ultimate judgement."

In 1951, President Truman, his wife, Bess, and daughter, Margaret, welcomed Princess Elizabeth, England's future queen, and her husband, Prince Philip, to Washington.

The 34th President
DWIGHT D. EISENHOWER
(1953-1961)

When Dwight D. Eisenhower was finally convinced to run for the presidency in 1952, the whole country seemed to be shouting "I Like Ike!" He liked hearing it, but it took a while to get used to the "Ike" part. It was the nickname attached to him as a boy, but he had long since outgrown it. During World War II, the guys in the foxholes referred to him by that name, but never when he was within earshot. His friends called him "Dwight," his associates "General." But neither had the right folksy ring to it, and there was no denying that to know him was to like him.

So "Ike" it was for the rest of his life. It was all part of the image, based on fact, that in spite of his impressive military accomplishments, he was still a regular guy. A guy like your father, many people said. And they were right, too. He had a warm, inviting manner that either reminded you of your father or made you wish your father had been like him. His smile defied description, though many tried.

It was boyish, but it was more than that. It was infectious, but that word didn't quite describe it, either. If the like of it ever comes along again, it will probably be described, simply, as an "Eisenhower" smile.

When he came back from the war, not many Americans knew much about him except that they adored him, and wherever he went they turned out by the thousands to honor the conquering hero. In New York, where the tonnage of tickertape topped even the amount poured down on Charles A. Lindbergh, a new measuring device rated the cheer that went up as he climbed the steps of City Hall as the equal of three-thousand thunderclaps. But even though he would later become a New Yorker for a time, he left town with the thought that it was a nice place to visit, but he wouldn't want to live there. A few days later, when he arrived back in his hometown of Abilene, Kansas, he told his former neighbors that "When I get out of this uniform, this is the country I'm coming back to." That same day, he told reporters, "I'm a soldier, and I'm positive that no one thinks of me as a politician. In the strongest language you can command, you can state that I have no political ambitions at all." He hadn't planned to become a soldier, either.

His family was poor when Ike was growing up in Abilene, and he and his brothers were often called upon to defend themselves against the taunts of other kids over their hand-me-down clothes. It wasn't as though the others didn't wear recycled shoes and shirts, but the Eisenhower boys occasionally appeared in their mother's made-over clothes. A thing like that can make a kid real scrappy.

At one point during his high school career, Ike was forced to drop out to go to work. But he went back and finished, and the family had developed a scheme to help him go on to college. His brother, Edgar, went off to the University of Michigan, and Ike worked to pay his expenses. The plan was for the two boys to switch places after two years and to continue the cycle until both had earned their diplomas. It seemed like a good idea until Ike stumbled on a better one. A neighbor had won an appointment to Annapolis and told him how easy it had been. All he had to do, he said, was

In his high school days, young Ike Eisenhower (center) towered over his brothers Milton (left) and Earl (right) to the obvious pride of their mother and father.

write to his Senator asking for an appointment and then pass an entrance exam. The best part was that it was free. He wouldn't even have to buy his own clothes. Ike took the suggestion and in 1911 became a cadet at the United States Military Academy. He would have preferred the Naval Academy, but by the time he got around to writing to his Senator he was twenty years old, and Annapolis wouldn't accept anyone past their twentieth birthday.

Because he was older than the average cadet, and bigger – he was six feet tall and weighed 175 pounds – he was tapped for the Army football team right away, and by his third or fourth game national sportswriters were telling their readers that he was the most promising halfback in college football. Unfortunately the promise was never fulfilled. A few days before the last game of his first season, he was sidelined with a knee injury and never played again.

But football was an important part of his army career. When he reported for his first assignment as a second lieutenant at Fort Sam Houston in Texas, his commanding officer suggested that it would be a good idea if he accepted an offer to coach the team at a nearby military academy, and throughout his career he was met with similar suggestions every time he was assigned to a new post. In fact, more than once transfers were held up until the end of football season.

He met and married Mamie Dowd while he was at Fort Sam Houston, too. And the new responsibility gave him a new resolve to put his career in the hands of the Army and "to do the best I could to make a creditable record, no matter what the nature of the duty." The English translation of that decision is close to the advice soldiers have been passing on to each other from the days of the Roman legions: "Don't volunteer for anything." But if making the best of a bad thing is good advice for foot soldiers, it's not always the best way for officers to advance their careers. In Eisenhower's case, he spent World War I moving from one stateside post to another, training men about to go to the front where he himself would like to have been. True to his resolve, he had become very good at the job even though it wasn't what he wanted to do. He finally managed to convince the Army to send him into the fight and he had orders to sail for France at the end of November, 1918. But before the ship was loaded, it was over over there, and the order was cancelled.

After the war he came to the attention of the top brass with some revolutionary theories about tank warfare, and Brigadier General Fox Connor, one of the most influential men in the Army, took him under his wing. In 1922, he made Major Eisenhower his executive officer, and during the next three years, when they were together in Panama, he gave him a liberal education on how to succeed in "This Man's Army".

Connor sent him on to the Army's Command and General Staff School, and when he finished he was accepted at the Army War College. Both were critical steps toward success for any officer. After graduation, he finally got to France as a member of the Battle

Monuments Commission. And when he came back after a year abroad, he settled down behind a desk at the office of the Assistant Secretary of War in Washington. The chief job of the office at the time was dealing with a commission charged with making rules for the mobilization of industry in time of war. The Army's interest in protecting its sources made the work quite important, especially to Chief of Staff General Douglas MacArthur, who was pleased with Major Eisenhower's efforts at keeping the "pacifists" at arm's length. No one was surprised when he was promoted to colonel and became the general's aide.

In 1935, when MacArthur went to the Philippines as adviser to the new government there, Eisenhower went along as his assistant. He was there when war broke out in Europe, and requested a transfer so that he wouldn't miss another chance to go into combat as he had in 1918. He had been in the Army for more than eighteen years by then, but had only served as part of a fighting unit for six months, and even then he hadn't seen any action. He was put in command of an infantry brigade and seemed on his way at last. But the War Department wasn't finished with him yet. He had no sooner become used to the idea of commanding actual troops than he was made Chief of Staff of the 3rd Division, and soon after that Chief of Staff of the IX Army Corps. The ink was hardly dry on those orders when he became Chief of Staff of the Third Army, and finally made a name for himself in combat, even though it was just a war game, by routing the Second Army in the largest peacetime maneuver in American history. It earned him a promotion to brigadier general, and newspaper copy desks began posting memos on the proper spelling of his name.

When the Japanese attacked Pearl Harbor in 1941 his years of service in the Philippines made him valuable to the War Department, and he spent the

Eisenhower's military career took a giant step forward when he planned and executed the Allied leap across the English Channel for the invasion of France on D-day, June 6, 1944.

next several months in Washington devising plans for waging war in the Pacific. Among the problems he dealt with was cooperation among the allies. The Dutch and the British were fighting in the Pacific, too, and it was obvious that their efforts needed to be orchestrated. After several false starts, the countries involved finally agreed to establish a committee to be called the Combined Chiefs of Staff, which allowed for the selection of a single commander of the allied armies. They also agreed that their best strategy was a land attack in Europe to try to end the war against Germany as quickly as possible and then concentrate on the Pacific theater.

Soldiers often scratch their heads about the wisdom of the top brass, and the next turn in Eisenhower's career was one of the things that mystify them. He was an acknowledged expert on the Pacific, and had spent his time drafting plans for the movement of men and material in the area. The plans were sound and well thought out, and it seemed logical that, if Eisenhower was actually going to get into the war, he'd rejoin his old boss, MacArthur, in the fight against the Japanese. But the logic was flawed. General Eisenhower would soon wind up in North Africa.

He had become Chief of the War Plans Division and it really seemed as though he was doomed to spend another war in the states. But General George Marshall, the Army Chief of Staff, had other plans for him. In 1942 he shipped him to London, where he and the British could get to know each other better, and planning began for a cross-Channel invasion of Europe. By midsummer he had been named commander of Operation Torch, an invasion of North Africa that would be the first step toward Europe. It was a touchy assignment that involved coordinating British and French forces, neither of whom had much respect for the other, and required political skills as well as military. General Eisenhower had plenty of both. The North African operation was successful and the allies were soon fighting their way up the Italian peninsula.

At the end of 1943, having been tested in battle and in the political arena, Eisenhower turned his attention away from the Italian campaign when he was appointed Supreme Commander of Operation Overlord, the coming invasion of France, and went to London to put the complex operation together. Six months later, the troops he commanded were inching their way across France and Belgium, taking the war to Germany itself. By fall, Eisenhower had been made commander of all Allied ground forces, and when the war ended, the victorious hero became commander of the American forces in Europe. Many years later, he wrote that his wartime achievement was his greatest

A few weeks before Ike's inauguration, the Eisenhowers took time out for a family Christmas. Left to right are Mrs. Elvira Doud, Mrs. Eisenhower's mother; Mrs. Mamie Eisenhower, holding her eleven-month-old granddaughter Susan; the President elect; four-year-old Dwight David Eisenhower II; three-year-old Barbara Anne, and close friend; and Mrs. John Eisenhower, mother of the three children.

At the beginning of the 1952 presidential campaign, neither candidate Eisenhower nor his running mate, Richard M. Nixon, had any idea of the rough seas that lay ahead.

accomplishment, transcending even his election to the presidency. He had been given a command that other officers with more experience and seniority might have killed for; and he had proven that it had been the right choice.

Soon after, he was brought home to become the Army's Chief of Staff, but his heart wasn't in the job, and he retired in 1947 to become President of Columbia University. Meanwhile, what the majority of Americans wanted was for him to become President of the United States. But he had another stop to make first. In February 1951, he left New York for Brussels to become Supreme Commander of NATO. Back in uniform, he seemed out of the running for the presidency.

But the bandwagon was already rolling. In the summer of 1952, the Republicans nominated the still-protesting General to be their standard-bearer. Harry Truman, who campaigned for the Democratic Candidate, Adlai Stevenson, gleefully predicted that Eisenhower would get his comeuppance at the polls. "He doesn't know any more about politics than a pig knows about Sunday," he said. But he was wrong. Ike's victory was a landslide of historic proportions. Not only that, but after a first term plagued with the uncertainty of the cold war, the red scares, the witch-hunting tactics of Senator McCarthy, and severe racial tension, not to mention the well-publicized poor state of his health, nearly sixty percent of the voters gave him a vote of confidence and a second term.

He was seventy years old when he eventually retired to his farm at Gettysburg, Pennsylvania, but though he would like to have spent the rest of his days painting and playing golf, he was still very much in demand as an elder statesman. It was a paradox. He kept the country at peace during a time when the whole world seemed on the verge of exploding, but his critics didn't have to dig very hard to find fault with his Administration. Harry Truman had been partly right, General Eisenhower understood politics, but the politicians around him were almost too much for him to handle. But if he was criticized, the people themselves weren't listening. Until the day he died, even until this day, the man in the street still liked Ike. They respected his decency and they saw him as a man they could trust. Even in the worst of times, the Eisenhower smile was reassuring. He had explained it himself in a London speech on the day the Germans surrendered in 1945: "I come from the heart of America."

When he died at the age of 78 he was given a simple military funeral and was taken back to Abilene, with only slightly more ceremony than had been given to the men he led. Of all the tributes that poured in, one of the most touching was one that would have made him proud. Bill Mauldin, the cartoonist who had created the character known as "G.I. Joe" all those years before, drew a representation of a battlefield cemetery with its endless rows of white crosses. The caption was, "It's Ike himself. Pass the word."

The 35th President

JOHN F. KENNEDY

(1961-1963)

Not long after his assassination, President Kennedy's widow, Jacqueline, was interviewed for *Life Magazine* by Theodore H. White. What she told him summed up perfectly how most Americans felt about the thousand days that had changed their world.

"All I keep thinking of is this line from a musical comedy," she said. "At night before we went to sleep, Jack liked to play some records, and the song he loved most came at the very end of this record. The lines he loved to hear were, 'Don't let it be forgot, that once there was a spot, for one brief shining moment that was known as Camelot.'"

Life Magazine had given some clues about what to expect from the Kennedy White House ten years earlier with a feature story they called, "Life Goes Courting With a U.S. Senator." The more serious *Saturday Evening Post* had recently said that "Kennedy seems to be at once preoccupied, disorganized and utterly casual – alarmingly so. For example, when he addresses the House with his shirt tail out and clearly visible from the galleries, many women have hopefully concluded that he needs looking after. In their opinion, he is, as a young millionaire Senator, just about the most eligible bachelor in the United States, and the least justifiable one. Kennedy lives up to that role when he drives his long convertible, hatless and with the car's top down, in Washington, or accidentally gets photographed with a glamor girl in a nightclub." *Life's* "courting" story was obviously a PR man's effort to polish up the Kennedy image after that, but it also parted the curtain on the Camelot to come.

The magazine said, "The handsomest member of the U.S. Senate was acting last week like any young man in love." A *Life* photographer just happened to be there when Senator Kennedy took his new fiancee to the family's summer home on Cape Cod. The future President was caught in the act of skipping stones

The Kennedy family in 1934. Left to right, they are Edward, Jean, Robert, Patricia, Eunice, Kathleen, Rosemary, John, Mrs. Rose Kennedy and Joseph P. Kennedy.

across the water, as catcher in a softball game and having his hair tousled by his bride-to-be. Two months later, *Life* took its readers to Newport, R.I., for the wedding of "Washington's best-looking young Senator to Washington's prettiest inquiring photographer" at the bride's mother's 300-acre Hammersmith farm. The magazine reported that the marriage of John F. Kennedy and Jacqueline Bouvier had been attended by "diplomats, senators and social figures," and said that the reception for 900 good friends was "just like the coronation." King Arthur and his Guenevere would have been envious.

Back then, it was easy to dismiss Jack Kennedy as the playboy son of a millionaire playing at politics. But he was an expert at the game. It was in his blood. Both his grandfathers had been forces to be reckoned with in the rough and tumble politics of the "Boston Irish." P.J. Kennedy, his father's father, had served in both houses of the Massachusetts Legislature, and his mother's father, John F. Fitzgerald, went from the legislature to the United States Congress, ran twice for the Senate and was the first son of Irish immigrants to become Mayor of Boston.

Along with Fitzgerald, Pat Kennedy was one of Boston's most influential men, part of an inner circle that decided who was elected to office and who got all the best municipal and state jobs. P.J. also had a flair for business, and when he went to the legislature, he sold the saloon that had established his political base and became a liquor wholesaler. He also owned a coal company, and two banks, all of which thrived with the support of the same people who gave him his political power.

By the time his son, Joseph P. Kennedy, was born he was a wealthy man, and the boy could easily have lived a life of leisure. But from the beginning, Joe liked making money for its own sake, and before he was a teenager he was already an entrepreneur. During his years at Harvard he owned a sightseeing bus, and two years after he graduated he became president of his own bank. A year after that he married the Mayor's daughter, Rose, and moved to Brookline, a suburb that was considered off-limits to the Irish. But, then, so was a Harvard diploma, and Joe Kennedy had one of those, too.

On the day his second son, John Fitzgerald Kennedy, was born he became a board member of the Massachusetts Electric Company, and if the likes of the Saltonstalls and Cabots still snubbed him, they were forced to rub elbows with this man they preferred to keep at arm's length. When the First World War broke out he became assistant manager of a shipyard, and when the war was over he joined the investment firm of Hayden Stone, where he learned how to make money work for him instead of the other way around. At the same time, he formed a partnership to buy control of a movie theater chain, which eventually led to the business of producing movies. In the meantime, convinced that proper Bostonians would never accept an Irishman into their society no matter how rich he became, he moved his wife and five children to New York, where nothing mattered except how rich he was.

When talking pictures arrived on the scene, Joe Kennedy joined forces with David Sarnoff's Radio Corporation of America and began producing talkies under the RKO name. He was also an active stock speculator, but by the time the market crashed in 1929 he had already taken his money and run from Wall Street. It was then that he decided to get into politics.

He had plenty of money and valuable business contacts, and believed that the road to real power was in supporting Franklin D. Roosevelt's presidential

The Kennedy family in 1960. Left to right are gathered Mrs. Robert Kennedy (Ethel), Steven Smith, Eunice Kennedy Shriver, Rose Kennedy, Mrs. Jean Kennedy Smith, Joseph P. Kennedy, John Kennedy, Jacqueline Kennedy, Robert Kennedy, Edward Kennedy, Mrs. Patricia Kennedy Lawford, R. Sargent Shriver, Mrs. Edward Kennedy (Joan) and Peter Lawford.

hopes and getting a Cabinet post in return. The new President turned his back on him, but his political contacts gave him inside information that Roosevelt was going to push for repeal of the Prohibition Amendment, and Joe Kennedy took advantage of the opportunity by arranging to become an importer of Scotch whisky. When repeal became a reality, he was ready with warehouses full of booze and was, for a while at least, the only game in town.

But the liquor business was only a waiting game. He was still hungry for a political appointment. He got his opportunity when Roosevelt established the Securities and Exchange Commission and made Kennedy its first chairman. Cynics said it was like putting the fox in charge of the henhouse, but this fox turned out to be a dedicated public servant and everyone was grudgingly impressed, especially the President. Other Government jobs followed, but Joe Kennedy got his big reward in 1937 when he was made U.S. Ambassador to Great Britain.

John Kennedy, Jr often upstaged his father, even before he was able to walk.

The Kennedy children matured during the family's London years. And though the head of the family often hinted in various feuds with Roosevelt that he was planning to run for President himself, it was obvious he had his eye on the job for his oldest son, Joe. But fate stepped in when Joe was killed flying an unusually dangerous mission as a World War II bomber pilot. His second son, Jack, who had dropped out of Harvard to join the Navy, was seriously hurt when the PT boat he commanded was rammed and sunk in the Pacific. But at least he was alive, and now he was the heir to his father's dream.

After he got out of the Navy, Jack went in an entirely different direction. At the beginning of the war, he had turned his Harvard thesis, *Why England Slept*, into a published book and decided he wanted to be a journalist. He drew some dream assignments from the Hearst newspapers and covered such events as the creation of the United Nations and the establishment of England's postwar government, but less than a year after taking the job he drifted back to Boston to take up the family tradition of politics. He hadn't lived in the city for most of his life, but his roots were there, and he had made it a point never to lose his distinctive Boston accent.

In 1945, he announced his candidacy for Congress and then he discovered that getting there was tougher than pounding a typewriter had been. It was generally agreed that any man with the names of both Fitzgerald and Kennedy wouldn't have to campaign very hard. But there was just one problem. Or rather, nine. It was a ten-man race. Worse, Jack Kennedy had probably never seen a tenement in his life, and that was the battleground. But if he found it distasteful to climb dingy stairs and shake dirty hands, he never let it show. In fact, the famous Kennedy smile never left his face, and the crowds couldn't help smiling back. They found him a fine broth of a lad, this grandson of the great Honey Fitz, and lest they forget, former Mayor Fitzgerald was on hand to tell them so. But it wasn't all fond memories. Kennedy recruited his college friends, his Navy buddies and his brothers and sisters to add fresh young faces and a new kind of enthusiasm to the job at hand. They all did their job well. Kennedy took forty percent of the primary vote, double the number of the next nearest contender. And in November he took the congressional seat by a two-to-one margin. He was twenty-nine years old and on his way.

He was reelected to congress twice and then decided to become a Senator. It wasn't a sudden move. He had been planning it from the time he shook his first hand on his grandfather's turf. But still, it was a bold move. His opponent was young Henry Cabot Lodge, Jr., a wealthy member of the Boston Establishment, a veteran Senator and a war hero himself. Lodge was better-known around the state, and for an added handicap Dwight D. Eisenhower was running for president in the same election, and his coattails were considered broad enough to get even mediocre Republicans elected along with him. To make matters worse, Kennedy and Lodge seemed to share the same views on the issues. But Kennedy had an edge. He was a fighter. And he had a new secret weapon, his brother Bobby, who had just graduated from law school and had signed on as campaign manager. He was a fighter, too. When it was all over and Lodge lost in spite of big Republican wins everywhere else, the former senator had probably predicted the outcome during the campaign when he said, "I don't have to worry about Jack Kennedy. I don't have to worry about the Kennedy money. But I do worry about that family of his. They're all over the state!"

"That family of his" was with him every step of the way to the presidency, and together they revolutionized American politics. He began marching toward the White House in 1956 with a bid for the second spot on the Democratic ticket. He didn't make it, but he made a good enough showing that party leaders began taking him more seriously. And it gave him four more years to look like a winner. He didn't waste a day. He used the time to build a professional staff, including several Ivy League professors, of young, fresh, eager and bright people. They put it to the test in his 1958 campaign for reelection to the Senate and passed with flying colors. He won the election by the biggest margin in the state's history.

Once he made it clear he wanted to be president, and that he could deliver the votes, only one thing stood in his way. No Roman Catholic had ever been elected President of the United States. And it was no accident of fate. Hardly a story was written about Kennedy in any newspaper or magazine that didn't mention his religion, though most agreed with a profile in *The Economist* that said, "Mr. Kennedy, like most of his rivals in both parties, is close to being a spiritually rootless modern man." But he still attended mass regularly, and even halfway into the twentieth century, Americans were still vaguely uneasy about the power of the Pope. Jack Kennedy had proven he could deal with handicaps, but this one was formidable. And when he formally announced his candidacy at the beginning of 1960, party leaders were visibly nervous. They relaxed a little when he beat the popular Senator Hubert Humphrey in the primary in heavily Protestant Wisconsin. But it wasn't enough for them. The political pros decided they'd wait to see if he could win in West Virginia, which they considered a hotbed of anti-Catholic sentiment. The Kennedy bandwagon fanned out all over the state, and when the trick was turned, it rolled on to win in five other states and very nearly gave him enough votes to clinch the nomination. The pros were convinced. And impressed. The victories were impressive enough in themselves, but how he accomplished them made the old-timers sit up and take notice. Kennedy had taught them how to use television, how to take advantage of polling, and even though the candidate had nearly unlimited funds, he showed them how to get the most mileage out of their money. Things we take for granted in modern elections were developed and refined by the Kennedys in their primary fights, and their techniques set the pace for the national campaign that followed. From that moment on, the politicians forgot their old-time religion. John F. Kennedy had taken politics into the twentieth century.

More people voted in the 1960 presidential election than in any other before it, but it wasn't a Kennedy landslide. He won by a slim two-tenths of a percent of the total, but it didn't cramp his style. He bounced into the White House with a verve the country hadn't seen since Theodore Roosevelt, and a cultured outlook that rivalled Thomas Jefferson. He was the youngest president in the country's history, and young people responded to his enthusiasm and his wit. Younger congressional candidates appeared on the scene and managed to get elected. Life in Washington changed and America's view of itself changed along with it. In the late 1950s, people had taken to wearing little buttons imprinted with smiling faces to remind them that they ought to be happy. With Kennedy, the smiles shifted to their own faces.

When he took the oath of office, Kennedy had said, "Let the word go forth from this time and place that the torch has been passed to a new generation of Americans, born in this century, tempered by war, disciplined by a hard and bitter peace …." The torch burned brightly through good times and bad until November 22, 1963, when the President was suddenly gunned down at the very height of his popularity. But the torch had, indeed, been passed to a new generation.

Even before Kennedy became President, his wife, Jacqueline, also sometimes upstaged him.

The 36th President
LYNDON B. JOHNSON
(1963-1969)

In November 1963, Lyndon Johnson was sworn in as President aboard the plane that had taken his predecessor to Dallas, Texas.

In 1928, when the Democrats met in Houston, Texas, to pick their presidential candidate, a young college senior sat transfixed in the press gallery as Franklin D. Roosevelt put the name of New York Governor Al Smith into contention. Lyndon Johnson didn't belong there. He was editor of the *San Marcos College Star*, but none of his readers had the right to vote. He had talked his way into the convention hall, and when he got back to school and was on the carpet for having violated a rule that restricted students to the campus, he talked his way out of that, too. Lyndon B. Johnson was good at that sort of thing.

When he enrolled at the Southwest Texas State Teachers College at San Marcos, he had every intention of becoming a teacher and, in fact, he did become one. He taught in a Mexican-American community during a break in his college career to earn enough money to continue; and when he graduated, he taught high school in Houston. But it was obvious from his first day at San Marcos that Lyndon would be something more.

His trip to Houston to watch the Democrats at work wasn't the only time he slipped away. His father had been a member of the Texas State Legislature, and one of the joys of Lyndon's boyhood was sitting in the gallery watching the lawmakers at work. At college, he went up to Austin as often as he could sneak away just for the fun of it. But he was having fun on campus, too, developing his political skills with slightly more enthusiasm than he brought to his studies.

He needed to work to pay for his education, and he began his college career on the campus trash detail. But he was able to talk his way out of it, and became assistant to the secretary of the school's president. It wasn't much of a job – he was a messenger really – but he managed to puff it up into something that at least seemed important. When he delivered a memo, he created the impression that a response sent back through him would get faster attention; and to reinforce the impression, he stationed himself at the door to the president's outer office so that anyone who visited there had to pass his desk. In a very few weeks, most of the faculty was convinced that Johnson had become assistant to the president. Even the president himself seems to have believed it. He began letting Johnson handle correspondence for him, and when he asked the boy to drive him to the State Capitol one day, he was impressed by the way he handled himself among the legislators, many of whom were old family friends. From that day until the day he graduated, Johnson served as the unofficial political adviser to the president of his college. The man had some advice for the student, too. "Don't become a teacher," he said, "become a politician." Lyndon Johnson had probably already come to the same conclusion.

He had used his political skills with the student body, too. Before he arrived there, campus life had been dominated by a faction of athletes organized in a fraternity called the Black Stars. When Johnson tried to join the club, they rejected him, but they eventually wished they hadn't. He was a new kid on campus, but that didn't stop him from organizing a new fraternity, which he called the White Stars, whose sole purpose was to end the dominance of the jocks. He made it a secret society and never allowed more than two members to be seen together at any one time, a rule that allowed them to infiltrate all the student groups to find out who shared their dislike of the Black Stars. It didn't take long to find out that it was nearly the entire student body. They resented that most of the money earmarked for student activities went into sports, and Johnson was able to use his position in the president's outer office to back up their suspicions with actual figures. White Star membership grew dramatically, and they began holding office in the student government. Then he used his influence in the president's office to distribute campus jobs. The best of them went to loyal White Star members, and jobs like his former post as trash collector went to Black Stars. By the time Johnson was a senior, a White Star became class president, and he owed every vote to Lyndon Johnson, who personally talked with every student with a plea to vote for his man. Lyndon had also found other ways to talk to people. He was editor of the school paper and an award-winning member of the debating team. He was also, in spite of all his extra-curricular energy, an honor student.

It's no wonder the college president encouraged him to get into politics. Even the college janitor could have recognized the talent.

During the summer of 1930, Johnson found the opportunity to run the campaign of a candidate for the State Senate, and the following year the new senator repaid the favor by recommending him to serve on the staff of Congressman Dick Kleberg. When he arrived in Washington to begin his new job as Kleberg's secretary he said later, "You just had to look around and it was very exciting to me to me to realize that the people, many of them that you were passing, were probably Congressmen at least, maybe Senators or members of the Cabinet. And there was the smell of power. It's got an odor, you know, power I mean." He never was able to get it out of his nostrils. But first, he knew he had a lot to learn.

He began by cultivating people he knew would be able to teach him how Washington ticked. He buttonholed anyone who looked like they had any influence at all, and though it seemed to everyone he met that he never stopped talking, Lyndon Johnson did a lot of intense listening. In a few months, one old pro said that he had learned more about what makes Washington tick than some people who had been on the scene for twenty years.

Fortunately, Congressman Kleberg didn't take his duties very seriously, and was pleased to let Johnson take care of the details. Among the details he took care of was dispensing patronage jobs in Washington, and Johnson put a new spin on the practice by requiring people he helped to help him in the Congressman's office after hours – not just in the evening but in the morning, too. It made Kleberg's office uncommonly productive, and it also freed Johnson to pursue his political education. The amazing thing was that none of the dragooned office help resented the long hours or the hard work. Lyndon Johnson was enjoying himself and the joy was contagious.

Part of the education process was a part-time job as doorkeeper at the House of Representatives. It was a job considered a cut or two below that of page, but to

A seasoned politician, Johnson steered legislation through Congress using his own style of arm-twisting.

Johnson it was a golden opportunity to get to spend time on the House floor, and to meet and mingle with Congressmen. Among the men he cultivated were Sam Rayburn and Wright Patman, fellow Texans who had known his father and who became impressed by Lyndon's eagerness.

He was a busy young man on the way up, but not so busy that he didn't find time for a whirlwind courtship of Claudia Taylor, known to everyone as "Lady Bird," whom he married in November 1934. A few months later they moved back to Texas for the next step in Lyndon's political career. He had been named Texas Director of the National Youth Administration, one of the agencies of Roosevelt's New Deal. He handled the job like he did everything else, and before long became known as the best administrator in the agency. And in his spare time he cultivated the friendship of important Texans who could help him later on. "Later on" came less than a year later when a Texas Congressman died, and Lyndon Johnson decided to run for his seat. He won by a two-to-one margin.

Before he left for Washington, though, he was invited to meet President Roosevelt, who was aboard the presidential yacht in the Gulf of Mexico. The Congressman impressed the President with a professed love of the sea, and Roosevelt responded by putting him in line for a spot on the House Committee on Naval Affairs, a juicy plum for a freshman Congressman. It also marked Johnson as a Roosevelt insider, which paid off in delivering Federal dollars to his home district. Within three years Congressman Johnson was ready to go on to bigger things. He ran for the Senate in 1941 and lost by a narrow margin, ironically because of his ties to Roosevelt, who had fallen out of favor in Texas. He was still a Congressman, though, but the day after the Japanese attacked Pearl Harbor, he joined the Navy. He was the first member of Congress to join up, and before he was returned to Capitol Hill by a special Presidential order a year later, he had earned a Silver Star for duty in the Pacific.

His life as a Congressman had become routine, and he used his spare time to start building a personal fortune, beginning with his purchase of a bankrupt

Austin radio station. It earned him a profit of eighteen dollars the first year he owned it, but within twenty years it was paying him a half million dollars a year, and he was investing the profits in Texas real estate, which made him one of the richest men ever to become President of the United States.

In 1948 he had another opportunity to run for the Senate and won by a margin of just 87 votes. His opponent challenged the result, of course, and the case went all the way to the Supreme Court, which refused to get involved in a local election, and the count was accepted as valid. They began calling him "Landslide Lyndon" after that, but he didn't care. He had his seat and he was going to make the best of it.

Within three years he was Senate Minority Leader, a man to be reckoned with. Two years after that, in 1954, when the Democrats took control of Congress, Johnson became the youngest Majority Leader in the history of the Senate. The man who had mastered the inner workings of the House of Representatives was in a position to dispense favors and earn the gratitude of a much more august body. He had the talent for it, and the will. His largesse extended all the way down the line to secretaries and janitors. No birthday went unmarked, no achievement unnoticed. He was a Dutch uncle to his colleagues and Big Daddy to their staffs. Everyone, it seemed, was indebted to Senator Johnson in one way or another. Meanwhile, his old mentor, Sam Rayburn, had become Speaker of the House of Representatives.

It was commonly accepted that Senator Johnson was the most powerful man in the United States in the 1950s, and Washington insiders agreed that the second most powerful was not President Eisenhower, but Sam Rayburn. Together, Johnson and Rayburn controlled the Democrats in Congress and made it look like their Republican colleagues were opposing the President of their own party.

In 1960, Johnson decided that it was time to push his power a bit further. He had served twelve years in

the House and another twelve in the Senate. He toyed with the idea of announcing for the presidency, but he knew that the Party would never accept a Southerner, even though he plaintively argued that he was a Texan and not a Southerner at all. When John F. Kennedy took the nomination and offered him the second spot on the ticket, he accepted immediately. When he was asked by an astounded friend why he's traded the job of Majority Leader for the relatively toothless position of Vice President, he answered, "Power is where power goes." Other Vice Presidents may have been toothless, but other Vice Presidents hadn't been Lyndon B. Johnson.

His instincts had been wrong, of course. President Kennedy wasn't a Senator any longer, and he didn't have to depend on Lyndon Johnson to get things done. "Every time I came into John Kennedy's presence," Johnson said later, "I felt like a goddamn raven hovering over his shoulder …. I detested every minute of it."

Power would fall on his shoulders again after the Kennedy assassination. He accepted it with the highest ideals. "I don't want to be remembered as a President who built empires or sought grandeur," he said. "I want to be the President who educated young children, who helped feed the hungry, who helped the poor to find their own way." He called his program "The Great Society." It was the program that gave the elderly Medicare and expanded their Social Security benefits. It gave minorities new pride and greater opportunities. It made industry accountable for what it was doing to the environment. It made the arts a beneficiary of Federal aid. It should have made L.B.J. one of our most revered Presidents.

But L.B.J. went to the White House with an albatross around his neck: the Vietnam War. No matter what he did, its spectre was always there, like a raven on his shoulder. He also suffered from a personal style that many people found charming, but others found offensive. He was a real "Down Home" Texan, big, brash, vulgar, informal to a fault. He had a passion for hard work, and he expected everyone around him to share it. If they didn't, he could be cruelly insulting. He once defended it by saying, "If I don't bawl you out once in a while, you ain't part of the family." But there were some who didn't want to be part of the family and, unfortunately for L.B.J., many of them were in the press corps. He wasn't a man who could take criticism gracefully, though he knew very well how how to use it constructively.

When he decided not to run for another term in 1968, he felt his efforts had been wasted. "How is it possible," he asked, "that all these people could be so ungrateful to me after I have given them so much?"

In his years of retirement in the Texas hill country, he found the affection and gratitude he had craved and worked so hard for. Some people did care after all. And when he died, a black man who said he remembered a time when he couldn't go to the movies in his own home town until President Johnson had made it possible, said, "I don't care what anybody else says. When it comes to presidents, he was my 'main man'"

Johnson's proudest moment, which he shared with Dr. Martin Luther King, was the signing of the historic Civil Rights Act into law.

by Margaret Connelly Nicholson

Bankruptcy!

When it's the smartest choice

As more women establish credit in their own name, they run the additional risk of facing personal bankruptcy: More than one million file every year.

Out-of-control debt is more than a personal problem—it's a legal issue. The courts frown on scofflaws who short-change deserving creditors or use bankruptcy to sidestep responsibilities, as happens too often in divorce cases. (This year, the Supreme Court is scheduled to decide if spouses can declare bankruptcy to avoid giving half the cash value of the family home to their ex.)

When to file

Deciding to get out of debt by declaring bankruptcy depends on the individual situation. If IOU's are mounting, creditors dunning, and you're in danger of losing a home, car or other possessions, bankruptcy may be a viable option. Once you do it, the panic and pressure is alleviated, debts are consolidated, and you have a chance to rebuild credit and your life.

Step one: Contact an attorney. Bankruptcy laws are complex, forms are confusing and too much is at stake to undertake it alone.

Step two: File a petition in federal court to obtain a discharge of debts and a 'fresh start.' After you've filled out the appropriate forms and paid a $60 fee, the court will issue an 'automatic stay,' which notifies the people you owe that all phone calls, threatening letters and repossession efforts must cease.

Step three: In exchange for calling off creditors, ownership of your property is transferred to the court's 'bankruptcy estate'—you'll need court approval before you can sell or give it away.

Types of bankruptcy

Of the two forms, Chapter 7 bankruptcy is faster. You can count on starting over, debt-free, in a matter of months. Chapter 13 bankruptcy can take years.

Under Chapter 7, your assets are liquidated by the court and the proceeds divided among creditors. It doesn't matter if your assets don't equal or exceed what is owed. The remaining debt is forgiven.

With Chapter 13, you keep your assets but promise to pay off all or part of the debt in three to five years. Anything left unpaid after this period is canceled. These terms are available only to individuals whose debt isn't gigantic.

The downside

Not sticking to the repayment plan can put you in worse trouble than before. And even after following the court's ruling to a T, companies can refuse you credit in the future. An agency such as TRW can list the bankruptcy claim in its records for up to 10 years.

Whether filing for bankruptcy under Chapter 7 or 13, some debts are inescapable: You're still responsible for making alimony, child-support and student-loan payments regardless of your financial status.

In the case of divorce or separation, property settlements are not considered part of alimony and can be used by the court to satisfy creditors.

If these considerations are outweighed by the need to make a clean start and you're able to curb future spending, going bankrupt may be right for you. Just look what it did for Pan Am. They're still flying high. ◆

No one could save her son

Because of an ill-conceived law, divers were prevented from pulling 12-year-old William from Lake Michigan

Imagine the horror of being told your child has drowned. Add to this the outrage of learning that those who might have saved your son were forbidden from plunging into the water for 20 minutes because they lacked proper authority.

Ollie Belle Ross of Waukegan, Illinois, doesn't have to imagine. On August 11, 1985, her 12-year-old son, William, and a friend were enjoying the Waukegan Lakefront Festival held on the shores of Lake Michigan. Suddenly, William slipped off a jetty and fell into the lake. His friend immediately ran for help. In less than 10 minutes they were back: Emergency personnel from the nearby festival, as well as two civilian scuba divers, prepared to attempt a rescue. But then a Lake County deputy sheriff arrived by boat and announced that Lake County had exclusive jurisdiction—no outside rescue attempts would be permitted. When the scuba divers said they would dive at their own risk, the deputy sheriff threatened them with arrest and positioned his boat so as to make their dive impossible.

Officially authorized divers arrived 20 minutes later and pulled William from the water. The boy was barely clinging to life. He died the next morning.

William's mother sued Lake County and Deputy Sheriff Gordon Johnson for unconstitutionally depriving her son of life. A federal district court dismissed Ross's complaint on the grounds that the county's policy was not unconstitutional.

On August 16, 1990, the U.S. Court of Appeals for the Seventh Circuit reversed the decision. Now the heartbroken mother can go back to district court and sue Lake County and Deputy Sheriff Johnson for the unnecessary loss of her son's life.

The 37th President
RICHARD M. NIXON
(1969-1974)

When he was mustered out of the Navy after World War II, former Lieutenant Commander Richard Nixon went home to Whittier, California, to pick up the pieces and reestablish the law practice he had left a few days after the war began. At about the same time an ad appeared in a local newspaper that said:

WANTED: Congressman candidate with no previous experience to defeat a man who has represented a district in the House for ten years.

The Representative the ad's sponsors were trying to unseat was Jerry Voorhis of California's Twelfth Congressional District, a man the Washington press corps had voted the "best Congressman west of the Mississippi." He was popular with the voters, too, but clearly not among the conservative businessmen who had written the want-ad.

One of them who knew Nixon approached him with two questions: "Are you a Republican?" and "Would you like to run for Congress?" The answer to both questions was "yes!" and the young lawyer with a pregnant wife and a good war record entered the world of politics as a candidate for Congress.

The campaign, one of the first to package and merchandise a candidate, began with six months of intensive schooling. Nixon learned his lessons well and began hinting, but never saying, that the incumbent was supported by people with Communist principles. Voorhis proved otherwise, but the principle of guilt by association worked against him. The deciding factor, which gave Nixon a comfortable margin, was a series of debates, prompted by the fact that Nixon couldn't draw crowds but his opponent could. By appearing on the same stage with Voorhis, the underdog was assured of listeners, and he had plenty to say. The master blend of innuendo and half-truth added up to doubt about Voorhis, and when it was all over he said it was "the bitterest campaign I have ever seen." Nixon ran unopposed for the seat two years later.

Nixon became a national figure as chairman of the House Un-American Activities Special Subcommittee investigating charges by Whittaker Chambers, an editor of *Time Magazine* and a confessed Communist Party functionary, that there were Communist spies in the Government. Among the accused was former State Department official Alger Hiss. Chambers eventually produced microfilmed documents he said had been concealed in a hollowed-out pumpkin on his farm, and Hiss was convicted of perjury.

Nixon had found his niche. "The Hiss case," he said, "for the first time, forcibly demonstrated to the American people that domestic Communism was a real and present danger." From then on, Nixon was never far from the issue. When he challenged Democratic Representative Helen Gahagan Douglas for the Senate, he defeated her by calling her "The Pink Lady," and printing all his anti-Douglas handbills on pink paper. The campaign had hardly begun when a local newspaper editorialized, "Tricky Dick Nixon is falsely accusing her … of being a Communist." Years after the campaign was relegated to history, and the name of Helen Gahagan Douglas forgotten, the name "Tricky Dick" was still with him.

Senator Nixon became a spokesman for the Republican Party and toured the country attacking Communists in general and the Truman administration in particular. He scored a coup when he was sent to Europe for a conference and made a side trip to Paris to have a chat with NATO chief Dwight D. Eisenhower. It put him in the forefront among Republicans trying to convince the General to become their Presidential candidate, and by the time Eisenhower agreed to run, Richard Nixon was in a position to become his running mate.

When the campaign began, a Gallup Poll noted that only 45 percent of Americans could name the GOP Vice Presidential candidate. Within a week, there was hardly a man, woman or child in the country who didn't know the name of Richard Milhous Nixon. And most of them had an opinion about him.

The New York Post had revealed that a group of California businessmen were contributing money to help cover Nixon's personal expenses that weren't paid by the Government. Nixon countered by saying that the contributions actually saved the taxpayers' money. But his own tactic, guilt by association, had caught up with him. Newspapers across the country began calling for his removal from the ticket, and before long the candidate himself volunteered to resign. But Eisenhower stayed cool and announced that he was convinced his running mate was "clean as a hound's tooth." Then he called on Nixon to prove it.

The suspense gave Nixon an audience for his televised speech of more than 58 million people. The speech they heard has often been criticized as something bordering on soap opera, and Nixon himself said it was "a flop" until the telegrams and phone calls began coming in. The Republican National Committee estimated that more than 300,000 "Keep Nixon" messages were sent to its Washington headquarters alone. General Eisenhower was impressed. "I'd rather have one courageous, honest man," he said, "than a whole boxcar full of pussyfooters."

After the election it was apparent that Vice President Nixon wasn't going to follow in the nearly invisible footsteps of his predecessors. He became the Administration's spokesman on political matters and campaigned for Congressional candidates, making as many as three speeches a day to elect an "Eisenhower Congress." His efforts, in which he accused the Democrats of treason or worse, failed, and after they took control of the 84th Congress in 1954, he was faced with the first defeat in his political career.

He was dealt another blow in September, 1955, when President Eisenhower was hospitalized following a heart attack. "I went dead inside," Nixon said. But the Vice President's grace under pressure impressed even his most hardened critics. It defused many of their objections to his becoming the President's running mate again in 1956, and when Eisenhower announced that he would run for a second term, he said he had left it up to the Vice President to

President Nixon considered his greatest legacy to be the reopening of relations with China, which began when he met with Chairman Mao Tse-Tung on February 21, 1972.

"chart his own course." In spite of tough opposition, the course Nixon chose was to be part of the ticket and "set the record straight."

The campaign was subdued, even dignified, and there was talk that a "New Nixon" had emerged. According to one source, when the Republican high command asked him to "engage in verbal street fighting," on behalf of nervous Congressional candidates, the Vice President responded, "I have no intention of becoming a political Jack the Ripper." Richard Nixon was working hard at appearing "presidential."

At the beginning of the second Eisenhower term, the President said that "no one in the history of America has had such careful preparation" as Nixon had for assuming the presidency. And Nixon's preparation was further enhanced by the state of the president's health. Eisenhower's 1955 coronary had thrust the Vice President into the center of White House activity. In 1957, after suffering a stroke, Eisenhower drafted a historic document that gave Nixon the power to assume complete presidential powers if necessary. No other Vice President had ever been given as much responsibility and power.

Nixon scored a political coup in 1959 when he was sent to Moscow. At one point during his tour of a trade exhibition with Soviet Premier Nikita Khrushchev, he managed to maneuver the crusty Communist leader into a debate on the merits of American kitchens compared to those found in Russia. The debate ended in a draw, but to a man like Nixon, anxious to establish himself as a fearless statesman, it was a stunning victory.

He came home a hero on an inside track toward the presidential nomination. And by the time the campaign began, polls put him well ahead of John F. Kennedy, the Democratic candidate. But when it ended he had lost the election, and for the first time in thirteen years Richard Nixon was a private citizen. It was an uncomfortable role for a man who had tasted the powers of the presidency, and in 1962 he ran for the governorship of California. He expected an easy victory and apparently planned to use the office to keep himself in the public eye. What he got was an embarrassing defeat, and in conceding the election he made it a point to blame his troubles on the press who, he said, "won't have Nixon to kick around anymore." His political career had, apparently, come to an end.

Keeping his word, the former Vice President moved to New York and became a Wall Street lawyer. Though he kept his political contacts, it seemed obvious to every observer that Richard Nixon's political career was, indeed, past history.

But history intervened in 1963 with the assassination of President John F. Kennedy. Though Nixon had repeatedly denied any presidential ambitions of his own, he became a campaigner again, and in the 1964 election he warmly supported the candidacy of Barry Goldwater. When Goldwater lost, Republican conservatives rallied around Nixon, and by the time they met to choose their candidate in 1967 he was nominated on the first ballot.

He and his running mate, Spiro T. Agnew, began the campaign far ahead in the polls and never lost their lead in the three-way race against Democrat Hubert H. Humphrey and Independent George Wallace. During the campaign, Nixon carefully avoided offering specific solutions to the problems the country was facing. He said he had a "secret plan" to end the war in Vietnam, and as President he quickly began to reduce U.S. involvement. At the same time he also expanded the fighting beyond Vietnam's border into Laos and Cambodia.

When Nixon had said that his first priority was to assume the role of peacemaker, he was thinking of more than Vietnam. America's European alliances were faltering. The Soviet Union represented a growing threat. There were severe problems in the Middle East, including a civil war in Jordan. Another war broke out between India and Pakistan, and Communist China seemed headed for superpower status, creating a new threat to peace. At home, the economy was in serious trouble with prices and interest rates rising and income stagnating. Crime had increased nearly 70 percent in a decade and the country was divided by fear. The mood of the Great Society had shifted to a call for law and order.

Nixon won approval for three major crime bills. He imposed wage-price controls and created a program to redistribute billions of tax dollars to state and local governments. In 1972, he became the first American President to visit Russia when he went to Moscow for a summit meeting with Leonid Brezhnev. But three months before, he had electrified the world by extending the hand of friendship to Chinese Premier Chou En-Lai and Party Chairman Mao Tse-Tung.

On February 21, 1972, Air Force One, the presidential jet, touched down in Peking and the hostility that had existed between the U.S. and China for a quarter century evaporated as President Nixon stepped out to be ushered to the home of Chairman Mao. Nixon had put aside his old hostility to Communist China when he supported its admission to the United Nations. He said he had no illusions about China's total dedication to Communism. "There will continue to be differences," he said, "the question is whether we are going to live with them or die for them."

By the time he returned from the Moscow summit, the 1972 presidential election campaign was warming up. Nixon faced little opposition, and the field of Democratic hopefuls was narrowed to Senator George S. McGovern. Nixon was far ahead in the polls and conducted a low-key campaign. But before it began, a burglary attempt at the Democratic National Headquarters in the Watergate complex in Washington, D.C. began a chain of events that became one of the most serious political scandals in American history.

In the aftermath, it was revealed that what the White House dismissed as a "third-rate burglary" was really just the tip of the iceberg. A special Senate Committee concluded that White House officials had authorized payment of hush money to defendants in the case. It also discovered that Nixon campaign officials had installed listening devices at the Democratic headquarters, that they had established a "dirty tricks squad" to keep the Democrats off balance, and that the White House had authorized a "plumbers" unit to plug leaks of damaging

Below left: the Nixon agenda was established in 1970 with his first State of the Union message. In the background are Vice President Spiro T. Agnew and House Speaker John W. McCormack.

Among the President's closest advisors was Secretary of State Henry Kissinger (below).

information. It was also revealed that the Administration had intended to use "Federal machinery to screw our political enemies."

The most damaging testimony came from White House counsel John Dean, who charged that the President himself had directed the cover-up. Meanwhile, more than a dozen Administration officials were sentenced to prison terms and the President was named an unindicted co-conspirator. The House Judiciary Committee approved impeachment proceedings against President Nixon, and on August 9, 1974, he became the first American President to resign from office. It was almost exactly ten months since his Vice President, Spiro T. Agnew, had become the first to resign from that office after a plea of no contest to a charge of income tax evasion. The presidency would pass to Gerald R. Ford, who had been appointed Vice President by Richard Nixon.

Nixon retired to San Clemente, California, where he maintained a low profile until September 8, when he once again made headlines with the news that he had been given a presidential pardon for "all offenses against the United States" during his tenure in office.

At the same time, former domestic affairs adviser John Ehrlichman went on trial for his role in the Watergate affair and angrily charged that the former President was responsible for all his troubles and had left him "twisting slowly in the wind." Judge John Sirica requested that Nixon take the stand to tell his side of the story but was rebuffed by a doctor's affidavit that it would "pose a serious risk to his health." The judge challenged the statement but it became a moot point when Nixon was hospitalized to remove a life-threatening blood clot. By the time he was released the trial was over, and Ehrlichman, along with former presidential chief of staff H.R. Haldeman and former attorney general John Mitchell, had been found guilty and were on their way to prison.

Though the former president had been spared telling his story in court, he was hard at work writing his memoirs, which eventually dominated the bestseller lists. And he agreed to a series of television interviews, during which he said "I let the American people down. And I have to carry that burden with me for the rest of my life."

Some time later he began receiving invitations for speaking engagements. Then in early 1980 the Nixons left San Clemente and moved back to New York City, where he quietly reentered the political mainstream as an elder statesman. As for the possibility of his making a comeback as a candidate, he explained: "I am the only native American citizen over the age of thirty-five who can't run for the presidency."

State secrets are not always serious matters as Soviet Party Secretary Leonid Brezhnev seems to be pointing out to President Nixon.

The 38th President
GERALD R. FORD
(1974-1977)

When Richard Nixon was reelected to the Presidency in 1972, he carried every state except Massachusetts and the District of Columbia. He didn't, however, carry a Republican majority into Congress, which prompted House Minority Leader Gerald R. Ford to abandon his dream of becoming Speaker of the House. He decided to run once more for the seat he had held since 1949 as Representative of Michigan's Fifth Congressional District, and then leave Washington to practice law. His plan would change dramatically.

Jerry Ford had originally gone to Washington more as the result of a dare than a plan. As a young lawyer in Grand Rapids, Michigan, he had been interested in politics, but the machinery was in the iron grip of a power broker who had little regard for idealistic young Republicans. Among his lieutenants was Congressman Barney Jonkman, whose strength was legendary, in spite of what many considered an appalling record in Washington. But everywhere Jerry Ford went, it seemed, the subject of what to do about Congressman Jonkman came up. He finally responded by announcing his own candidacy. The incumbent didn't seem to care a bit, and when Congress was called into special session just before the election, Jonkman cheerfully went back to Washington, confident that a campaign wasn't necessary.

It left the field wide open for Ford. By the time Congressman Jonkman came home again, it was too late. Ford won the primary by a two-to-one margin, and went on to win the election easily. Ford said luck had taken him to Washington, but until then he hadn't seemed like a man born under a lucky star. He was born Leslie L. King, Jr. in Omaha, Nebraska in 1913. When his parents were divorced, his mother took him to Grand Rapids, where she married Gerald Rudolf Ford, who adopted the boy and renamed him Gerald R. Ford, Jr. The family was poor, but not destitute, and young Jerry had an "average" childhood. His grades at school were called "average," too, but he had other interests. He played center on the city championship football team and was captain of the team that won the state championship.

He played football at the University of Michigan, too, and before he graduated he had offers to play professionally from both the Green Bay Packers and the Detroit Lions. They were tempting offers, but he decided he'd rather study law. When he was offered the jobs of boxing coach and assistant football coach at Yale University, he thought he had found a way. He enrolled in Yale's law school and kept the coaching jobs at the same time. When he graduated in 1941, in the top quarter of his class, he went home to establish a law firm. But before the firm was a year old, the United States entered World War II, and counselor Ford entered the Navy.

Almost from his first day in the House of Representatives, Jerry Ford dreamed of becoming House Speaker and concentrated on learning the workings of Congress and getting to know the people who served there. He became well-known as a "Congressman's Congressman," and became active in the national Republican Party. In 1963, President Lyndon Johnson appointed him to the Commission investigating the Kennedy assassination. It gave Ford more national recognition and strengthened his already high standing among his colleagues.

When President Johnson won the 1964 election he pulled in a strongly Democratic Congress along with him, and the GOP began looking for new leadership. When the Eighty-ninth Congress convened in January, 1965, Gerald Ford had been elected Minority Leader. With a little luck, if the Republicans could get a majority in the next Congress, he would become Speaker. They gained forty-seven seats in the next election, but were still short of a majority. Three years later, when the GOP came up short again, Congressman Ford decided to retire.

His chief reason for the decision was his wife, Betty, who was in almost constant pain from a pinched nerve compounded by arthritis, which wasn't helped by the damp Washington climate. Ford was devoted to her and his four children, and he often said they made him "as happy as a man can be." But he didn't become a family man until he was 35 years old. He said he had been too busy for such things. And he claimed he may not have married at all if his mother hadn't been so persistent in her suggestion that he "settle down."

He began dating Betty Warren, a former dancer

and model, who was a fashion coordinator in a local department store. He decided to marry her at about the same time he made his decision to run for Congress, and when they were married just two weeks before election day, Jerry arrived for the ceremony directly from a campaign speech. Their honeymoon lasted one weekend, during which time he took her to a football game and then on to a rally to hear a speech by Presidential candidate Thomas E. Dewey. They never really "settled down."

In October, 1973, when Vice President Spiro Agnew resigned, Ford was called to the Oval Office, where President Nixon offered him the job. Ford later wrote: "The Vice President didn't have much to do.... On the other hand, the Vice Presidency would be a splendid cap to my career." He also said that he felt he could be valuable to the President, whose policies he had consistently supported. Since he had no designs on the Presidency, he would be able to keep his promise to Betty that they'd retire in 1977.

But even before confirmation hearings could begin, the Watergate scandal boiled over, and as Ford's name was submitted to Congress, no less than twenty-two bills in the House were calling for the impeachment of President Nixon. The hearings took on a special importance as a result, and Ford's life was scrutinized more than any other candidate in the history of the country. Confirmation was overwhelmingly approved and on December 6, 1973, the man who wanted to be Speaker of the House

All the world loves a lover and the obvious love affair between President Ford and his wife, Betty, was an inspiration to all America.

became President of the Senate and the Vice President of the United States.

Eight months later, President Nixon himself resigned, and on August 9, 1974, Gerald R. Ford was sworn in as President. "Our long national nightmare is over," he said. But the job of healing the wounds of that nightmare had fallen squarely on his shoulders. One of his first acts was to tell the members of the Nixon Cabinet that he wouldn't accept their resignations. He also told them that he was going to give them more control over their departments and would to leave the details of management to them, a policy that broke completely from the previous Administration. Then he went to the Capitol to address a joint session of Congress. "I don't want a honeymoon with you," he told them, "I want a good marriage." And then he went back to the White House to look at the realities. Among the most pressing was that he needed to appoint a new Vice President.

The man he eventually chose, former Governor Nelson Rockefeller of New York, was a man with a liberal record, which would anger some of Ford's constituency. Even though Rockefeller had rejected a Republican offer to run for Vice President in 1960 and Democrat offer in 1968, he accepted Ford's offer, and the Congressional confirmation process began. It took four months before the Senate finally gave its approval.

In the meantime, in spite of the dismal state of the economy, and of the world, everyone was asking, "What will Ford do about Nixon?" The new President said he felt the issue should be left up to the Courts. But no one was going to let him off the hook that easily. Part of the controversy was over the issue of Nixon's papers and tapes, which he claimed were his personal property. President Ford was expected to rule on it, but found himself in a morass of conflicting legal opinion. The legal question of whether he could pardon Mr. Nixon was clear enough, but if he did, would there be a backlash of public opinion?

And Ford had another opinion to consider. The Special Prosecutor estimated that if Nixon were ever brought to trial, it would be at least a year before jury selection could begin, and that the trial itself could take years longer. Faced with that prospect, President Ford decided to give Richard Nixon a full pardon. When he did, his Gallup Poll rating dropped from 71 to 49 in less than a week, thousands of letters of protest arrived at the White House, and newspapers that had been friendly began turning on him. His own press secretary resigned rather than make the announcement. Ford never fully recovered.

Before the month was over, Soviet Foreign Minister Andrei Gromyko arrived at the White House for talks on the Middle East and indicated that the Soviets were ready to talk about other matters as well. The machinery for domestic talks on the economy went into gear and Ford completed assembling his own White House staff. But the furore over the Nixon pardon refused to die. The House Judiciary Committee asked Ford if any deals had been made. "There was no deal, period, under no circumstances," he told them.

Ford's problems increased at the beginning of 1975,

when Republican losses prompted the Democrats to boast that they had accomplished a "veto-proof Congress." The state of the economy was deteriorating at a faster rate, the automobile industry was closing plants and laying off workers by the thousands, and the Administration was forced to admit that the country was in the grip of a recession. And Ford soon discovered that the problem had a twin. The cost of foreign oil had skyrocketed but production of domestic energy, not just oil, but coal and natural gas as well, had dropped almost as dramatically. It was clear that demand needed to be curbed and production increased, but the Administration and Congress disagreed on how to do it.

Ford asked for a $16 billion tax cut to stimulate the economy, and higher taxes on oil and gas to encourage conservation. He also called for drastic cuts in spending and caps on pay raises. Congress called the President "misguided," and its leaders went to work bottling up his proposals. Ford, who had been so proud of having been called "a Congressman's Congressman," was clearly not a Congressman's President.

The following month, a different kind of problem presented itself when an American merchant ship, the *Mayaquez* was captured in international waters by the Cambodians. Ford ordered a naval squadron into the area, then airlifted marines into Thailand. Two days later they attacked, and in a daring rescue recovered the ship and her crew. Although more than 40 Americans were killed in the operation, it was a needed morale booster for the country as well as for the President.

The economy was improving by then, too. And in July Ford had another opportunity to shine on the world stage. The occasion was a summit meeting at Helsinki, Finland. The result was a perceptible easing of East-West tensions that had existed for thirty years. The trip gave world leaders a chance to know each other, and it gave Ford an opportunity to make progress with the Soviets on a Strategic Arms Limitation agreement that had been stalemated.

Ford was jubilant as he set out for the West Coast in September for some political speechmaking on the subject of crime. He had sent a proposal to Congress calling for strong handgun legislation. But the laws hadn't been passed. On the morning after his speech, he noticed a woman in a red dress in a crowd of well-wishers. Her hand was extended toward him and as he reached out to shake it, he saw she was pointing a handgun at him.

The would-be assassin was Lynette Alice "Squeaky" Fromme, a follower of the infamous murderer Charles Manson. She was later sentenced to life imprisonment for the crime. Because of her Manson connection, the incident was considered isolated. But two weeks later Ford went to the West Coast again, and as he was leaving his hotel a shot rang out from across the street. It was fired by a radical named Sara Jane Moore. Her bullet missed Ford by a few feet.

The President refused to alter his public schedule

Two assassination attempts in as many weeks were made on President Ford in September, 1975.

133

saved enough to buy four houses to rent. He sold them in 1946 to buy a diamond ring for Rosalynn Smith, who became Mrs. Carter not long after he graduated from the United States Naval Academy at Annapolis. Two years later, they moved to the submarine base at New London, Connecticut. In 1951 he was reassigned to the nuclear submarine program and his future seemed assured. It was only a matter of time, he was certain, before he would become commander of one of the new atomic submarines. The Carters had come a long way and the future looked bright.

But in July 1953 James Earl Carter, Sr. died. He left his widow, Lillian, and her four children more than a thousand acres of land, but almost no cash. Jimmy resigned his commission and went home to take over the family business. In addition to running their own farms, they sold seed and fertilizer to other farmers and bought their crops – mostly peanuts. It was a business that depended on the weather, and as a result of a major drought in their first year back home, Jimmy and Rosalynn netted $200 for a year of 15-hour workdays. But the following year more than made up for it and they began expanding. Before long, the Carter holdings extended to some 3,000 acres of farm and timberland with an annual gross income of more than $2.5 million.

As his business grew, so did Jimmy Carter's status. He began as a deacon of one of the local churches and then became active in the state Lion's Club. He was elected to the local school board not long after the Supreme Court ruled that schools should be integrated, and he began making speeches throughout the county in favor of building a model high school open to everyone. It was an unpopular stance in Southwest Georgia and he lost when it came to a vote. Carter decided then to run for the State Senate. Though it was 1962, long after such practices were considered a thing of the past, he lost in an election he later proved had been weighted against him with the votes of people long dead and others who were serving prison sentences. When the fraud was revealed, a judge ordered a new election and Jimmy Carter was an easy winner. It was his first step on the road to the White House.

In the 1978 Middle East Summit at Camp David, President Carter brought Egyptian President Anwar El Sadat (left) face to face with Israeli Prime Minister Menachem Begin (right).

On the way, he often said, "The American dream endures." And as the new President and his family left their official car to walk the last steps to the White House, they seemed to be living proof. But there were nightmares ahead. Within a few days of his inauguration, a blizzard roared across the Central States into the Northeast. Combined with bitter cold, it created a shortage of natural gas that closed schools and businesses and put more than two million out of work. The new President told Congress that their decisions on solving the energy crisis constituted "the moral equivalent of war." It was the beginning of a battle that would dog him for the rest of his Presidency. With the exception of adding an Energy Department to the Cabinet, the first session of the 95th Congress adjourned without approving any energy legislation at all.

During his first summer in the White House, Carter was accused by black leaders of not caring about the needs of minorities. Congress had rebuffed him on tax reform, on welfare reform and on a national health program. Carter later reflected, "There was really very little in the list to attract constituents, but much to alienate special interest groups." He was learning the hard way about the world of Washington and, as some other Presidents before him had done, he turned to the international scene as a means of finding his place in the sun. He worked on new initiatives in Africa and the Middle East, the Far East and Russia. But the Soviets rejected his initial ideas on Strategic Arms Limitation and the Chinese at first refused to send a delegation to Washington to talk with him.

Against that background, he was faced with the problem of resolving a dispute with Panama over the treaty that had been signed in 1903 to make the Panama Canal possible. Presidents Johnson, Nixon and Ford had all wrestled with the problem without success, but during the 1976 Republican Primaries, Ronald Reagan hit hard on the issue, saying as often as he could that the Ford Administration was giving in to "blackmail" from Panama. "We built the Canal, we paid for it," he said, "and we are going to keep it."

He said it so often that the issue was very much alive when Carter took office. His negotiating team came up with a compromise that suited the Panamanians, but getting Congress to agree was quite another matter. Debate dragged on for more than two years before legislation was finally in place to make the treaties effective. Carter later said that the debate over Panama was "the most difficult political battle I have ever faced, including my long campaign for President."

The day after the first Panama treaty was approved, an event on the other side of the world set the President on a course toward another battle. When the Palestinian Liberation Organization attacked an Israeli bus, killing more than 30 civilians, Israel responded with a full-scale invasion of Lebanon, killing more than a thousand civilians and leaving more than one hundred thousand without homes. In an attempt to defuse the situation, Carter invited Egypt's President Anwar el Sadat and Israeli Premier Menachem Begin

to meet with him in the neutral ground of the presidential retreat at Camp David, Maryland.

Carter said that he thought they would be secluded there for "one week at most." The Egyptian foreign minister predicted that the talks would break down "after a few days." Begin had indicated he could walk out at any time without losing politically. The meetings lasted thirteen days, and they all left together. On September 17, they announced an agreement that would lead to an Israeli-Egyptian peace treaty.

Carter went to Vienna in 1979 to sign an agreement on Strategic Arms Limitation with Soviet Premier Leonid Brezhnev. When he came home to push ratification through Congress, he ran into opposition that made his battle over Panama pale by comparison. In the midst of it, the Soviets attacked Afghanistan, and any question of the SALT pact becoming official vanished.

By then, Jimmy Carter was already well into what he would call "the most difficult period of my life." The Shah of Iran, faced with dissension marked by bloody demonstrations and strikes, went into exile. It was a signal to the Ayatollah Khomeini to end his own fifteen years of exile and return to Teheran. The militant Moslem leader had kept in touch with his followers and had never missed an opportunity to condemn the Shah and the American "foreign devils" who supported him. But, surprisingly, in spite of the outpouring of hate Khomeini's supporters didn't at that time seem interested in harming Americans. In fact, when a mob held the United States Embassy under siege, the rioters were dispersed by the Ayatollah's followers. A month later, Khomeini sent a pledge of friendship and cooperation to Washington.

But the message didn't reach the mobs in the streets of Teheran, and Khomeini didn't miss any opportunity to tell his followers that the U.S. was to blame for everything that was wrong with their country.

On November 4, 1979, the American embassy was overrun and hostages taken. The religious leaders hailed the demonstrators as heroes, and though they didn't seem to have any clear purpose in seizing the embassy in the first place, they clearly enjoyed the limelight and showed no signs of wanting to leave, demanding the return of the Shah and all his money as ransom. By the end of the month their demands included an apology by the United States for crimes against the Iranian people and, in addition to the Shah's assets, the Ayatollah said the U.S. should pay financial damages.

The hostages had been imprisoned for more than six weeks when the 1980 presidential election campaign opened. President Carter announced that he would seek a second term, but he also pledged not to make political appearances while hostages were held in Iran. But there seemed to be almost no hope that the crisis could end any time soon.

Carter retaliated by threatening stronger sanctions against the Iranians and they responded by saying they were ready to transfer control of the hostages from the militants to the government. Days went by,

and when nothing happened Carter decided to take them by force. Three days after it began, the elaborate operation was aborted after a series of unpredictable mishaps and the loss of six men.

After the rescue attempt was made public, the Iranians moved the hostages from the embassy and kept moving them from place to place to make future rescue attempts impossible. Then Iran moved on to its own election, announcing that there could be no decisions until it had a new government. It was a signal to Carter that he was free to leave Washington and take part in the election campaign he hoped wouldn't result in a new government for the United States.

His campaign began in Alabama, a source of his strength four years before. When it was over, he lost its nine electoral votes to Republican Ronald Reagan. In fact, Carter lost all but three states south of the Mason-Dixon Line, including his home state of Georgia. His conservative Christian constituency abandoned him as well, amid accusations that he had been soft on Communism, that he had given away the Panama Canal and that he was trying to destroy the American family by supporting the Equal Rights Amendment. And blacks, who had voted so heavily for him, also abandoned him, as they felt he had abandoned them.

Just after losing the election, Carter noted that he was still President until January 20, and he began the final desperate round of negotiations that would result in freedom for the hostages on the last day of his presidency. He wrote of that day, "I was overwhelmed with happiness – but because of the hostages' freedom, not mine."

Rosalynn and Jimmy Carter worked together fifteen hours a day to build a failing family business into a multi-million-dollar enterprise. That sense of partnership worked well in their White House years.

The 40th President
RONALD REAGAN
(1981-1989)

When former actor Ronald Reagan announced that he was seriously considering running for President, he said:

"I remember the movie *Santa Fe Trail*. I played George Custer as a young lieutenant. The captain said, 'you've got to take over.' My line was 'I can't.' And the captain said, 'but it's your duty.' And that's how I feel about this. I'm going to run."

Many people began deriding his acting career as poor experience for the nation's highest office, but his critics didn't take into account that he had served two terms as Governor of California and had been elected President of the Screen Actors Guild eight times. He appeared in more than fifty movies and as many television episodes in his career, but his work with the Guild was a full-time job as well.

By the time he became Guild President in 1947, the industry had been rocked by a series of sometimes-violent strikes. One of Reagan's first assignments was to help negotiate its first new contract in a decade. It gave him new insight into what he called "high-altitude bargaining." Before the smoke cleared, an industry committee had been formed to look into accusations that Communists had infiltrated the Hollywood community. It led to a special hearing by the House Sub-Committee on Un-American Activities, at which Reagan was characterized as a friendly witness. Though Reagan was accused of "red-baiting" by some, his appearance provided him with a national forum to present himself as something more than a glamorous movie star, and with an introduction to the Washington scene, which fascinated him from then on.

In 1954 Reagan was one of the first Hollywood stars to become a television personality as the host of a series for the General Electric Company. His experience as a spokesman for the Guild was GE's primary reason for choosing him. In addition to a TV host, the company was looking for someone to tour its plants and make personal appearances as part of its employee and community relations programs. During the next eight years, Reagan visited 135 different GE plants in 40 states as corporate ambassador. The company also frequently arranged for him to be the principal speaker at dinner meetings of chambers of commerce and other civic groups. He averaged fourteen 20-minute speeches a day and learned how to keep each one of them fresh. But in addition to making speeches, he signed autographs, toured assembly lines, and learned a great deal about a segment of America he believed was underestimated by the country's leaders.

What those GE employees discovered about Ronald Reagan was that he was one of them. He was born on February 6, 1911, in Tampico, Illinois, a lusty ten-pound baby his father, Jack, immediately began calling a "fat little Dutchman." He was nicknamed "Dutch," a name that has followed him all his life.

The family arrived in Dixon, Illinois, when Dutch was nine. It was a small town with a half-dozen factories surrounded by farms. It wasn't much different from hundreds of other prairie towns that lured farmers for Saturday night shopping, where the

In Ronald Reagan's teenage years he worked so hard at his lifeguard job that he even rescued people who did not need saving. The image of a modern-day Sir Galahad followed him to Hollywood.

circus visited once a year and where Chautauqua pitched its tents for two weeks every summer providing lectures and seminars and other forms of cultural uplift.

Downtown Dixon consisted of a hotel, a couple of luncheonettes, a drugstore, a movie theater, and a row of retail stores including the Fashion Boot Shop, owned by Jack Reagan. It was probably the least successful business in town. In the 1920s, Midwesterners felt that owning more than two pairs of shoes was an extravagance. Jack's own son, Dutch, didn't have much to wear that hadn't been handed down by his brother, Neil. The boys' mother, Nelle, coped with hard times and turned to the Fundamentalist beliefs of the Christian Church of Dixon for inspirational help, and both her sons were also active in the church. She gave her younger son speech lessons, and he followed in her footsteps as one of the most dynamic speakers in the congregation.

When he was fifteen Dutch convinced the concessionaires at a local park that they needed a lifeguard and that he was the man for the job. He was signed on at $15, and all he could eat, for seven 12-hour days a week. He had already earned a reputation for charm as a Sunday School teacher, but this was a different stage. He worked at the park for seven summers and not one person drowned. He admitted that he "saved" a great many who weren't in any danger, but if they weren't overcome with gratitude, they were pleased with the attention of this handsome young man who seemed to like everybody and enjoyed having the affection returned.

Swimming was clearly his sport, but he dreamed of being a football player. Even though he couldn't see very far without glasses, his enthusiasm outweighed his nearsightedness, and the football coach at nearby Eureka College got him an athletic scholarship for half his tuition. The money he had saved from summer jobs covered the rest of his expenses, at least for the freshman year. Later he got a job washing dishes at the Tau Kappa Epsilon fraternity.

Eureka College was established by the Christian Church and nearly all its students, like Reagan, were church members. But it was 1928 and campus life was changing all over the country. Change hit Eureka, too, in the form of a student protest calling for the resignation of the school's president, and freshman Dutch Reagan was selected to make the speech announcing a student strike. It was his first political speech and he admitted it was "heady wine."

He graduated in 1932 in the midst of the Great Depression, in debt and with no prospects. He hitchhiked to Chicago, where he didn't know a soul, intent on becoming a radio sportscaster. A few days later he was riding his thumb back to Dixon. He finally struck paydirt at WOC in Davenport, Iowa, where the station owner, like the Eureka football coach, was impressed by Reagan's enthusiasm. He challenged the young man to recreate a football game in words "that will make me see it." It got Reagan a job announcing a real game the following week and an assignment to do three more. By the time the season was over, he had a full-time job.

The station was later consolidated with the larger WHO in Des Moines and Dutch Reagan became its chief sports announcer, making him a celebrity all over the Midwest. But he had his eye on a bigger prize. In 1937, he convinced WHO to send him to Los Angeles to cover the Chicago Cubs' spring training. While he was there he went for a screen test at Warner Brothers, secured a seven-year contract and went back to Des Moines to say good-bye.

He worked regularly after that, and appeared in an average of five films a year for the next five years. He became a certified star in 1942 in *King's Row*. Among the people who granted such certification was Louella Parsons, movie columnist for the Hearst newspapers.

Ronald and Nancy Reagan brought a new kind of elegance to Washington, and they never seemed happier than when they were together.

In 1947, Reagan discovered the heady glow of a Washington spotlight – as a friendly witness (right) before the House Un-American Activities Committee.

She, like Reagan, was from Dixon, Illinois, and took him under her wing. In addition to promoting his career, she engaged in marital matchmaking when she signed Reagan to acccompany her on a national vaudeville tour. Among the others who went along was actress Jane Wyman. She and Reagan were married in 1940. But their careers and interests went separate ways, their relationship deteriorated and they were divorced eight years later.

About the same time, a young actress named Nancy Davis appeared in Hollywood. She was looking for a career in movies, but didn't mind saying that she was also looking for a husband. After meeting Ronald Reagan, his name led her list of eligibles, even though he had other things on his mind. He managed to stay single for some time, but no one was surprised when they were married in 1952.

In 1960 the problem of television reached showdown proportions. Reagan was appointed head of a delegation to negotiate with the movie-makers at a meeting that ended in stalemate. The union responded with a six-month strike. In the end the producers won the right to sell TV rights in return for a contribution to the union. Reagan's membership, though happy to see the long strike over, felt they had been sold out. He resigned as the Guild's president and Nancy resigned from its Board.

He had a different kind of politics on his mind by then. In his corporate tours for General Electric he had developed an electrifying speech against the evils of Communism. He ended it with a call to action: "Freedom is never more than a generation away from extinction. We didn't pass it on to our children in the bloodstream. It must be fought for, protected, and handed on to them to do the same, or one day we will spend our sunset years telling our children and our children's children what it once was like in the United States when men were free."

Reagan's speeches inspired many to think of him in political terms, but he denied that he had political ambitions. He said, "One serves where he feels he can make the greatest contribution. For me, I think that service is to continue accepting speaking engagements, in an effort to make people aware of the danger to freedom in a vast permanent government structure so big and complex it virtually entraps Presidents and legislators." Two years later he announced he was running for Governor of California.

In his campaign he told the voters that he was "sick of the sit-ins, the teach-ins and the walk-outs," that were taking place on California's college campuses. "When I am elected governor," he said, "I will organize a throw-out." And when he was elected, he kept the promise. He shunned professional politicians, seeking instead the advice of businessmen "who have to show a profit," and accountants to "keep an eye on the bureaucrats."

When he ran again in 1970, he won in a landslide. His critics said he was only interested in Sacramento as a stepping-stone to the White House, and they may have been right. He spent his first term building a staff and an organization that would eventually follow

Exactly forty years later, he was on the world stage, standing between (left to right) Belgian Prime Minister, Alfred Martens; Jacques Delors, President of the EEC; Japanese Premier, Yasuhiro Nakasone; British Prime Minister, Margaret Thatcher; Italian Prime Minister, Amintore Fanfani; French President, François Mitterand; West German Chancellor, Helmut Kohl; and Canadian Prime Minister, Brian Mulrooney.

him to Washington. But while they were getting organized, a former California Governor, Richard Nixon, won the 1968 presidential election. There seemed no doubt that he would remain in the White House until 1976, by which time Governor Reagan would have been a private citizen for two years.

But by 1976 the incumbent President was Gerald Ford and not Richard Nixon. Reagan decided to fight him for the nomination and kept his campaign alive until the Republican National Convention. When it was all over, Ford had the nomination and the loyal support of Ronald Reagan, who had his eye on the 1980 election, even though he would be sixty-nine years old by then.

The most critical issue in that election was inflation. The country was experiencing its worst economic crisis since the 1930s, and Reagan's message was simple: "Are you better off today than you were four years ago?" The program he presented, which became known as "Reaganomics," grew, in part, out of a theory known as supply-side economics, based on the time-honored principles of supply and demand, but concentrating on the idea that supply creates demand rather than the other way around.

In the first two years of his Administration, the country went through its worst recession in four decades. But the recovery was dramatic. By the 1984 election, the economy was booming and Reagan swept into a second term, in part because the electorate felt they were better off than they had been four years before.

The problem of international terrorism put Reagan to the test in June, 1985, when Lebanese Shiite Moslems hijacked an American plane. Seventeen days later, all the hostages were released without any of the terrorists' demands having been met. Reagan had often promised "swift retribution" in such crises, but met this one with cool patience instead.

After the Israeli assault on Beirut in 1982, American marines were sent to Lebanon to act as peacekeepers. But when 241 of them were killed, the survivors were quickly withdrawn. Two days later another U.S. armed force attacked the Caribbean island of Grenada in reponse to a threat from what the President called "a brutal group of leftist thugs." But Admininistration critics charged it was sabre-rattling at best, and at worst a public relations ploy to distract attention from events in Beirut.

Reagan had been cool to the idea of a face-to-face meeting with the Soviets, but in November 1985 he arranged a meeting in Geneva with Mikhail Gorbachev, General Secretary of the Soviet Communist Party. It was the first superpower summit in six years. They met again a year later in Reykjavik, Iceland. The general feeling after the Reykjavik talks was negative, but Gorbachev finally went to Washington in December 1987 for another round of meetings, which were considered the friendliest ever held between the leaders of America and the Soviet Union.

At the end of his presidency, Ronald Reagan's popularity had hardly changed. His opponents often called him the "Teflon President" because neither negative fallout from his policies nor the sometimes less than honorable actions of his appointees ever stuck to him personally. The most serious challenge to his credibility came when it was announced that the United States had sold missiles to Iran in return for a hoped-for release of U.S. hostages in Lebanon. Then it was disclosed that the money had gone to support the anti-Communist efforts in Nicaragua, and the Administration became embroiled in a scandal known as the "Iran-Contra Affair." When public hearings ended, President Reagan said, "I let my preoccupation with the hostages intrude into areas where it didn't belong …. I was stubborn in my pursuit of a policy that went astray." He retired to a new home in California provided by his supporters in the business community there without having accepted any responsibility, or even knowledge, of the events that led to the scandal that shadowed his last days in the White House.

But as his Administration drew to a close, most Americans agreed that they were better off than they had been when it started. And in spite of the unanswered questions he left behind, his ratings in opinion polls indicated that Ronald Reagan was still an extremely popular President.

One of Reagan's favorite roles as a movie actor was that of George Gipp in the film, *Knute Rockne – All American*. On the hundredth anniversary of Rockne's birth, President Reagan took a sentimental journey to the University of Notre Dame, where he told an enthusiastic audience, "There is a will to succeed evident in our land. I happen to have always believed in the American people. Don't ever sell them short."

When Mikhail Gorbachev became the Leader of the Soviet Union in 1985, the Cold War began to unravel, and President Reagan was pleased with the thaw.

The 41st President
GEORGE BUSH
(1989-)

If you were to ask George Bush where home is, he would answer without the blink of an eye, "Texas!" But in a country where image is often considered as important as substance, most people usually think of men like Lyndon Johnson and say, "Funny, you don't look like a Texan."

Even if President Bush was never successful in cultivating the image of a 'good ole boy,' he is as much a Texan as any of them. He called the Lone Star State home for more than forty years. And if that doesn't qualify him as a son of Texas, remember that Sam Houston was Governor of Tennessee before he got the Texas spirit, and that Moses Austin, who led the first American families into the territory, was born in Connecticut. And though he himself was born in Massachusetts, Connecticut is where George Bush came from, too. His father, Prescott Bush, served as a United States Senator from Connecticut for ten years, in fact, though he grew up in Columbus, Ohio.

The five Bush children, including the second eldest, the future president, grew up in Greenwich, Connecticut, but their favorite place during those growing-up years was the family's summer home in Kennebunkport, Maine, which had been owned by Mrs. Bush's father, George Herbert Walker, a St. Louis businessman. Even as President, the house remains one of Bush's favorite places. It is filled with memories of his boyhood days when he explored the rocks, hunted for starfish and collected treasures from tidal pools; and of the wonderful, long summer days when he was allowed, at the age of nine, to handle his grandfather's lobster boat all by himself, even if it was under the watchful eye of his eleven year-old brother.

Six months after the Japanese attack on Pearl Harbor in 1941, young George graduated from the prestigious Phillips Academy in Andover, Massachusetts, and it was expected he would follow in his father's footsteps by going on to Yale University. But when he announced that he had decided to join the Navy instead, his family backed his decision, and not long after his eighteenth birthday, George Bush was learning to fly. When he got his wings, he was the youngest pilot, not to mention the youngest-looking officer, a mere boy in 'This Man's Navy.' To make

matters worse, his girlfriend, Barbara Pierce, was even younger. To upgrade his image, he asked her to lie about her age.

George met Barbara, whose father was publisher of *McCall's Magazine*, at a dance while he was in flight school. Her family lived in Rye, New York, not far from his family's home, and she was a student in South Carolina, not far from his Navy base. But they were attracted to each other by more than just the convenience of geography. He was in advanced flight training when they decided to become engaged in 1943, but at the same time he was assigned to a carrier-based torpedo squadron scheduled for active duty in the Pacific, and the wedding date was postponed for the duration of the war.

Weddings were the farthest thing from Lieutenant j.g. George Bush's mind on the morning of September 24, 1944. The target for the day was a Japanese communications center on Chichi Jima, part of the island chain that includes Iwo Jima, where the Marines landed six months later. As his TBM Avenger, a three-man torpedo bomber, began its dive over the Chichi Jima radio tower, it was hit by anti-aircraft fire. His cockpit filled with smoke and flames licked the wings of his dive bomber, but Bush kept on diving. He released all four of his 500-pound bombs and destroyed his target before heading for the open sea. Then, after his crew bailed out, Bush jumped. He was slightly injured when his parachute ripped on the way down, but he was still intact when he hit the water, where he floundered in a rubber raft for nearly two hours without a paddle and drifting slowly in the direction of the enemy-held island. Finally, an American submarine broke the surface and the ordeal was over. The only bad news that day was the discovery that his two crewmates had been killed. Bush was awarded a Distinguished Flying Cross for his efforts to save them, and for succeeding in his mission in spite of the smoke and flames.

He was back in action again after a few weeks, and after completing fifty-eight combat missions he was finally ordered home. He arrived back in Connecticut on Christmas Eve, 1944, and he and Barbara were married two weeks later. Their plan to wait until the war was over was scrapped and Barbara dropped out of Smith College to become Mrs. Bush. During the next few months, his squadron was being readied for the anticipated invasion of Japan, but the Japanese surrender came before he was scheduled to leave, and George and Barbara Bush were more than ready to get on with their lives.

He enrolled at Yale and, like so many students in the 1940s, lived off campus with his wife and their son, George, who had been born in 1946. Every couple in the house's thirteen apartments had at least one child, and one had twins. It was a far cry from the typical Yale life his father had known. But family obligations notwithstanding, George Bush still found time to follow in his father's footsteps as captain of the University's baseball team and then did even better as its star first base man at the College World Series two years in a row. He also earned a degree in economics in just two-and-a-half years, and a Phi Beta Kappa key in the bargain. And before leaving New Haven, he became a member of the elite Skull and Bones, an honor reserved for the brightest and best Yale undergraduates.

It was expected that his next logical step would be to join Brown Brothers, Harriman, the New York investment banking firm where his father was managing partner. But George Bush is fond of the unexpected. When the job was offered, he turned it down. He wanted to be his own man. A family friend suggested that the best place for an ambitious young man to make his mark was in the oil fields of Texas. When he backed up the advice with a job offer, George and Barbara packed the baby into an old red Studebaker and headed for West Texas and his new job as a clerk with a company selling oil rig equipment.

They settled down in a one-bedroom "shotgun house," whose rooms were connected to each other with no hallway, in Odessa. They learned the lingo there, developed a taste for chicken-fried steak, and beer from long-necked bottles, and followed local football as passionately as any native-born Texans.

In a little less than a year, Bush was promoted to salesman and transferred to California, but when they eventually went back to Texas, he knew he had come "home." There was an oil boom there in 1950, and the Bushes waded right into the center of it, buying a tract house in Midland in a neighborhood that was filling fast with young people who were all, like George, ambitious to make money. The subject even came up at backyard barbecues, and after one of them George teamed up with John Overby to form an independent oil company. Overby, the Bush's neighbor across the street, was as enthusiastic as he was bright, and it seemed like a perfect opportunity for twenty-six year-old George Bush. It was. Together, they developed oil fields as far from Texas as Montana, and Bush's financial contacts back East, combined with an unusual amount of luck, made them highly-successful wildcatters. They sunk 128 wells and never once hit a dry hole. The company operated in the black for the entire three years of its existence, a rarity among independents in the rough and tumble oil business.

In 1953, Bush and Overby joined forces with two other neighbors to form an even bigger company, which they named Zapata Petroleum for a Mexican rebel played by Marlon Brando in a movie they all had just seen. The company was split into two separate entities five years later and the Bushes moved to Houston, where he took charge of Zapata Off-Shore, the new subsidiary they had created, and pioneered a radical new type of three-legged off-shore oil drilling rig that eventually became the industry standard.

After Zapata's first off-shore rig began pumping crude, George Bush seemed destined to join the pantheon of self-made Texas oil millionaires. But something new had entered his life. Of all the things Texans get passionate about, politics is among the highest on the list, and in 1962, Texan George Bush got passionate about politics himself. The traditionally Democratic state had begun to show Republican leanings during the 1950s, and Bush was approached by GOP leaders in the Houston area to take advantage of the trend and help them build a new organization. It was an opportunity as important to him as the new oil rig design he had gambled on a few years earlier. He agreed to become their county chairman right away, and two years later he became their candidate for the United States Senate. He lost the election, but not the fever. On the theory that his campaign had suffered because his business interests were taking away some of his energies, he sold his stake and severed his connection with the company in 1966. Zapata kept growing even without him, and later became part of the highly-successful Pennzoil Company. If he had kept his interest in Zapata, he could easily have become a billionaire. But George Bush had found a new interest that seemed more important than money, and he never looked back.

Britain's Prince Charles and Princess Diana were among the hundreds of world figures George and Barbara Bush knew well even before George became President.

The same year he got out of the oil business he was elected to Congress from Houston's newly-created Seventh District, and his new career officially began.

After serving four years in the House of representatives, where he was regarded as something of a rising star and was made a member of the powerful House Ways and Means Committee, Bush followed the advice of President Nixon, and an avuncular hint from President Lyndon Johnson that it might be a good idea, and ran for the senate again in 1970. He lost the election, not because he had been given bad advice, but because rural Democrats turned out in record numbers to vote down a referendum to sell liquor by the drink. The loss was hard for him to take, but before the year ended Bush was named Ambassador to the United Nations, where he served until 1973, a period that included the admission of the People's Republic of China to the organization.

When he went back to Washington, President Nixon offered him the chairmanship of the Republican National Committee, explaining that after his recent landslide victory in 1972 the Party needed a strongman to build a new coalition. Bush accepted the challenge, but no one knew at the time what a tough assignment it would be. The Watergate scandal broke a few months later and the challenge for the committee members was less to build a new coalition than to keep the old one from crashing down on their heads. And Chairman Bush was given the job of asking President Nixon to resign for the good of the Party.

During the Ford Administration, Bush was offered his choice of posts as Ambassador to Great Britain or to France, but he turned down both and held out instead for the job as head of the newly-created U.S. Liaison Office in China. As though he hadn't been challenged enough in recent months, he said that he wanted the job because he and Barbara were looking for "a challenge, a journey into the unknown," as they had all those years before when they headed for Texas in an old Studebaker.

George and Barbara and the family dog set off on their journey into the unknown in 1974. They lived and worked in Beijing for fifteen months, during which time "the Bushers," as the Chinese called them, became part of the local scene. They rode around the city on bicycles as the natives do, even though they had a car and driver at their disposal. As the unknown became familiar, they were reluctant to leave, but in 1975 duty called them home again when President Ford designated George Bush the new head of the Central Intelligence Agency.

The CIA was under investigation at the time by two Congressional committees for alleged abuse of power, and the job of restoring its image seemed to Bush, and everyone else, to be as thankless as his chairmanship of the republican National Committee had been. But he rose to the occasion, and by the time Jimmy Carter was elected President, agency personnel had regained their self-respect and the image of the CIA had been restored again. On the other hand, George Bush was out of a job. But he had his sights on a better one. On May 1, 1979, he announced he was going to run for president.

He last his bid, but made a strong enough impression on Ronald Reagan, his opponent in the primaries, to be offered the vice presidential nomination. He accepted the offer. His duties in the Reagan Administration went well beyond those normally assigned to a vice president. He headed the Presidential Task Force on Regulatory Relief, a key agency in Reagan's economic recovery program; and he was made the Administration's chief spokesman on the entire recovery effort. Later he was put in charge of a task force to find remedies to the problems of crime and rampant drug smuggling in South Florida, which later expanded to include all of the country's borders. As Vice president, Bush traveled to 74 different countries as Reagan's personal representative. He said he was treated "almost as an equal" to the president himself, and he became one of the most loyal members of the Reagan team. His service was rewarded with the vice presidential nomination again in 1984, and finally with the presidential nomination and his election to the highest office itself in 1988.

When they moved into the White House, George and Barbara Bush noted that it was the twenty-ninth time they had moved in four decades. Over those years, from his days of building a business to serving in Congress, at the UN, in China, at the CIA, in the Reagan Administration and into his own presidency, he has accomplished enough to make any man proud. But when he was asked what single accomplishment made him proudest of all, George Bush responded, without the blink of an eye, "the fact that our children still come home." And when they all get together, it adds up to quite a crowd. The Bush family includes four sons and a daughter and ten grandchildren.

Though they are at home on the world stage, President and Mrs. Bush are just as much in their element at down-home Texan barbecues.